RIO DE JANEIRO

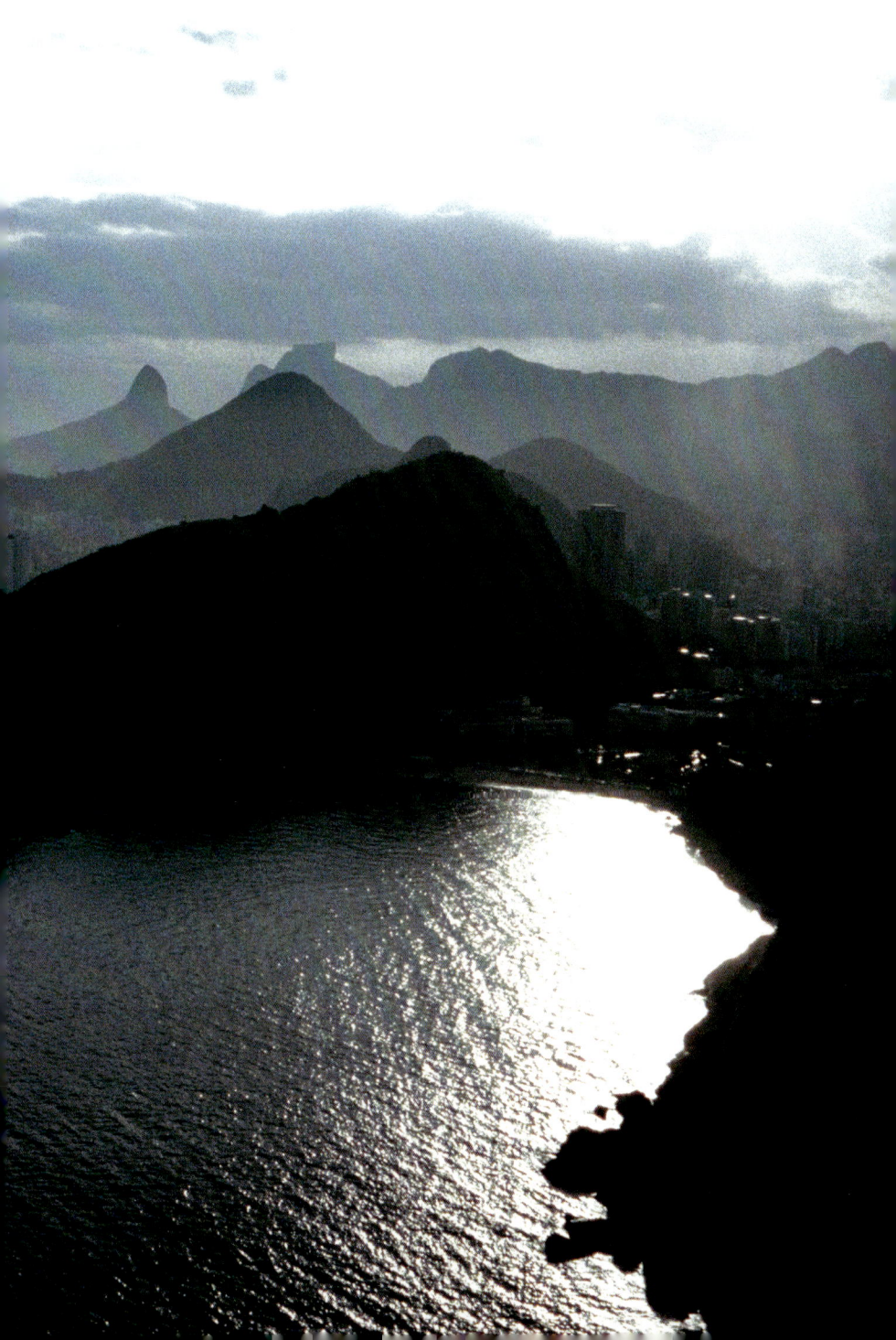

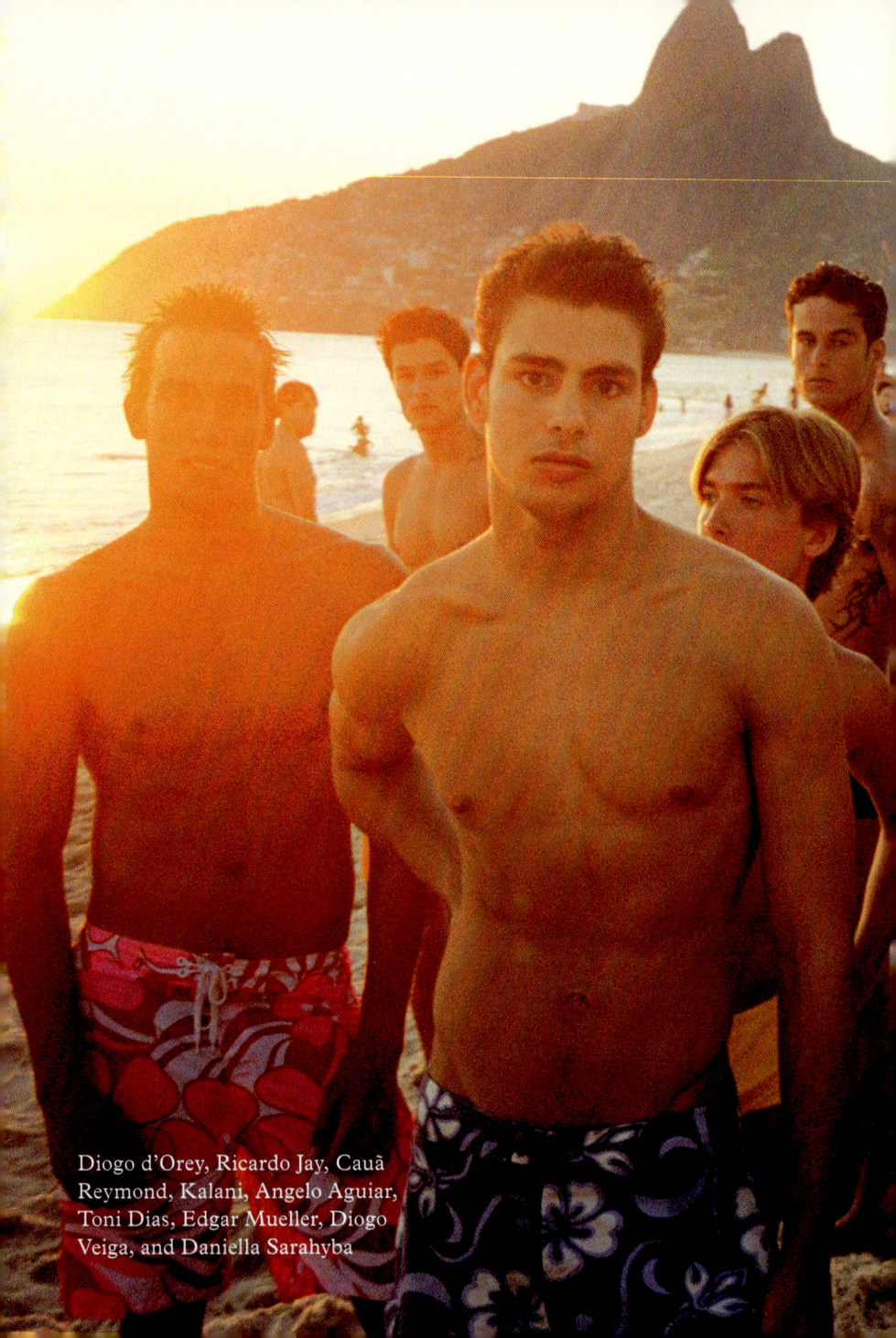

Diogo d'Orey, Ricardo Jay, Cauã Reymond, Kalani, Angelo Aguiar, Toni Dias, Edgar Mueller, Diogo Veiga, and Daniella Sarahyba

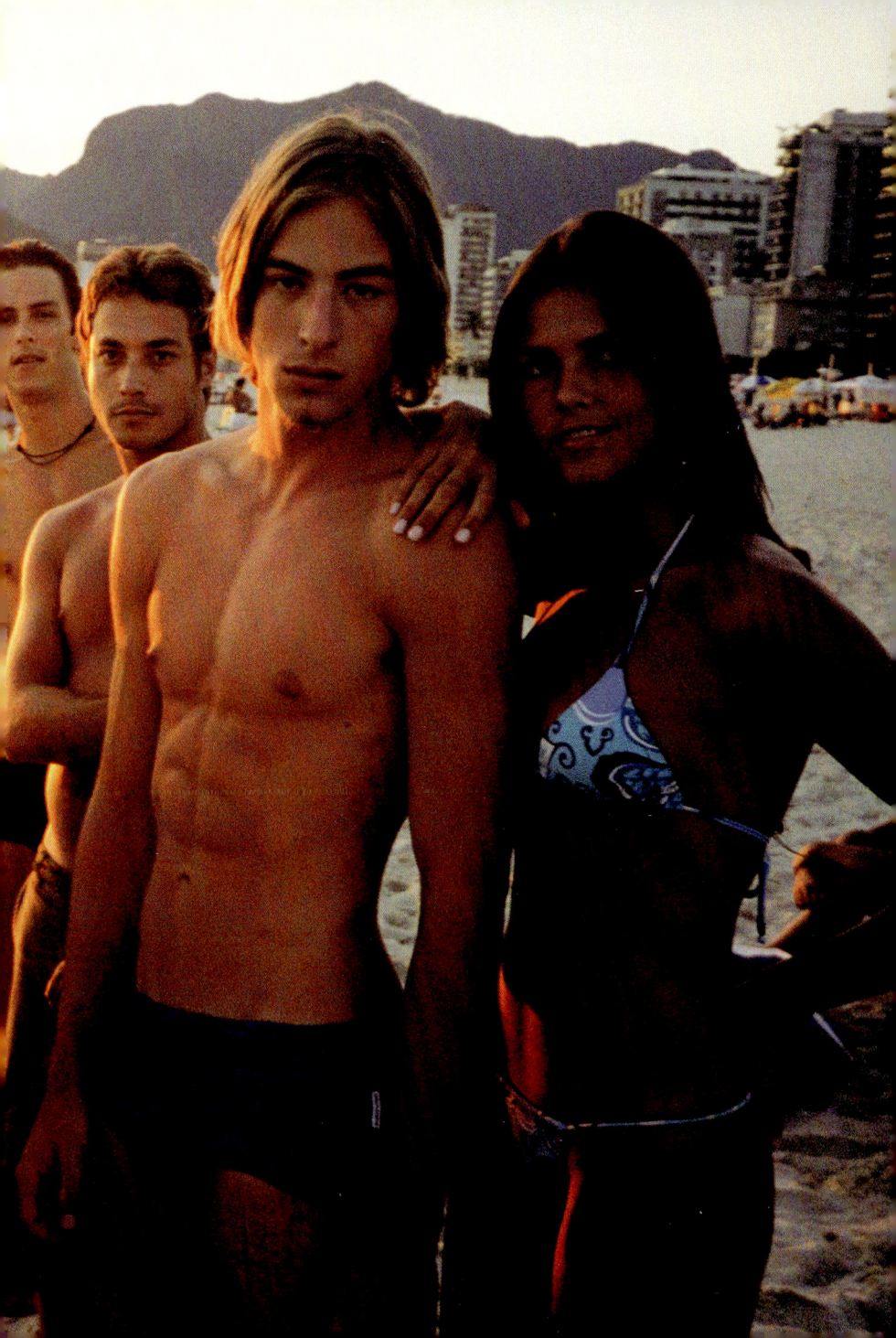

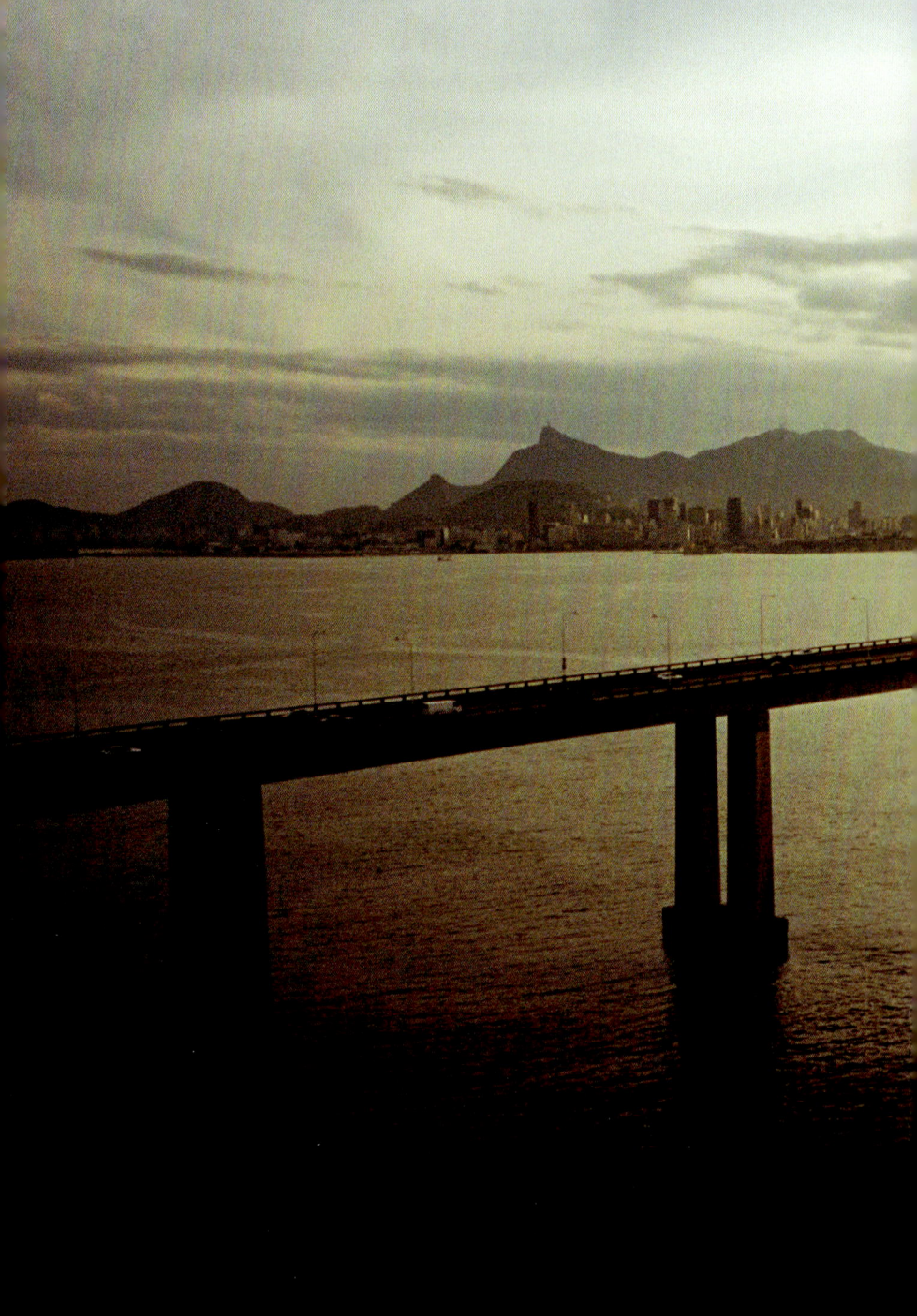

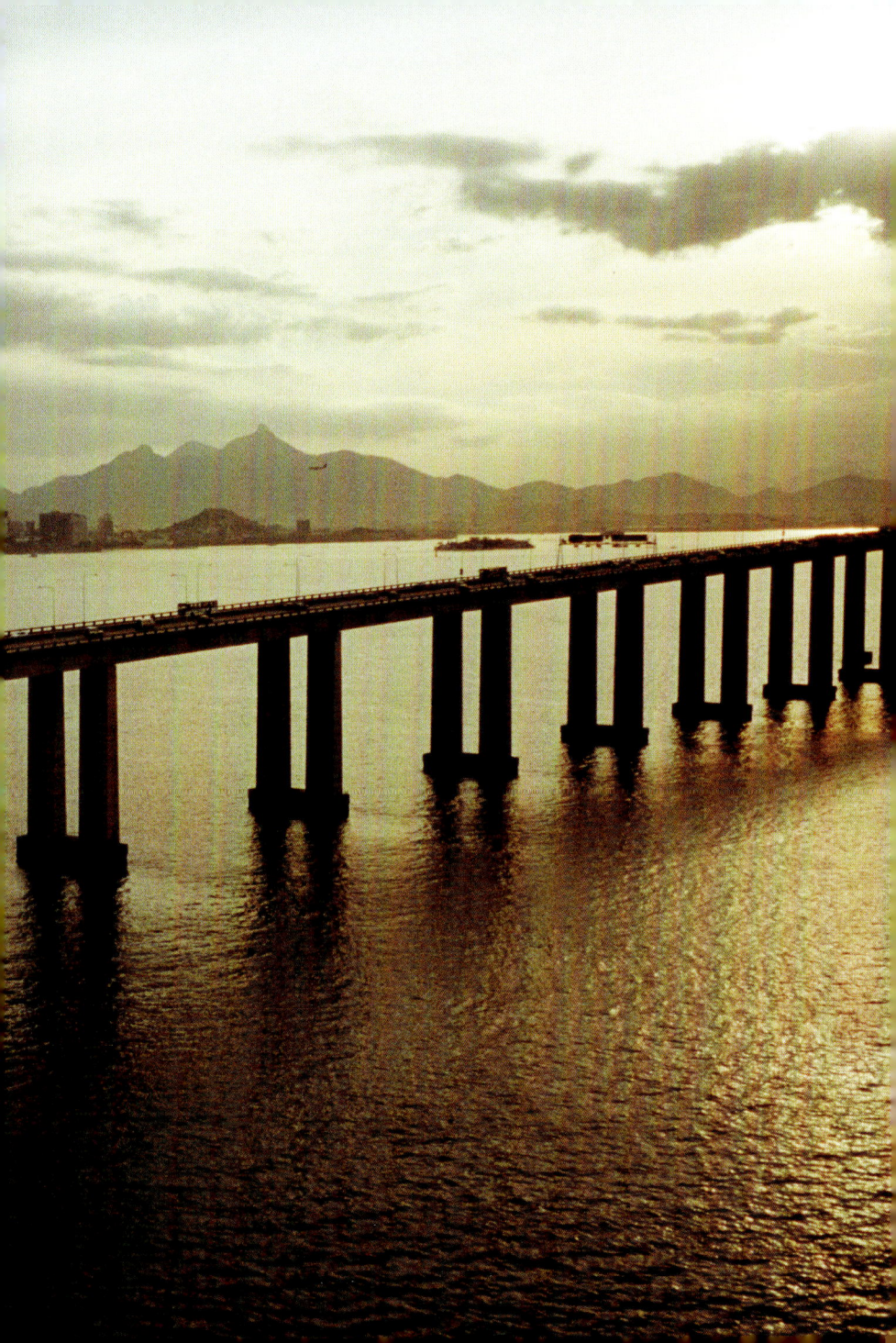

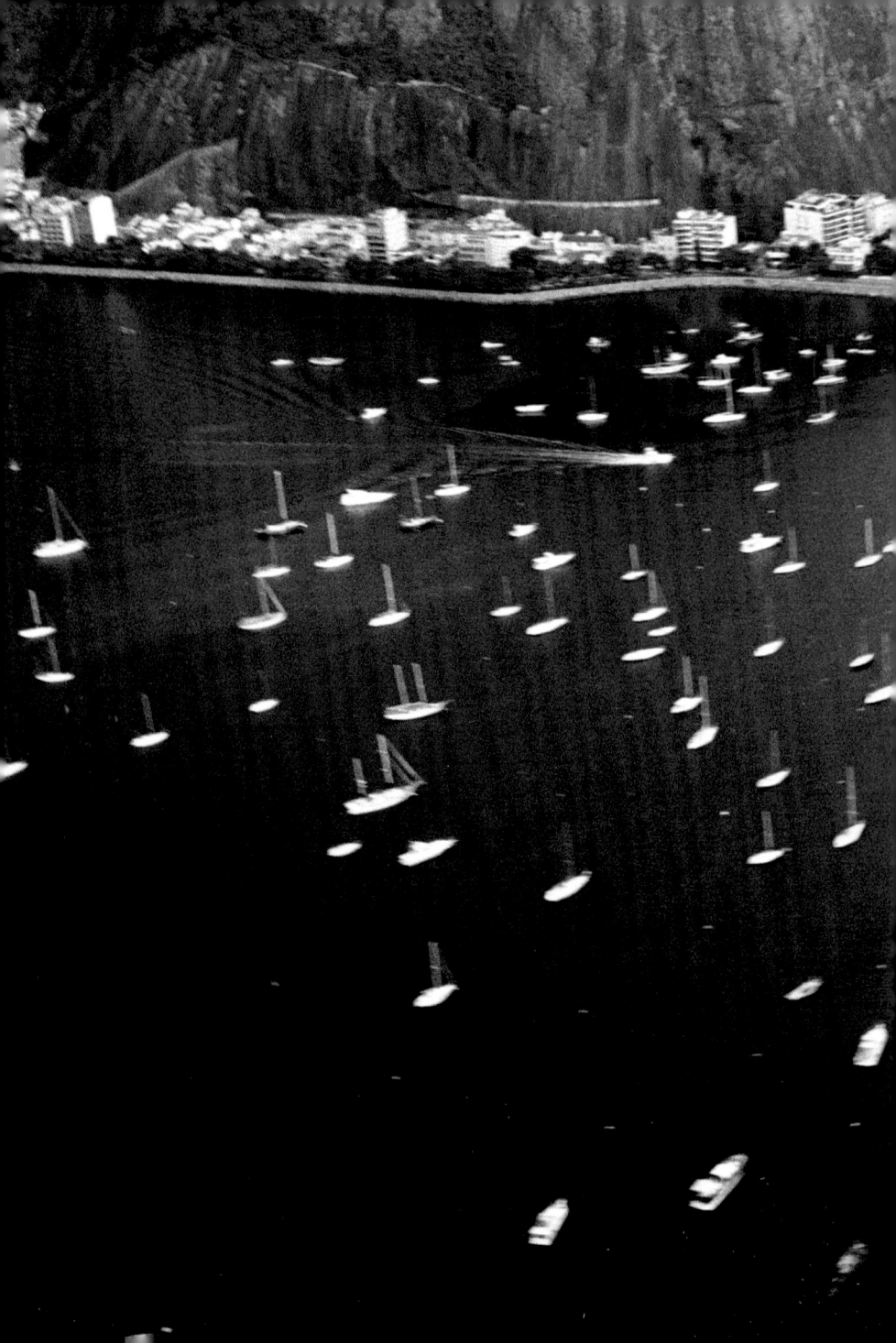

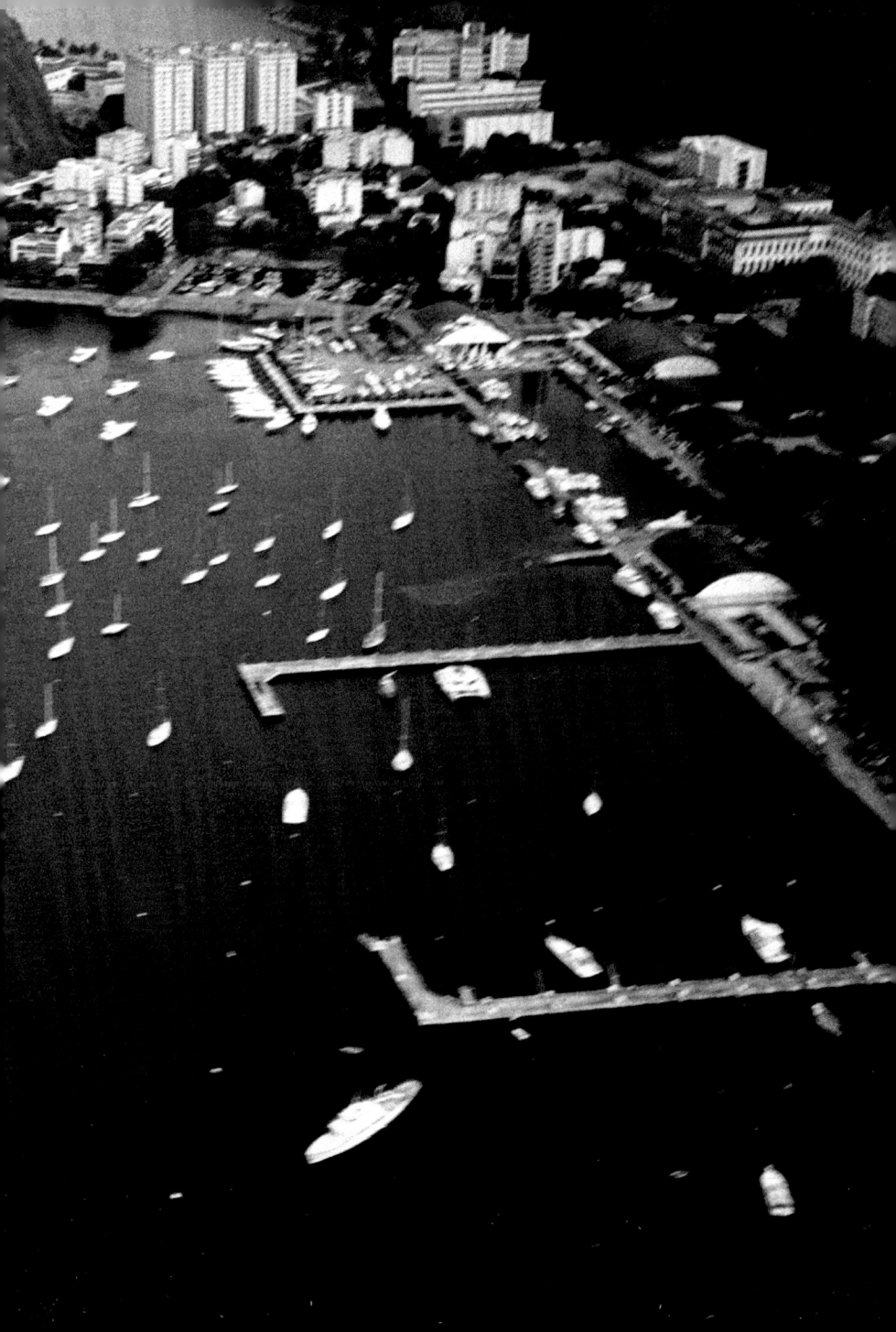

FOREWORD

BY CAETANO VELOSO

Rio de Janeiro has cast its own unique spell, even on those with a reputation as conjurers: Paul Gauguin deemed the bay to be even more stunning than Tahiti's, and Cole Porter said on several occasions that it was the sight of the city as he first anchored his yacht here that provided the inspiration for writing the languid "It's De-Lovely." And although Claude Lévi-Strauss considered it ugly, numerous photographers have trained their lenses on Rio, and some have devoted whole books to the city. What makes Mario Testino's photographs stand out from those of other inspired visitors is that Mario captures the city's essential inner being. His superior inspiration is borne out by the fact that he isn't merely a visitor. Mario had become a *Carioca* long before he became the worldwide celebrity he is

now. His camera is guided by a pair of eyes that live at the top of the world, but his eyes are guided by the insights received when, as a young man from the beautiful and complex city of Lima, he experienced for the first time the daytime and nightlife delights of Rio. Whenever Mario captures the beauty of a glamorous woman, a sexy hunk, or a loving couple with his camera, in that vision he distills the awe—the unbridled enthusiasm of delight—that he, as a young South American, felt when he first encountered the sensuality and carefree attitude of the *Carioca* lifestyle. He also conveys the satisfaction he feels today as he sees this impression reconfirmed after decades of global experiences. Not only does Mario have Rio imbedded in his own name, he has Rio's urban landscapes—and the friendliness of its inhabitants—embedded within his soul. Several times I have heard Mario mention the amazing modernity of Rio de Janeiro. He does not reminisce about Rio de Janeiro without its buildings and asphalt. On the contrary, each time he frames the skin of a beautiful girl—who's usually his friend of many years—he is sure to include the corners of a "modernist" window, a hackneyed balcony, or an elegant façade. The inhabitants of Rio, too, recognize themselves immediately in Mario's photographs. A foreigner's view can be utterly revealing; it can create wonders not previously imagined by those within. But the view of an outsider—albeit one from a place not so distant—who has melded into the scene and then projected himself onto the world's top trendsetting genres can

excite the city's myriad subtle connotations, giving them the warmth and texture of living, breathing things. The impression left by Mario's photographs of Rio is that of a complex, rich and multilayered love, overflowing with intimacy and the lucidity of dreams brought to life.

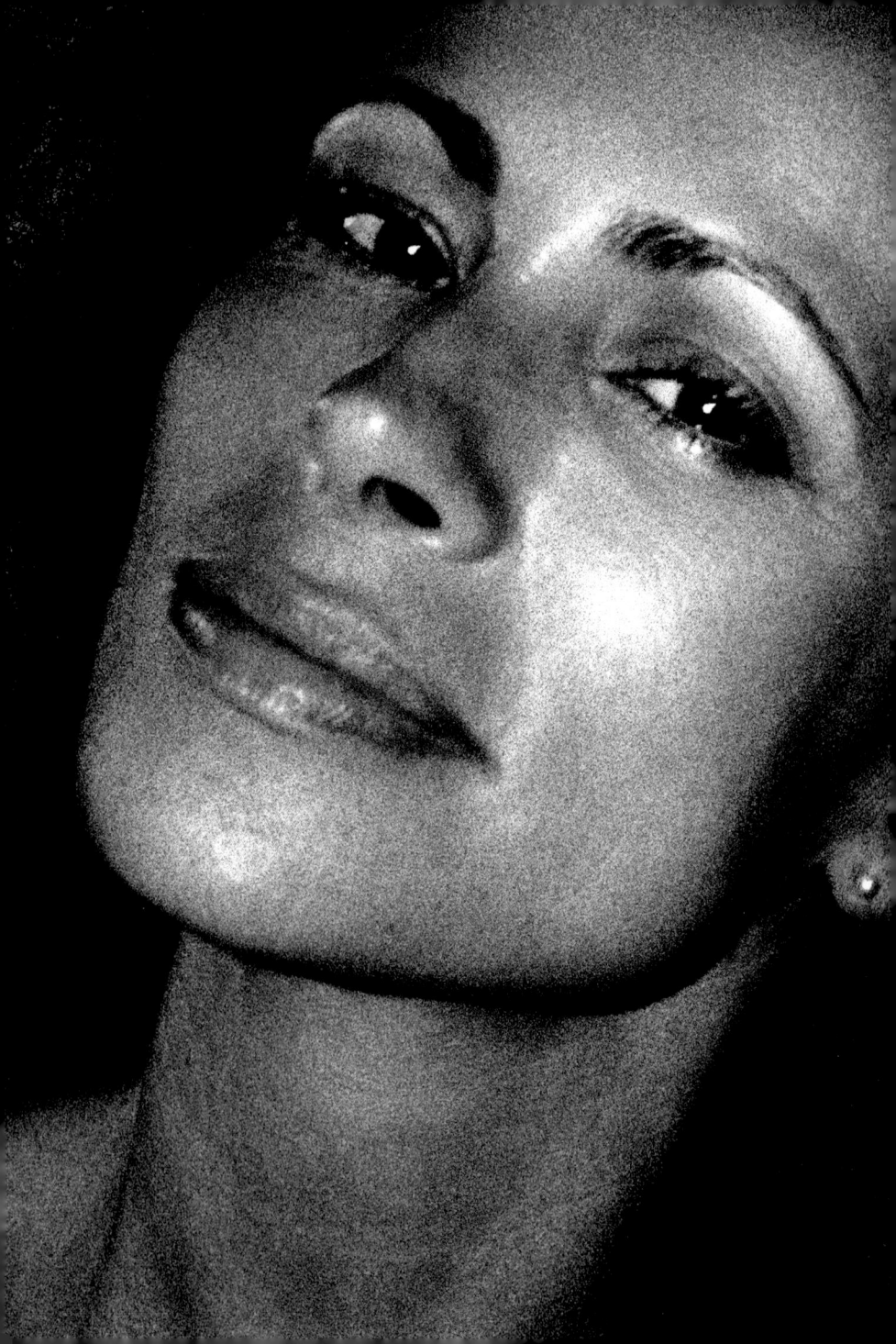

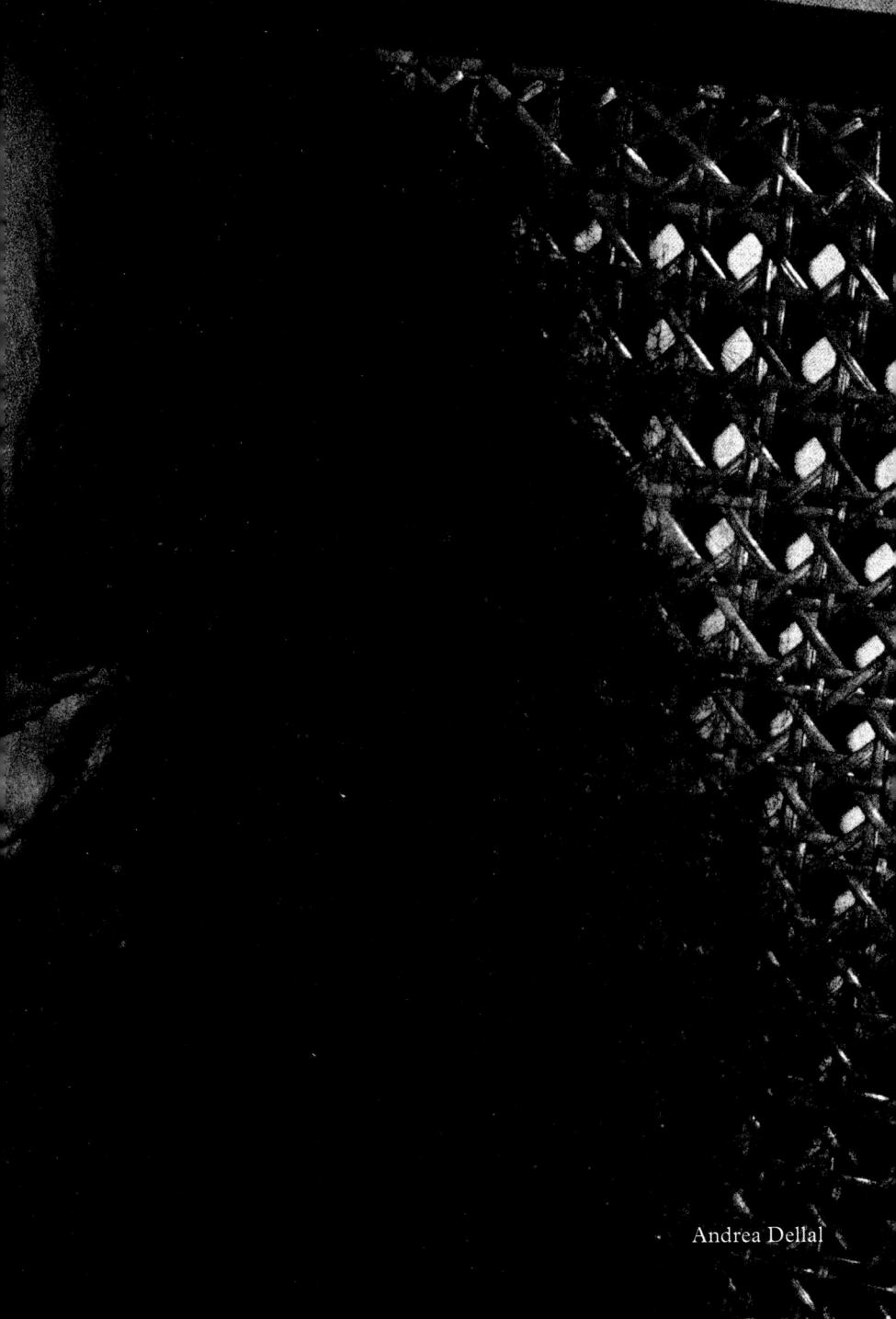

Andrea Dellal

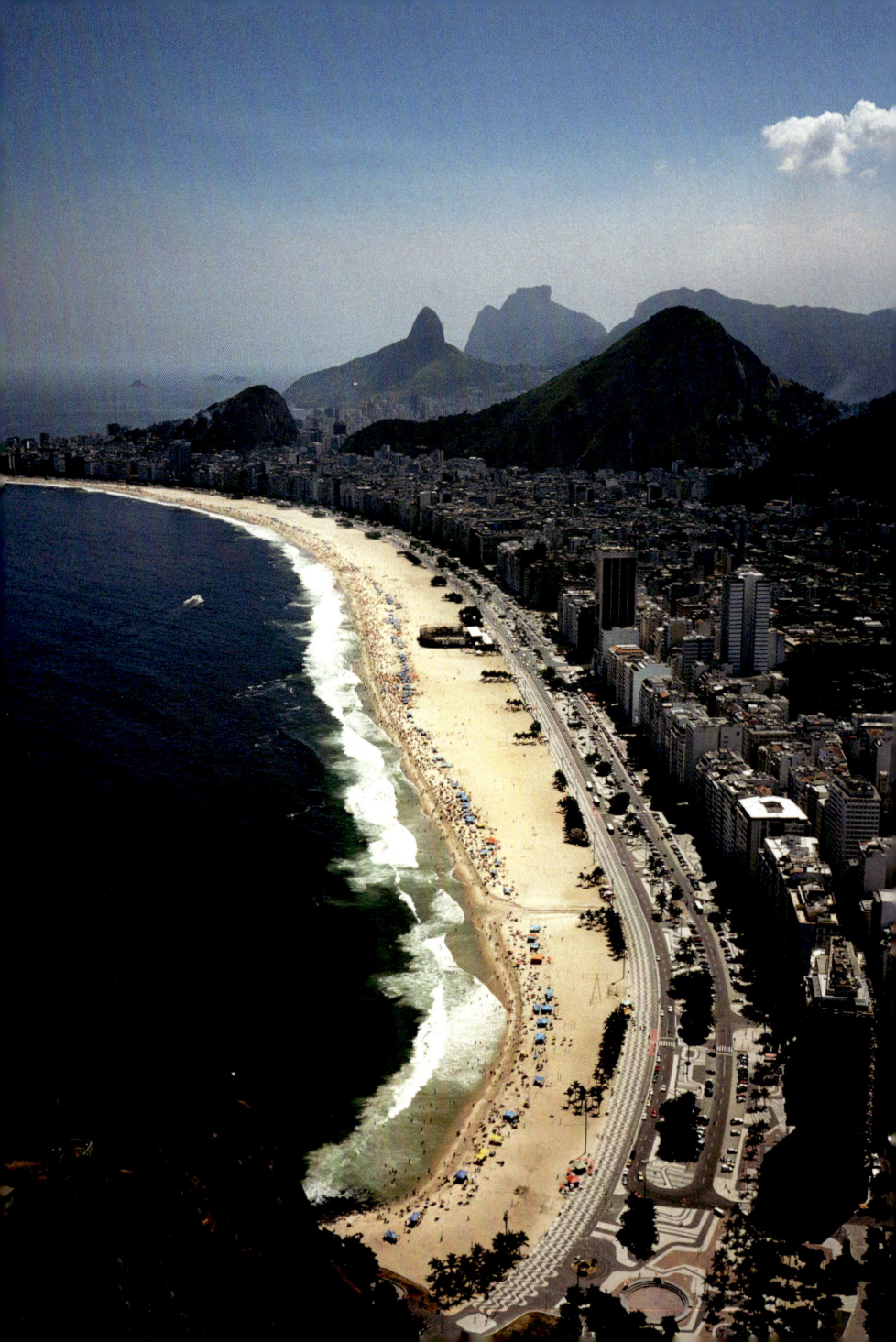

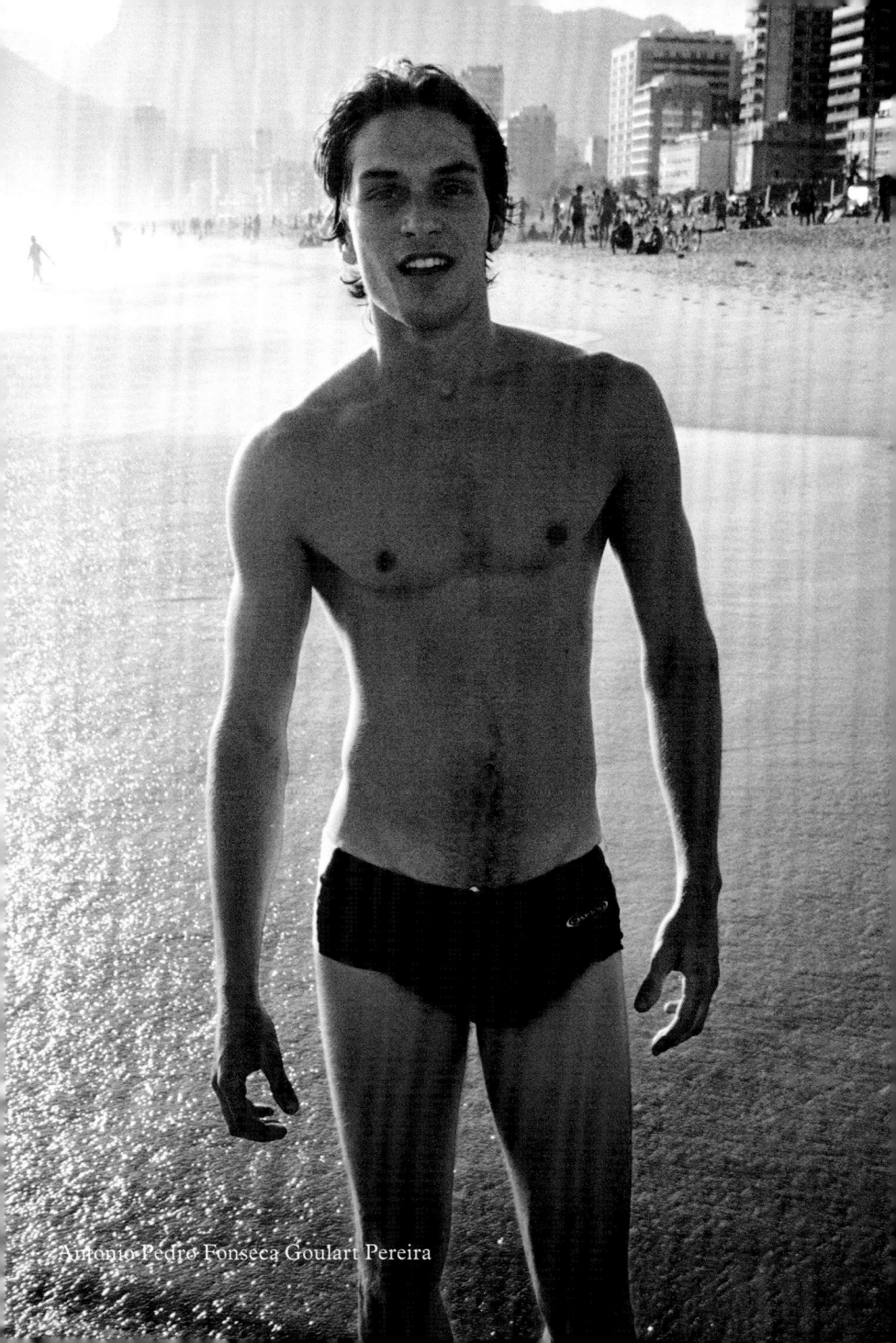

Antonio Pedro Fonseca Goulart Pereira

INTRODUCTION

BY REGINA CASÉ

I am *Carioca*. I was born and raised in RIO, so I am part of it… and it's part of me. One day I woke up to the sound of someone calling my name. I looked out the window and the person shouted, "Regina! Can you throw me some change so I can buy some coconut water? I've got no money on me!" It was MaRIO, wearing nothing but a *sunga*,[1] with a *frescobol*[2] racket in one hand and a rubber ball in the other. The moment MaRIO sets foot in RIO, as soon as he steps out of the airport, jet-lagged or not, he becomes one of us. He is one of us. He knows how delicious the *Cariocas* are. He knows how exciting it is to stay at the beach until the very end, when the light of sunset acts as a natural makeup and makes everybody beautiful, even those who aren't as pretty as the boys and girls in this book.

People wait for this moment to make a move: to gently slide the hand farther up the partner's thigh, to smile in a subtly different way, to take someone home and… MaRIO knows how good it is when the sun sets and the breeze, just slightly cool, prompts us to ask for a hug to warm up; a hug from behind, with a wet swimsuit… a hug that lingers without parting for fear of revealing the increased volume of its contents; a hug from the front, the breeze giving you goose bumps all over, as your taut nipples press hard against the bikini top. He knows how this sensation continues later, in the apartment, and how everything around us encourages the feeling. It's in the architecture and in nature. Everything helps, even the omnipresent Atlantic Forest, which is so close by and has so many kinds of trees in such a small area! All those elements are combined and blended together, and everything is so luscious! Even the rocks display bromeliads with big red phalluses. Amazing orchids exhibit their clitorises, their tiny little pussies in shades of pink and lilac. That's how it is for us. It is part of our nature. MaRIO knows that lust here doesn't hide at the bottom but floats on the surface. It is everywhere. Lust is not hidden at the bottom of the *Lagoa*,[3] it may very well be at the top of the building that blocks our view. It's not only in the darkness of the forest but also in the potted fern at the *churrascaria*.[4] Horniness doesn't languish at the bottom of the ocean but flows freely over RIO. Our common friend Caetano—who's from Bahia—always says, "Gisele is from the South and Mario is from Peru, but they're all *Cariocas*, just like me." That's how RIO is. And that's where I'd like MaRIO to live, because I like him very much.

1 Brazilian-style swimming briefs, or a Speedo
2 Brazilian beach sport
3 Short for Lagoa Rodrigo de Freitas, a lagoon in the southern zone of Rio de Janeiro.
4 Barbecue restaurant

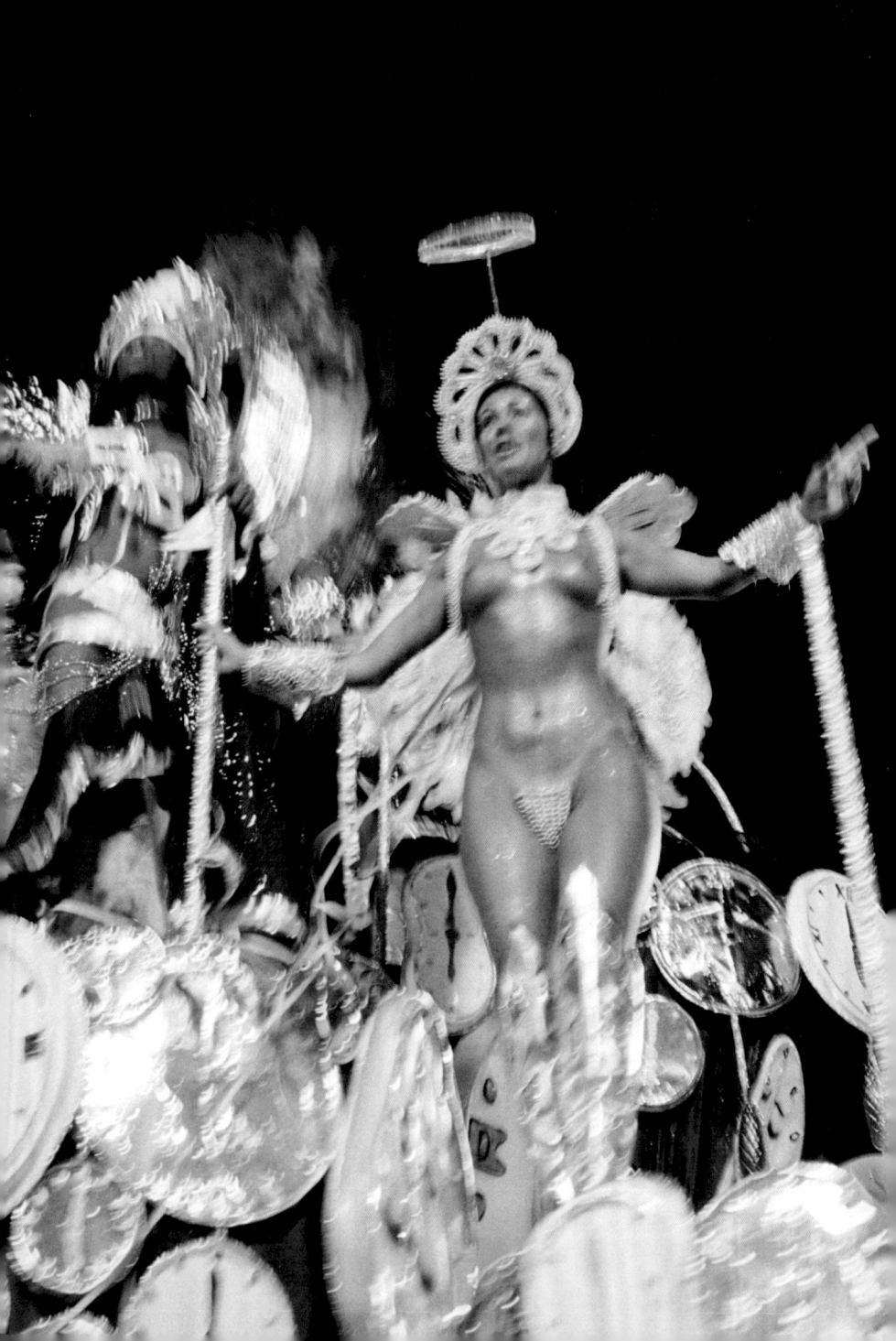

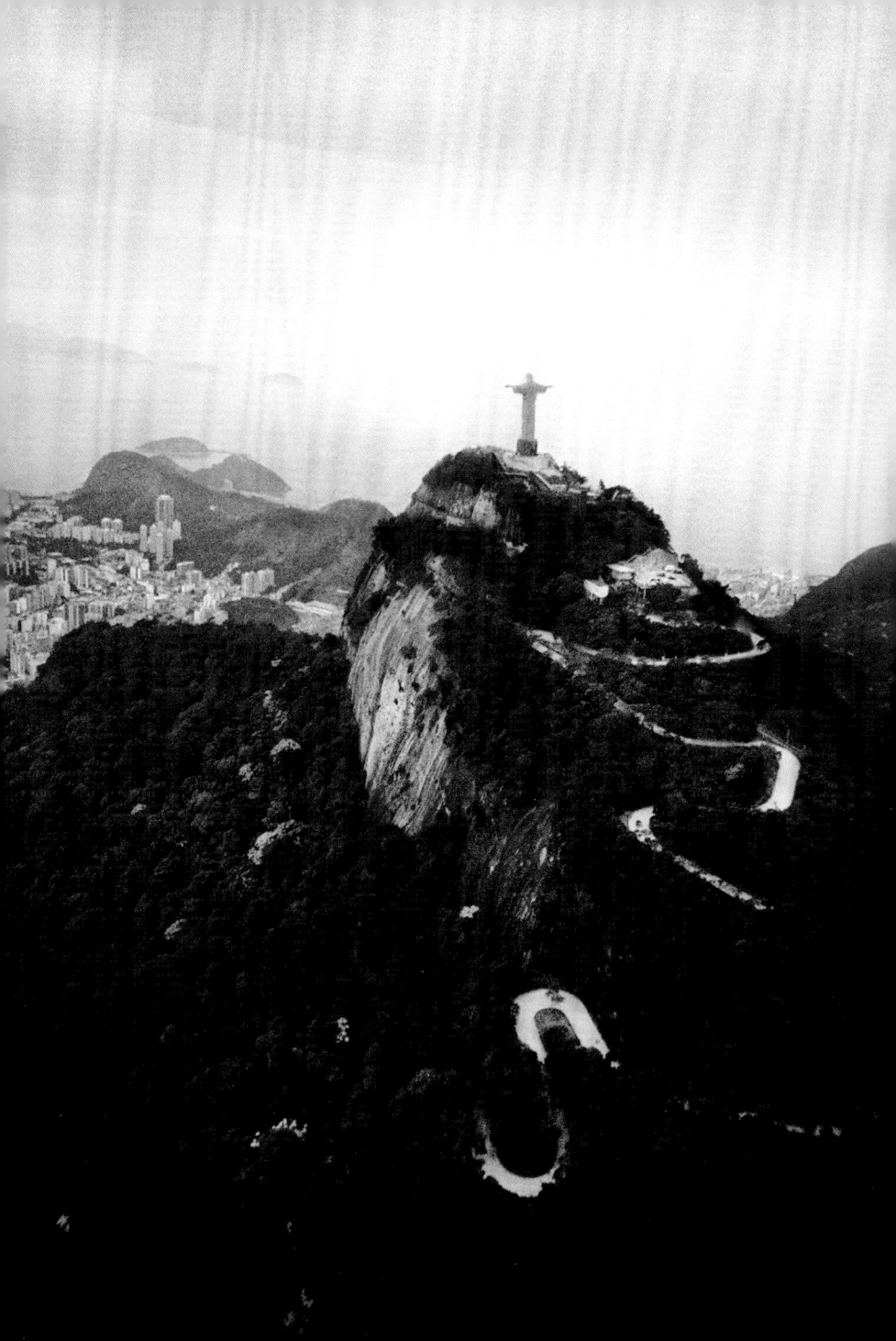

RIO AND MARIO

BY GISELE BÜNDCHEN

I am from Horizontina, a small town in southern Brazil. I'm from a big family and we never traveled to Rio because it was so far away—a journey of six hours in the car followed by a three-hour plane ride—too long of a journey for all eight of us. I was 13 when I first had the opportunity to go to Rio and it happened at a very special time in my life. The trip was planned as an excursion by the modeling course I was on in Horizontina. There were about 50 of us girls traveling together, including my mom and two of my sisters, and it took us 28 hours by bus to get to Rio, with one stop on the way in São Paulo. It was in São Paulo, while I was walking around in a shopping mall, that I was discovered as a model. I was so happy about this; so thrilled. And to top it all, what lay beyond São Paulo was Rio! I couldn't have been more excited.

Rio existed in my head long before I ever went there. Soap operas are huge in Brazil, and Rio is where they are made. When I was young my absolute favorite TV show was called *Xuxa*. I loved the show's heroine of the same name so much that I named my dog after her. Of course she lived in Rio. So for me Rio was this magical place where Xuxa lived, and though I left home to live in São Paulo when I was 14 and grew up fast in many ways, I was still young on that first trip to Rio, and those associations were very important to me. But it was also a real place. How cool was that?

The reason for the trip was to visit the statue of Christ on Corcovado Mountain overlooking the city, and to watch the famous talk show *Domingão do Faustão* being filmed. I was already ecstatic about the idea of Rio, but nothing prepared me for its beauty. The way it is laid out geographically, in nature, right on the ocean with lagoons and many little coves, and with mountains rising up behind it, is truly a gift from God. It's so beautiful, I just thought, it couldn't be true. I found it magical.

But however much I fell in love with Rio, I couldn't go there whenever I wanted to, because it was simply too far away. And so Rio is important to me for many reasons. Plus, for any Brazilian it is shrouded in a kind of historical romance because up until 1960 it was our capital city, and so it has a certain importance, and yet it's always been the city of glamour. São Paulo is regarded as a business center, but not Rio! For me Rio was like this stage set kind of place where soap operas were made, where Xuxa lived, and where healthy people ran on the beach every day and drank coconut water. It's this dream-like place, only you can go there for real and it doesn't disappoint.

For me, a perfect day in Rio would be to start with a coconut for breakfast, and then to get out on to the beach and play some volleyball. Plan things? You don't have to plan *anything* in Rio. It's more like, you just arrive and say, "Hey, let's have fun." That's the thing about Rio: it makes you want to be outside, playing sports, running on the beach, drinking coconut water, eating the delicious *coxinhas* that are sold everywhere. Or if you're not in the mood to run around, then just bring a good book and some sunblock, and sit on the beach with your delicious coconut water and you'll be in heaven. Every so often you'll look up from your book, look around and you'll be like, oh wow!

For me, Rio and Mario are strongly connected. I met Mario in New York City when I went to his studio on a go-see for a job, but the first time I traveled with him for work was to Rio, when I was 17 and we were doing the *Allure* shoot with the fashion editor Polly Mellen. It was incredibly exhila-rating for me because Mario was a big photographer, and the first person that saw something in me, who felt that I was this girl, and that we could really work well together. We had a connec-tion. So of course Mario occupies a very special place in my heart. He has been there with me from the beginning.

But more than that: we understand each other. You know what I mean? I understand what he wants, and I think he understands what I want. He is very respectful of my boundaries, and yet at the same time no one pushes them like him.

Mario is always saying, "Oh, Rio is amazing, it's fantastic!" I'm like: "Hey, I'm the Brazilian. *You're* the Peruvian, and yet I've got to go to Rio with you! What's going on here?!" Whenever I've been in Rio with Mario, it has always been unbelievably fun. Mario is more *Carioca* than anybody I know. What is *Carioca*? Well, to me *Cariocas* are very… how to put it? Imagine your daily life goes kind of like this: you wake up in the morning and even though you live in the city, you are right there on the beach and everybody is half dressed or hardly wearing any clothes. That's your everyday reality. That sort of living and attitude builds the foundation for the way you feel about yourself. A *Carioca* woman, for example, is very

comfortable with her body. She's voluptuous, athletic, and strong. Most of all, she is confident about herself and her body.

Mario is Peruvian by blood, but I think his heart is Brazilian. The way he's comfortable in his skin; the way his spirit expresses itself; the way he's a bit *safadinho*—you know, a little bit naughty and mischievous. He's like a little kid in some ways. I love that about him, and that playfulness shows in his pictures. So imagine what Rio, this incredibly sexy place, does to him. It brings all those qualities into even sharper focus.

Likewise, Mario is brilliant at capturing Rio; the sensuality of its people and their happiness in their bodies—the fact that they are at ease with their sexuality, and not afraid to reveal everything about themselves. I don't just mean in terms of wearing few clothes, though that too, but more the way they are authentic and upfront about who they are. I think Mario is like that himself, and that's one reason why he is so great at capturing the people of Rio.

If someone else asked me to do some of the things Mario does, I would say no way. But Mario, with that clever way of his, is like, ah, Gisele... and the next thing I know we're doing some picture with my butt sticking out. But what can I do? It's hard to say no to Mario. He has this way of being his sweet, friendly little self while getting his way. But at the same time, he'd never do anything to expose you in a bad way. He's just not interested in that. What he's interested in is getting you to do things you'd never do for another photographer, and the result is shown in his great work.

As you can see in this book, for example, I went to visit Mario in his hotel room after work. We were just hanging out when a friend of his, a young guy, dropped by and Mario asked if he could just take some quick snapshots of him with me. I was in my bathing suit, with no make up on, and totally unprepared for a photo shoot, but it's hard to say no to Mario. He snapped away for about 10 minutes... and the images are now in this book.

But my experiences of Rio with Mario have not just been about work. The first time I went to Carnival, I made sure to bring all my sisters with me. We were singing and dancing and hanging out when all of a sudden I saw this big smile coming towards me. I was like, "MARIO!" You cannot imagine what your first Rio Carnival is like. It is as if your fingers are in a socket and you are experiencing a continuous electric shock. It's like being plugged into life. And who was there dancing with me all night? At my first Rio Carnival? *Carioca* Mario.

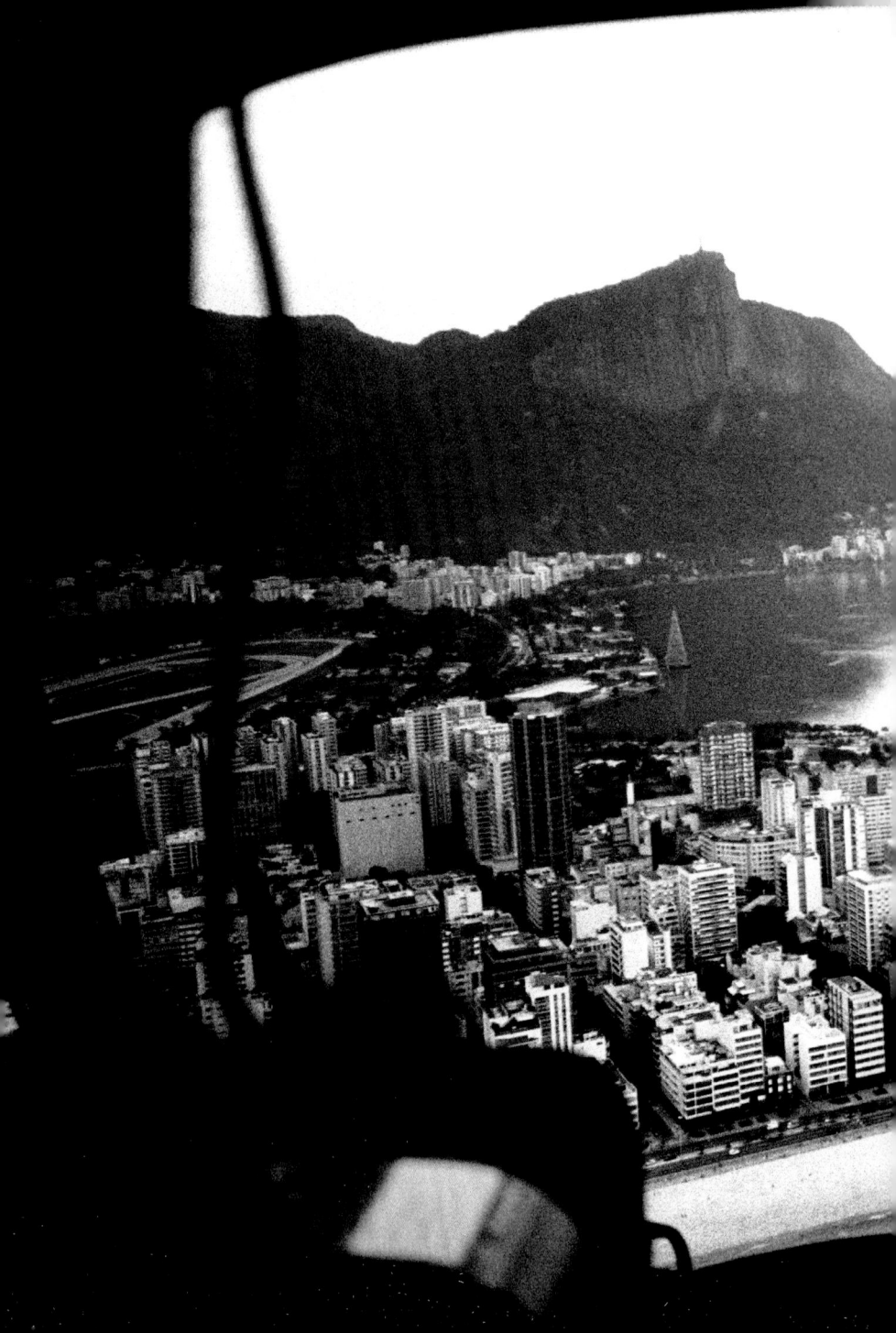

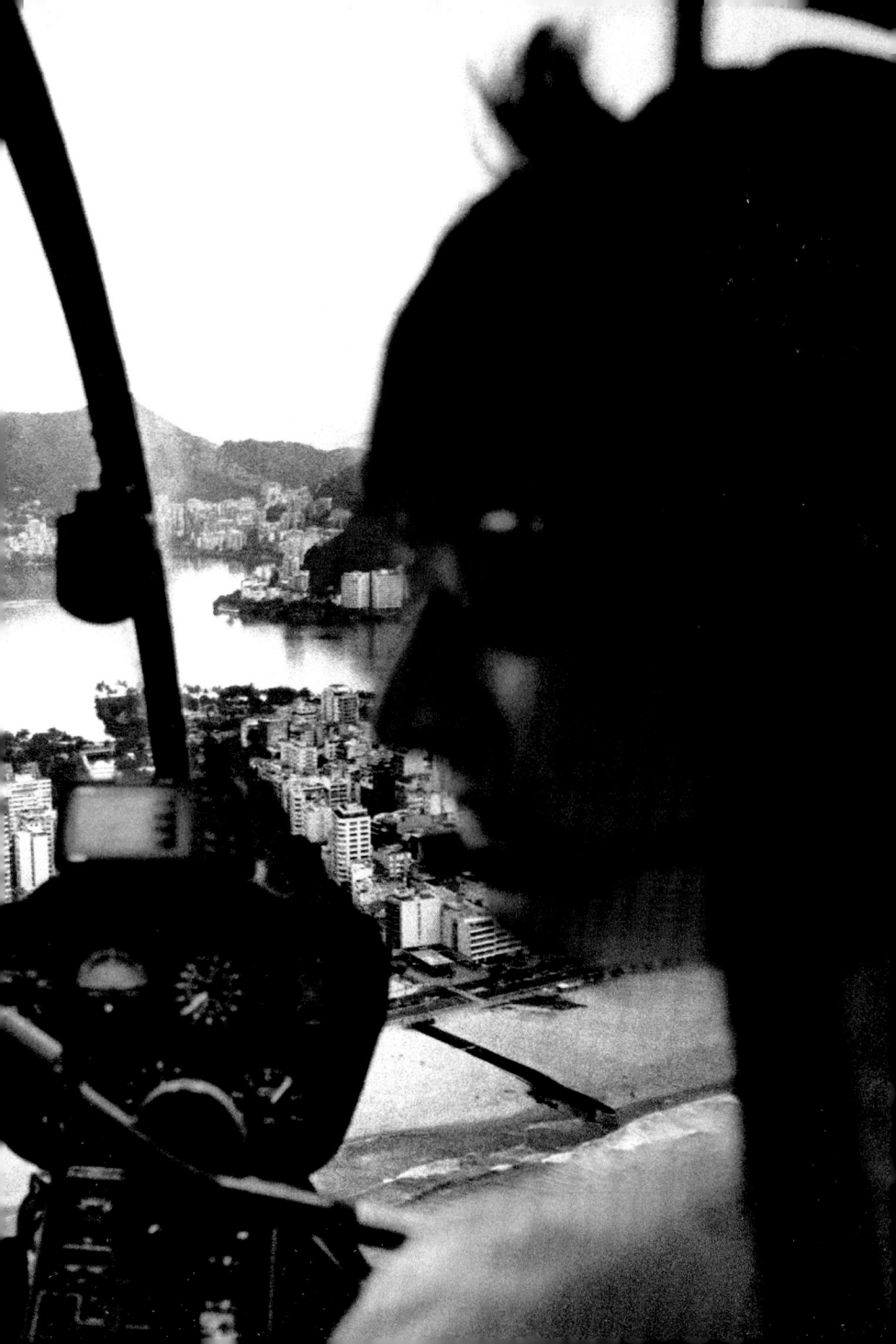

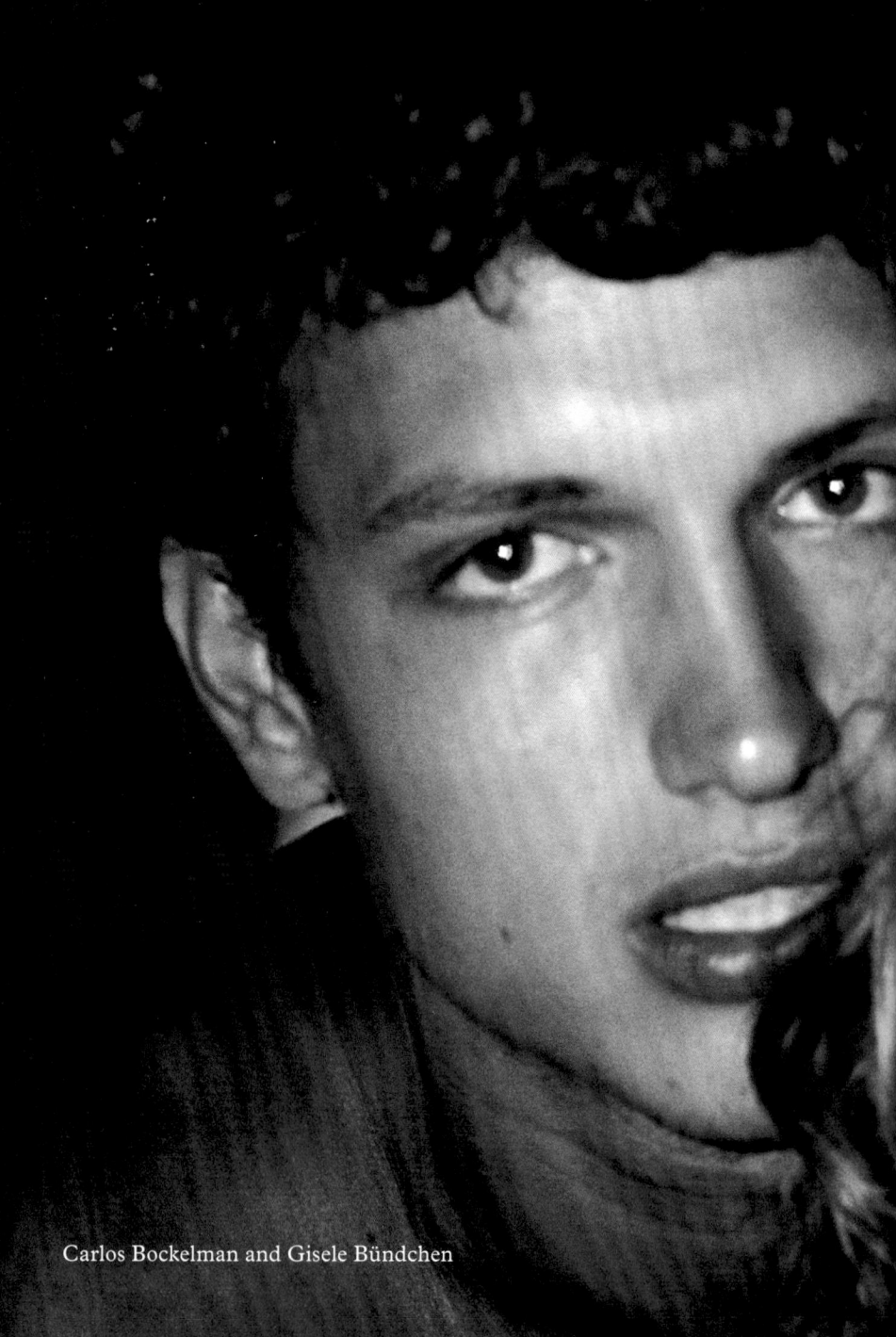

Carlos Bockelman and Gisele Bündchen

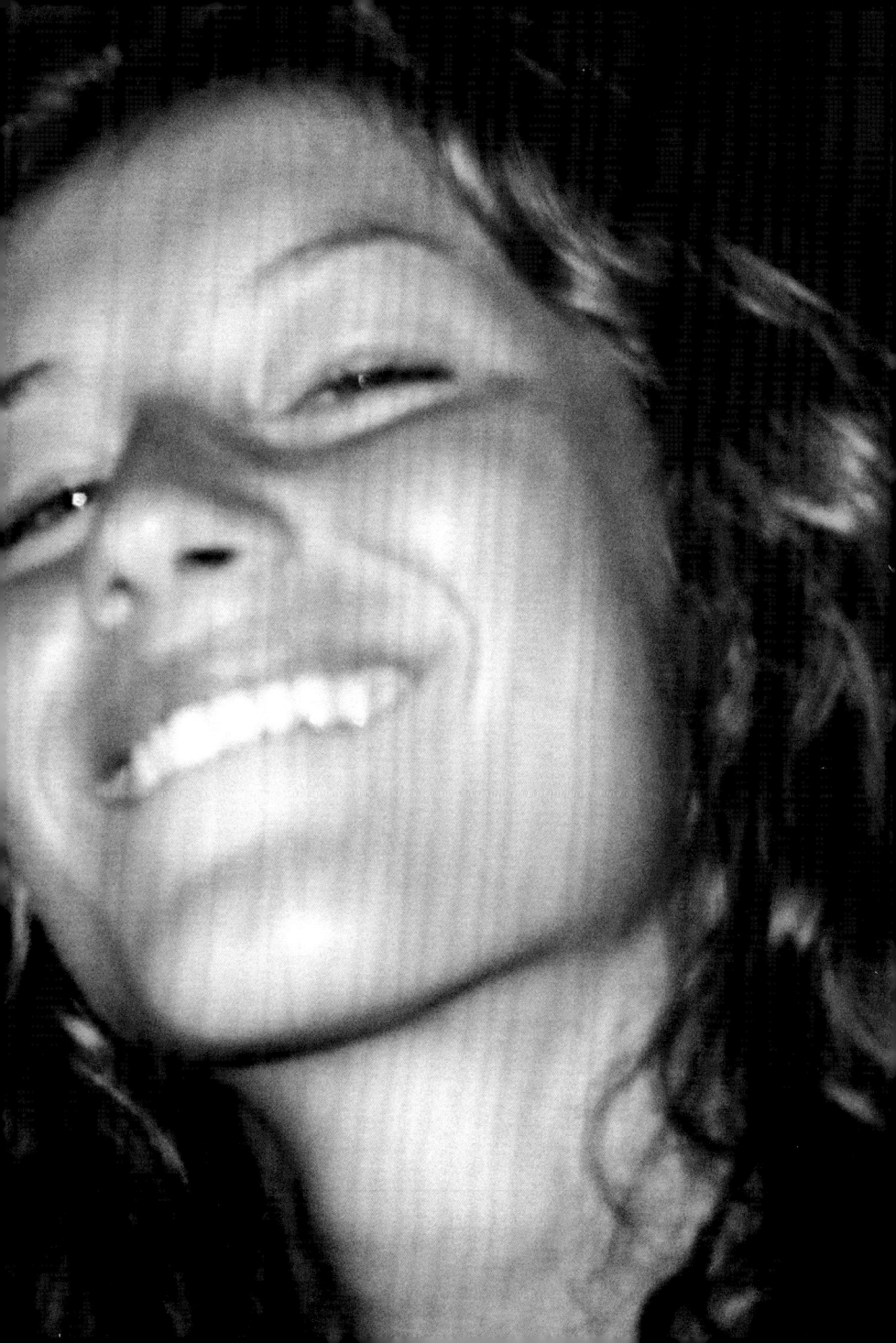

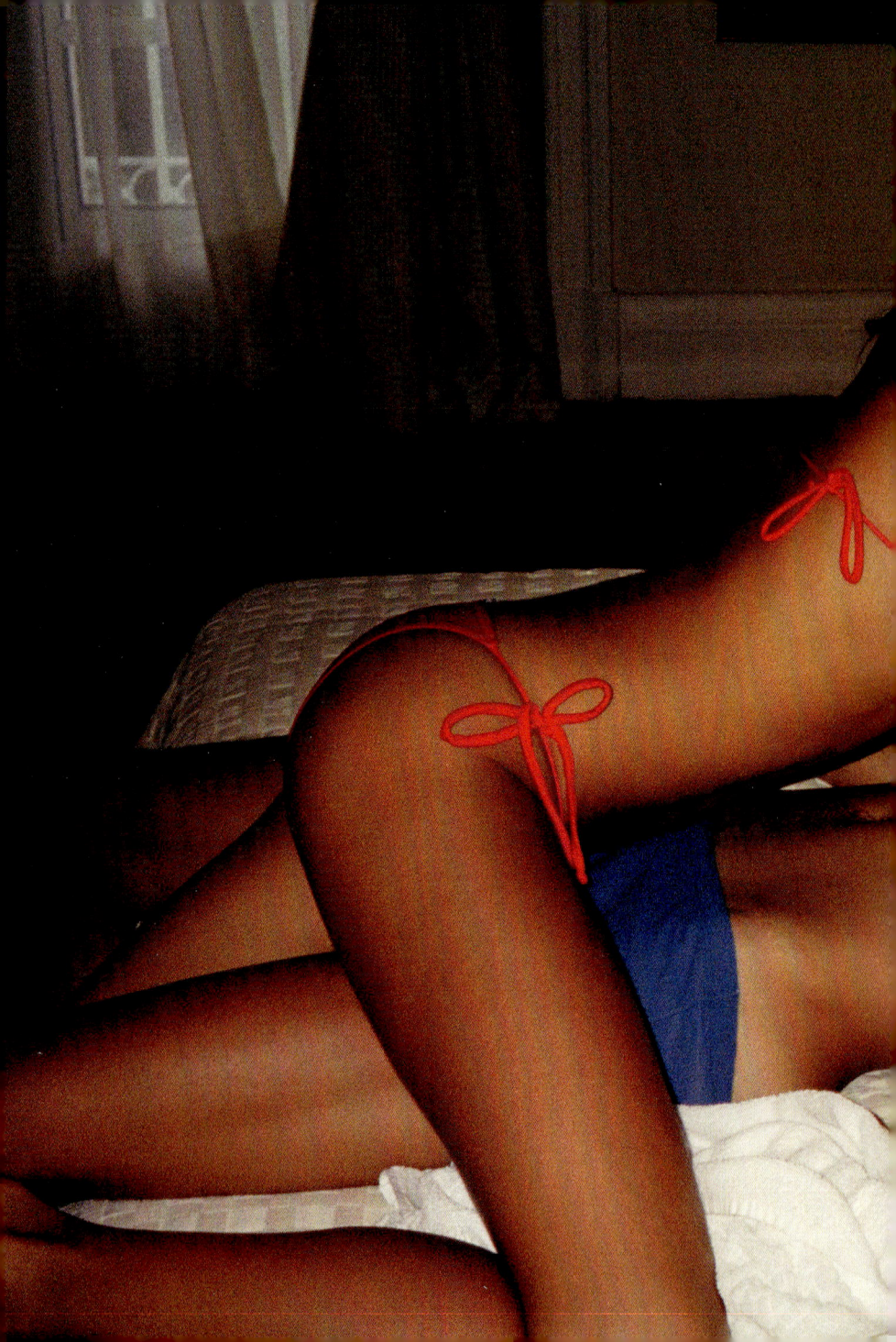

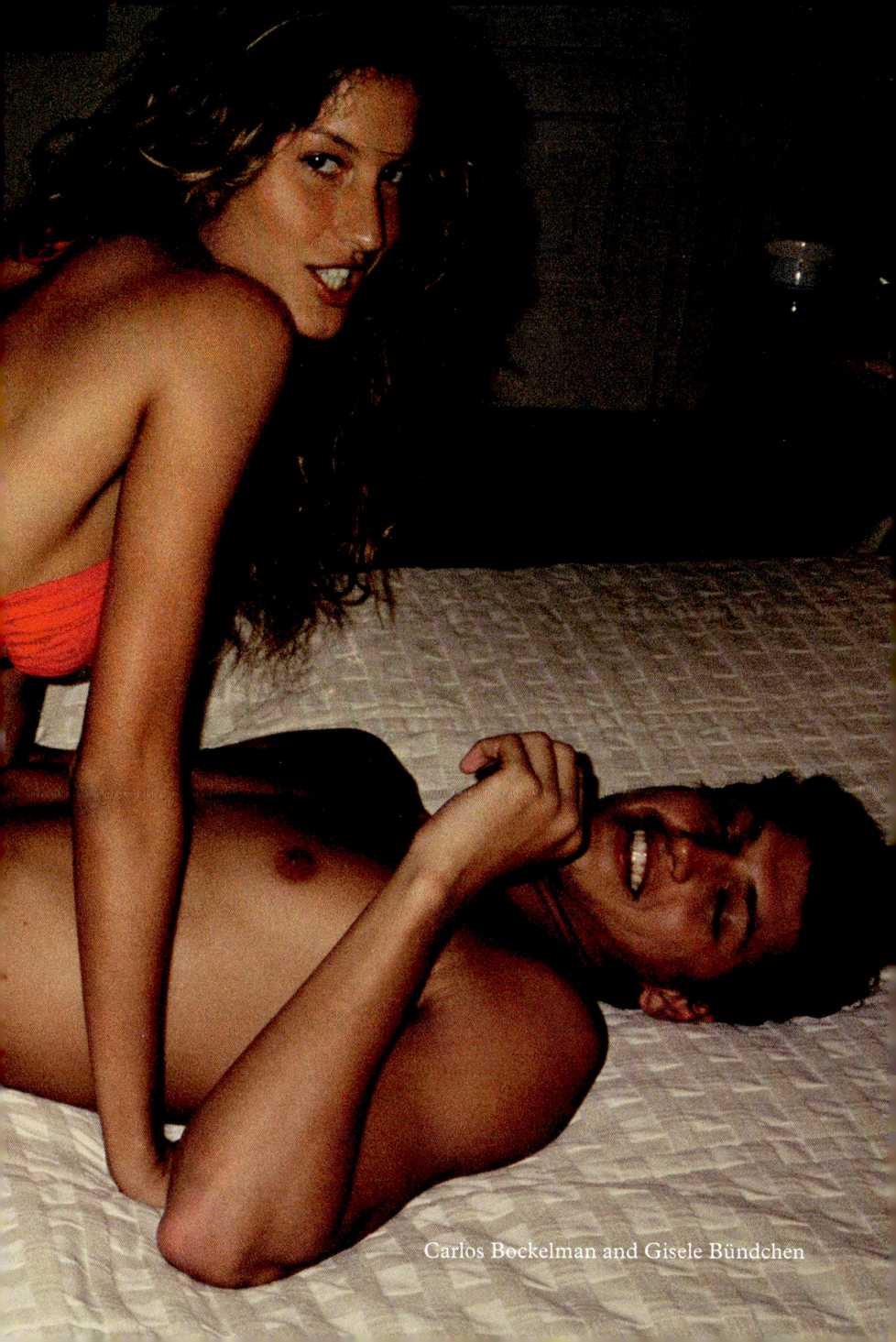

Carlos Bockelman and Gisele Bündchen

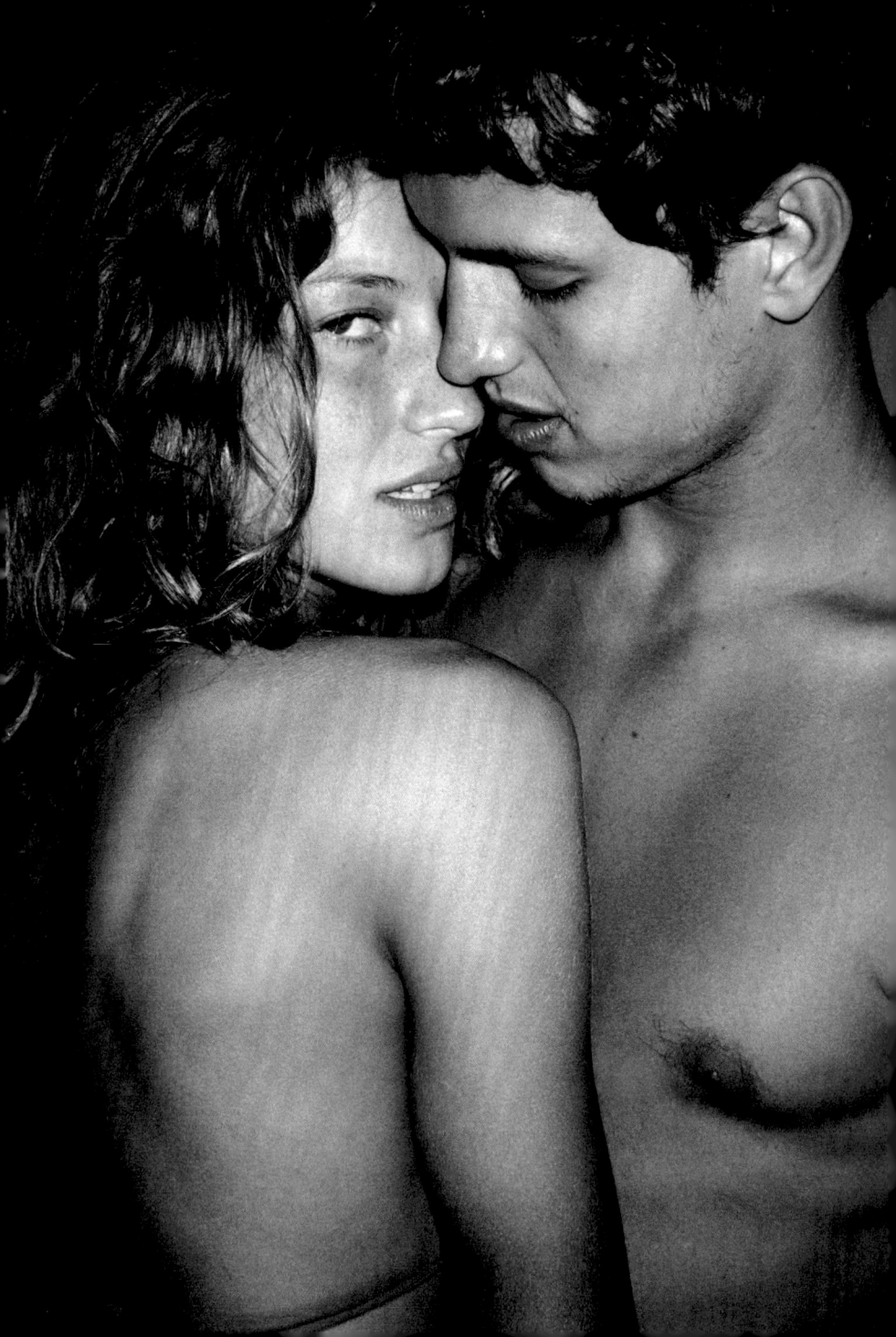

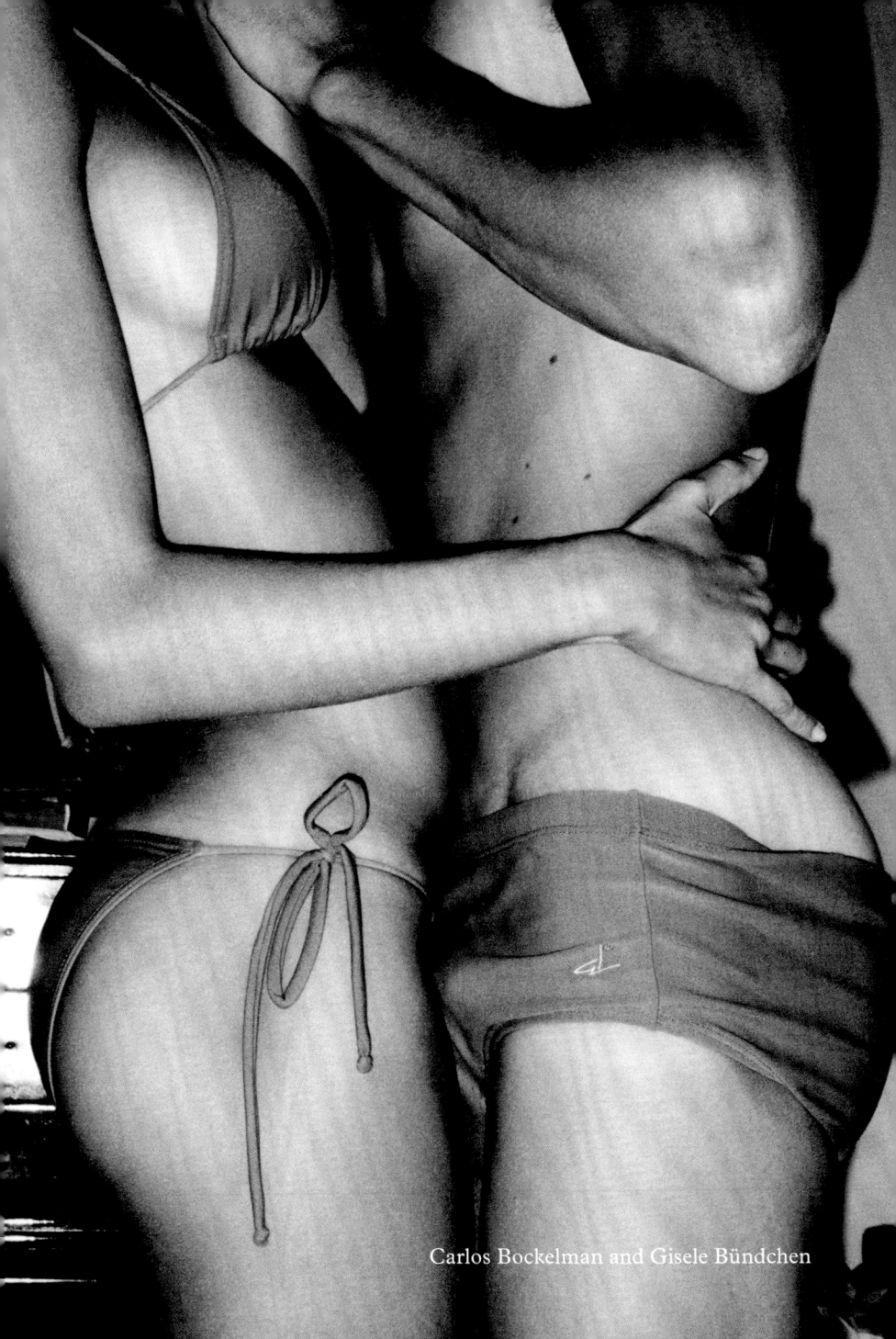

Carlos Bockelman and Gisele Bündchen

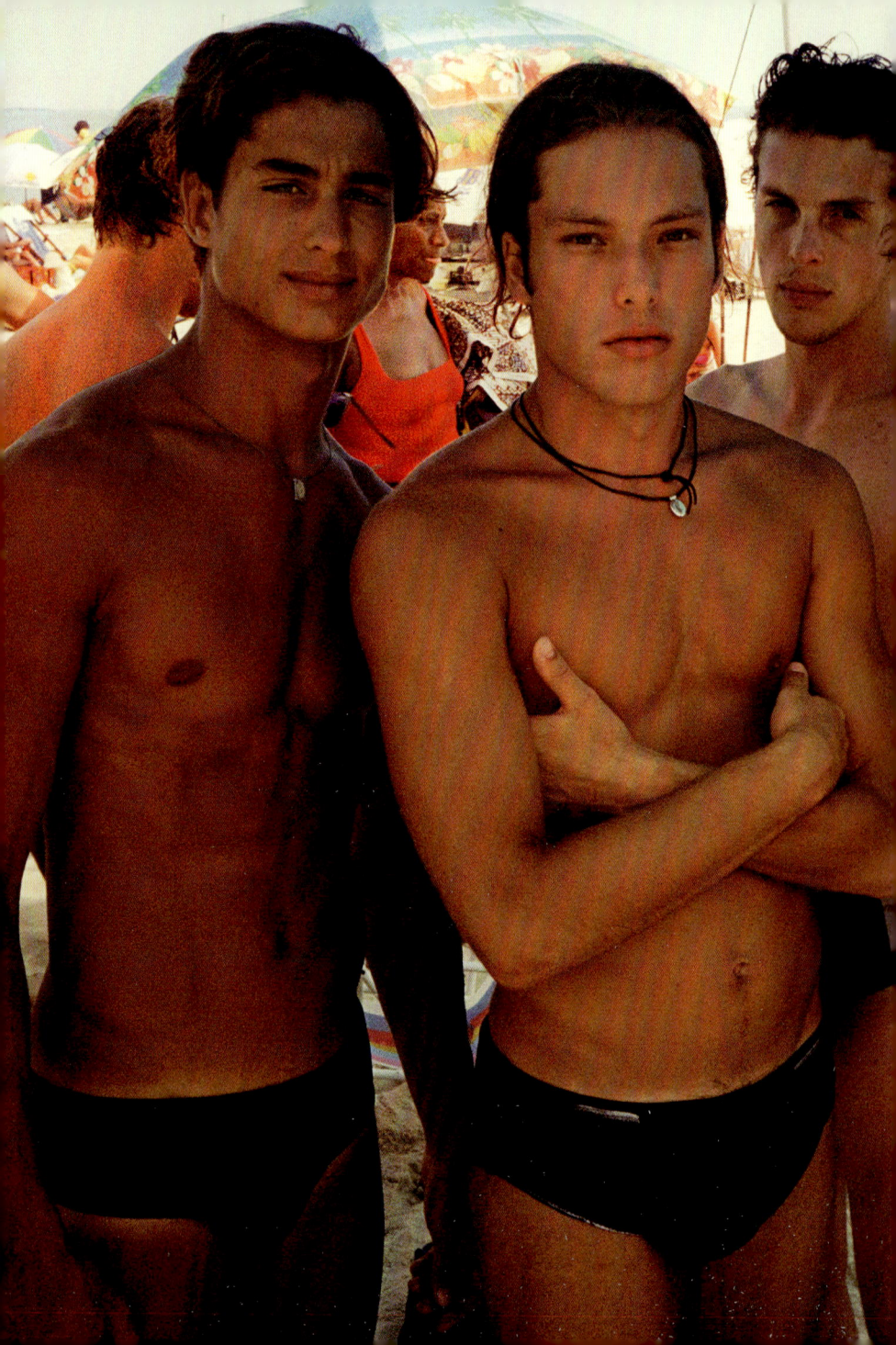

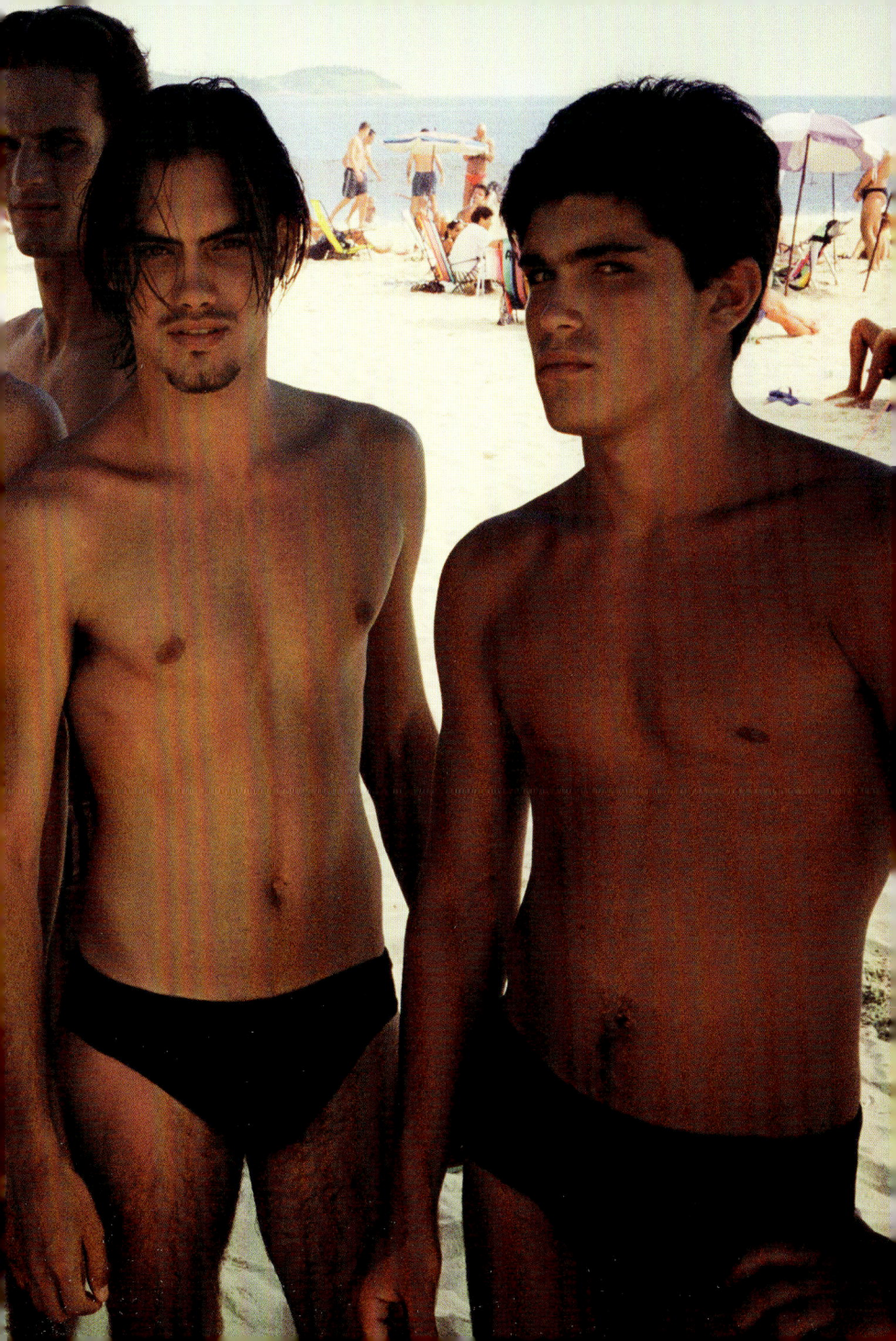

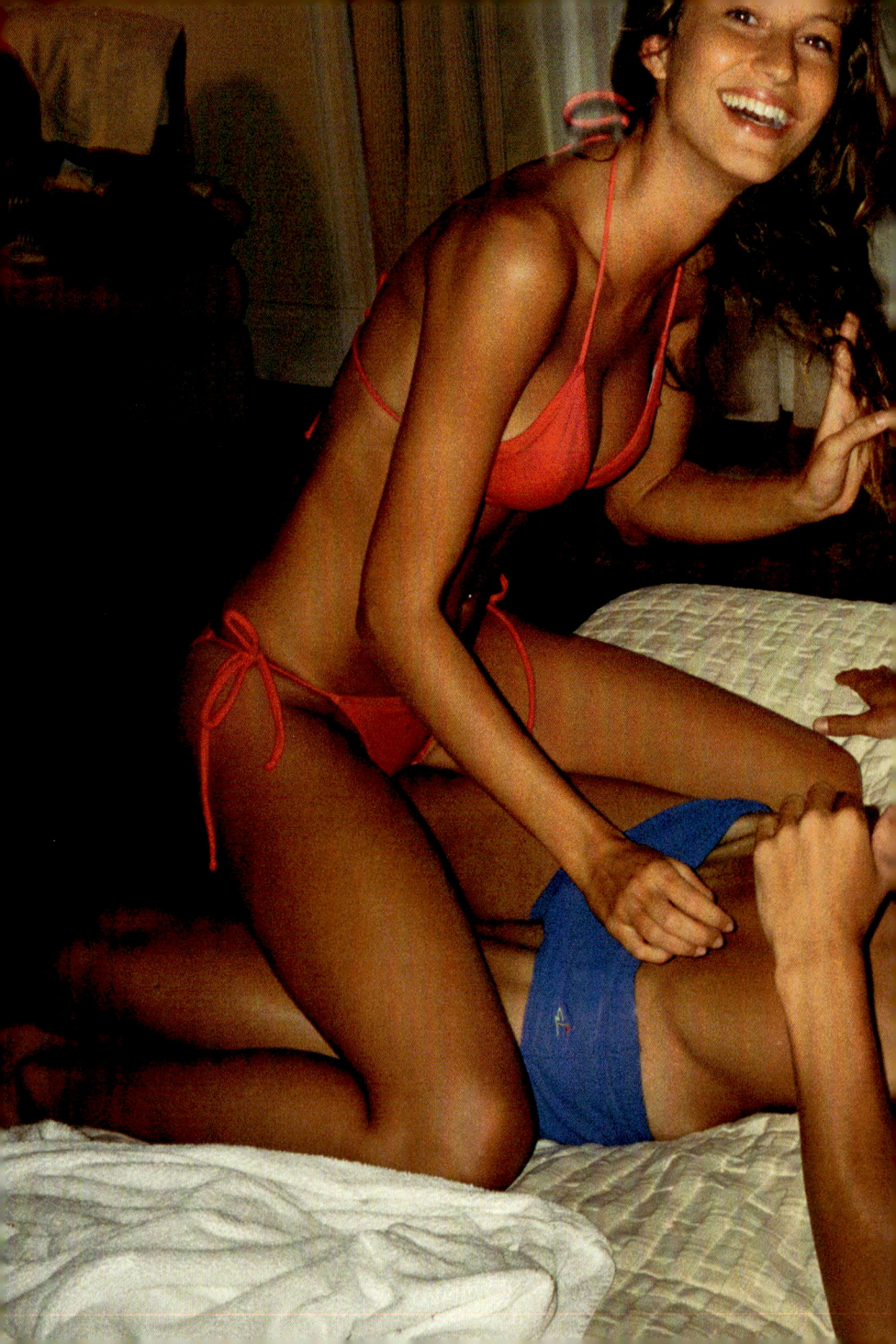

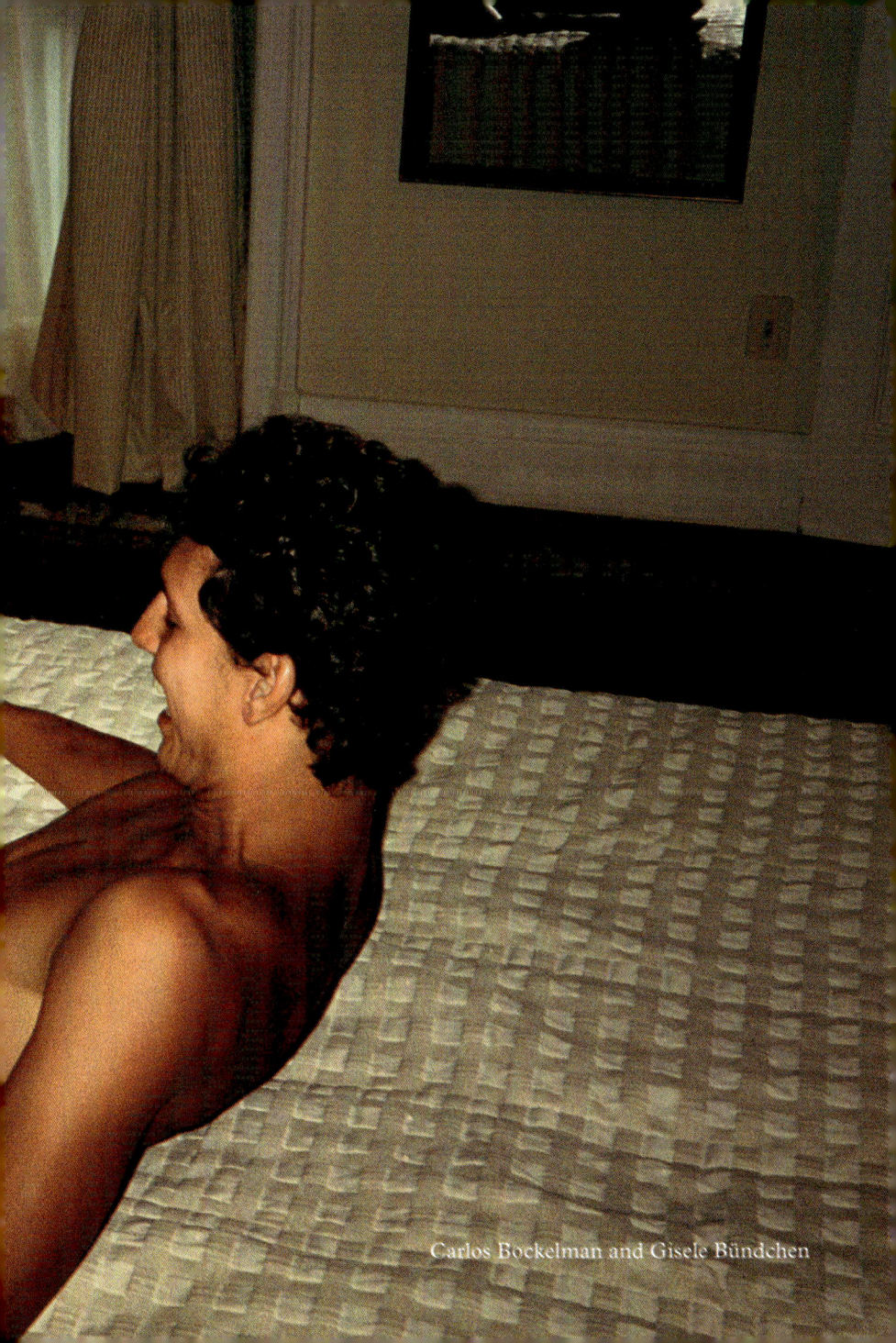

Carlos Bockelman and Gisele Bündchen

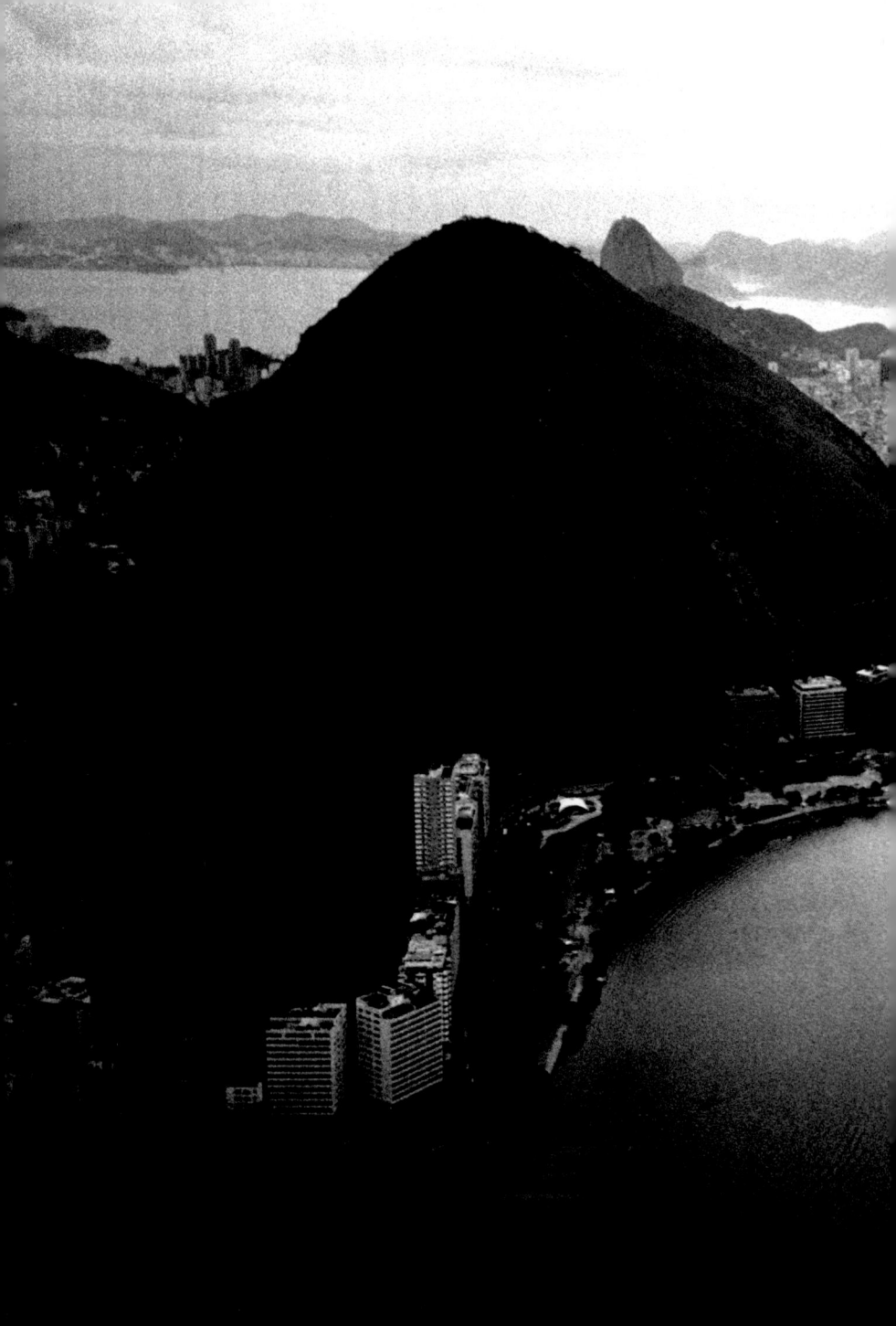

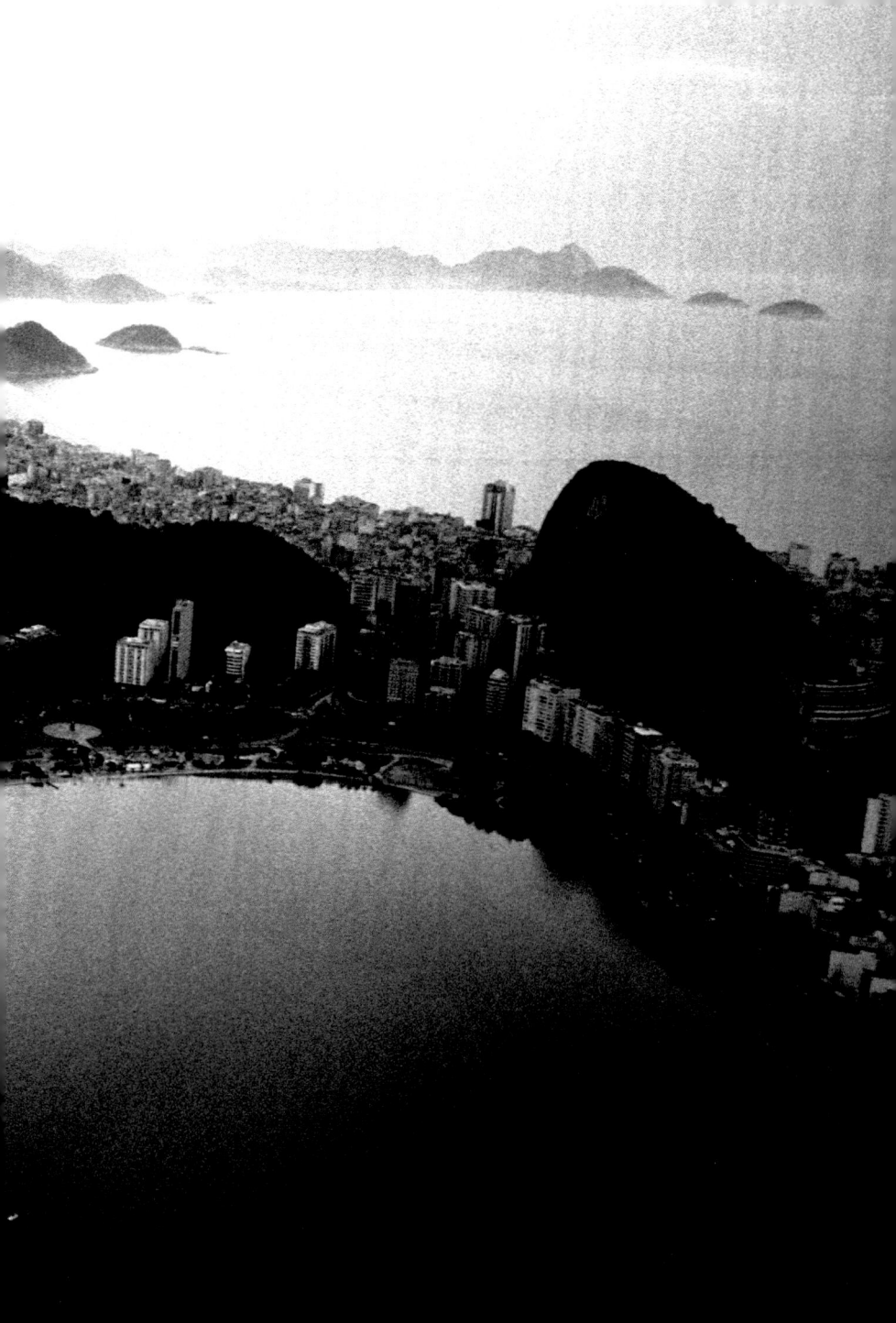

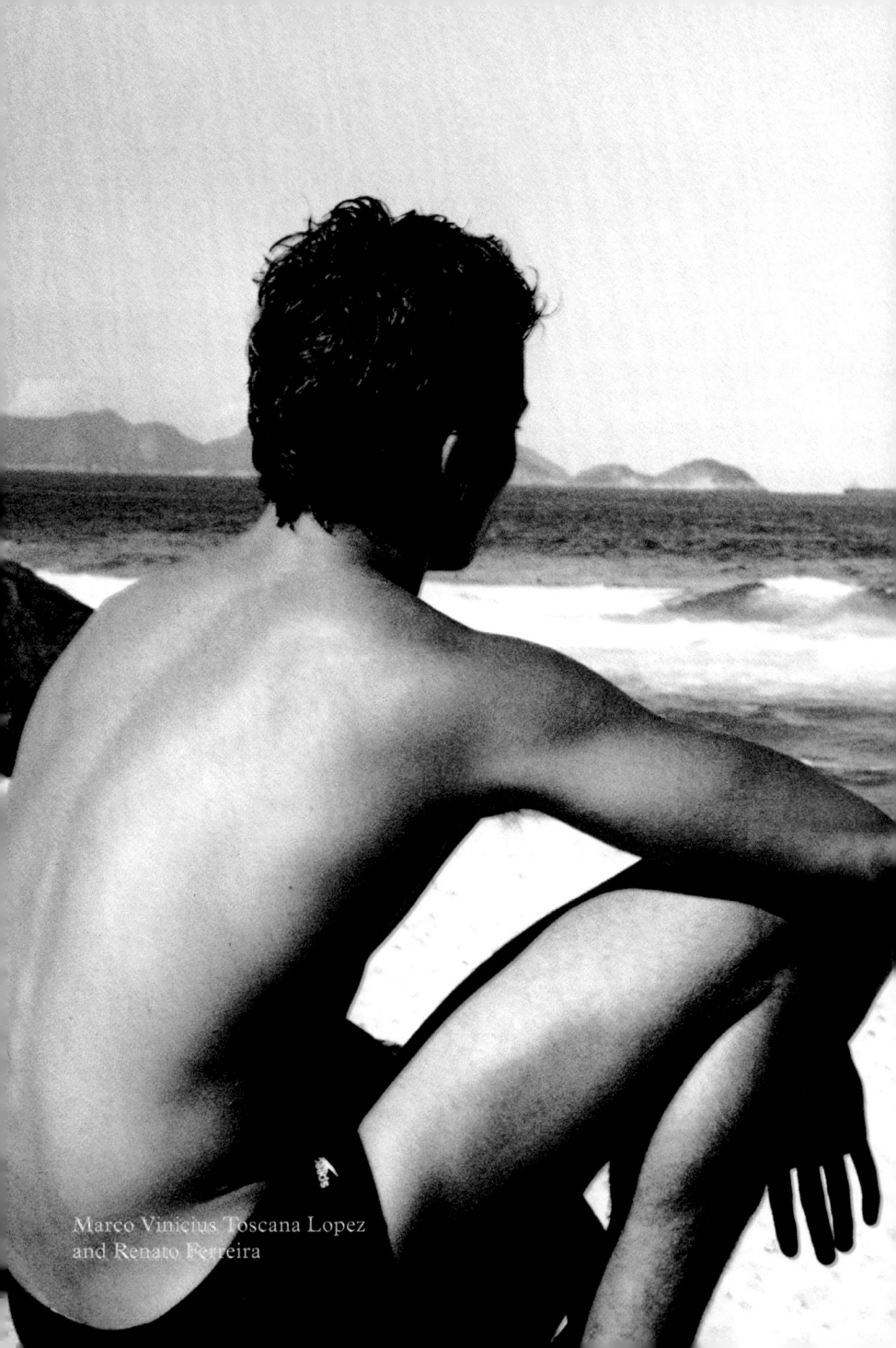

Marco Vinicius Toscana Lopez
and Renato Ferreira

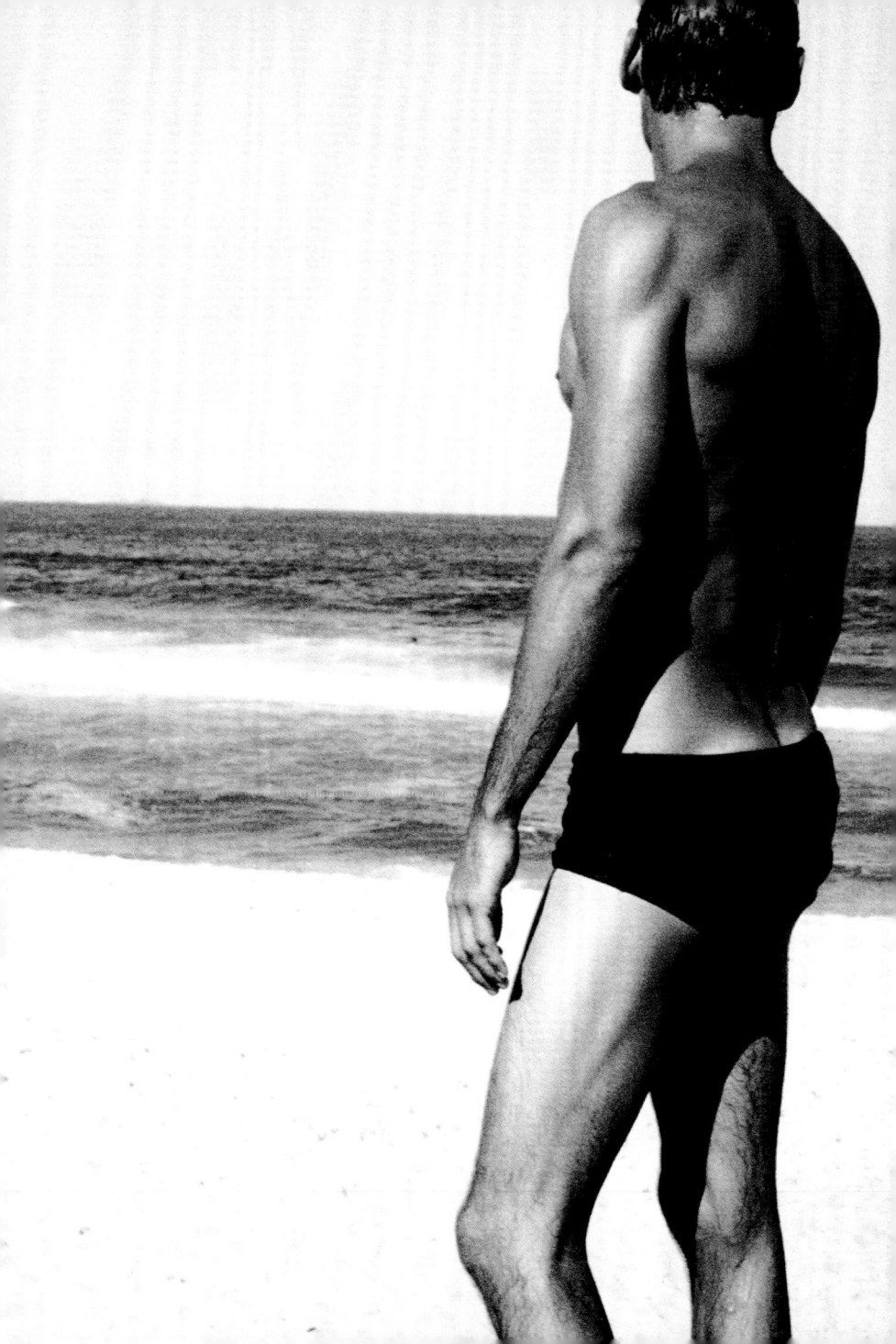

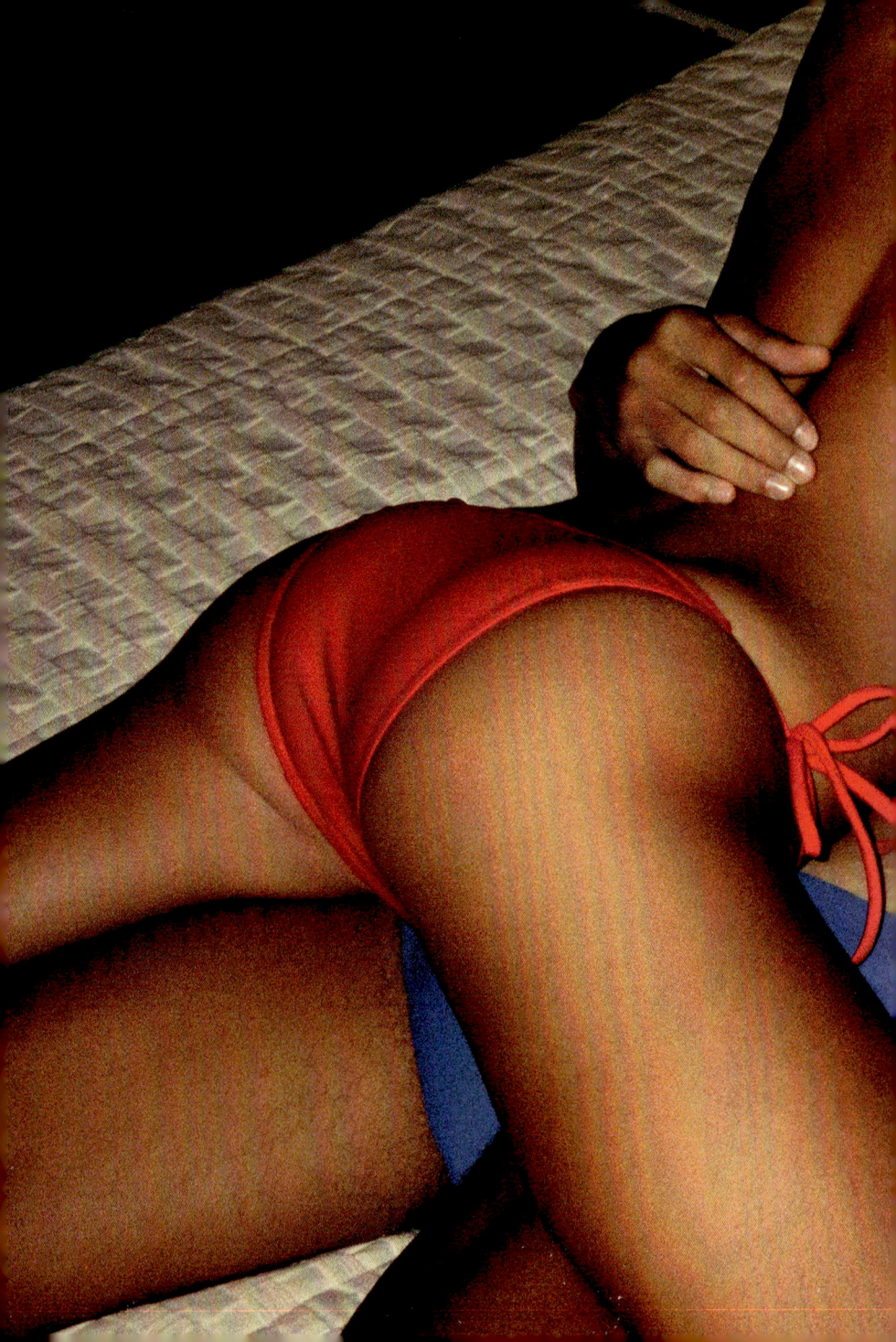

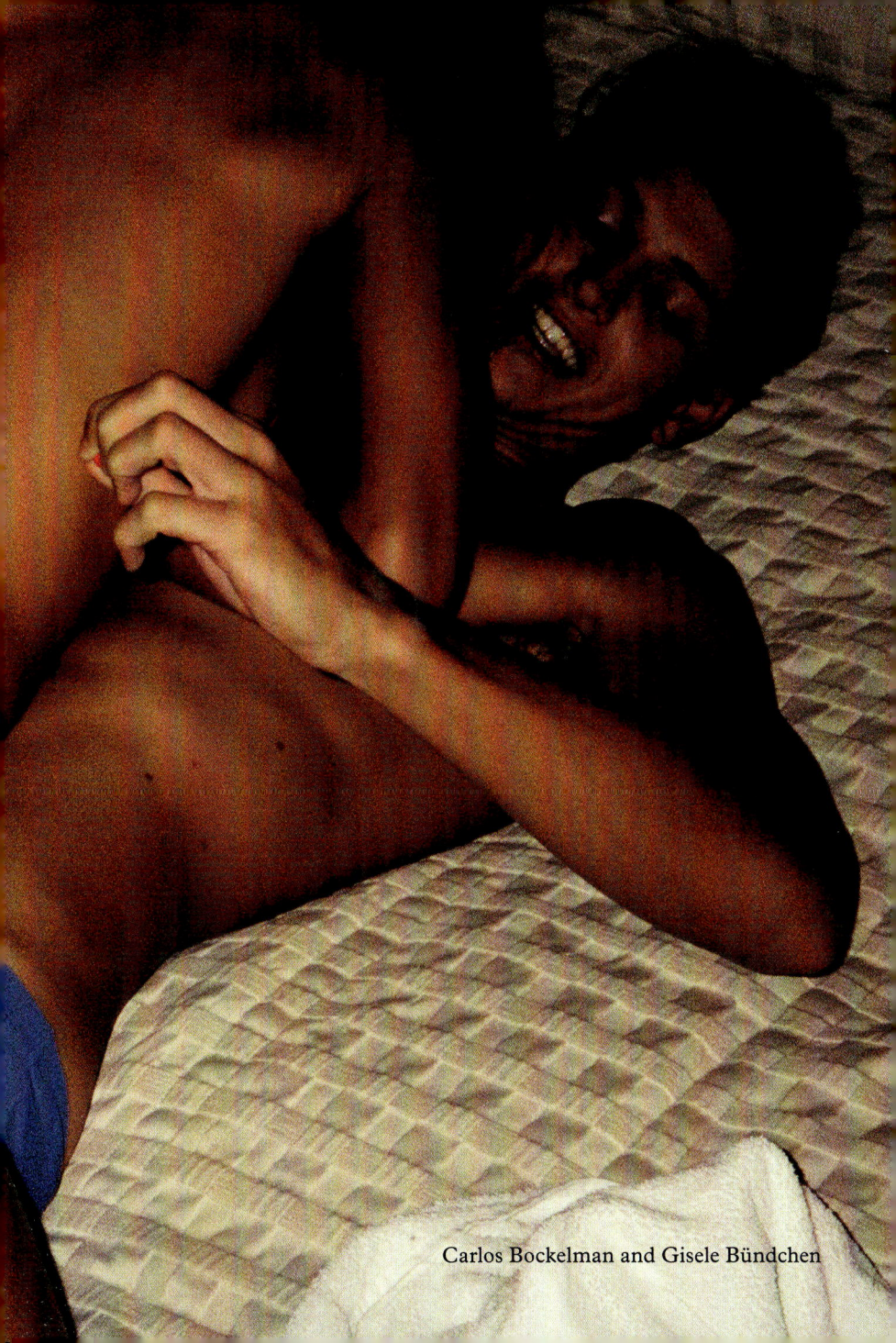

Carlos Bockelman and Gisele Bündchen

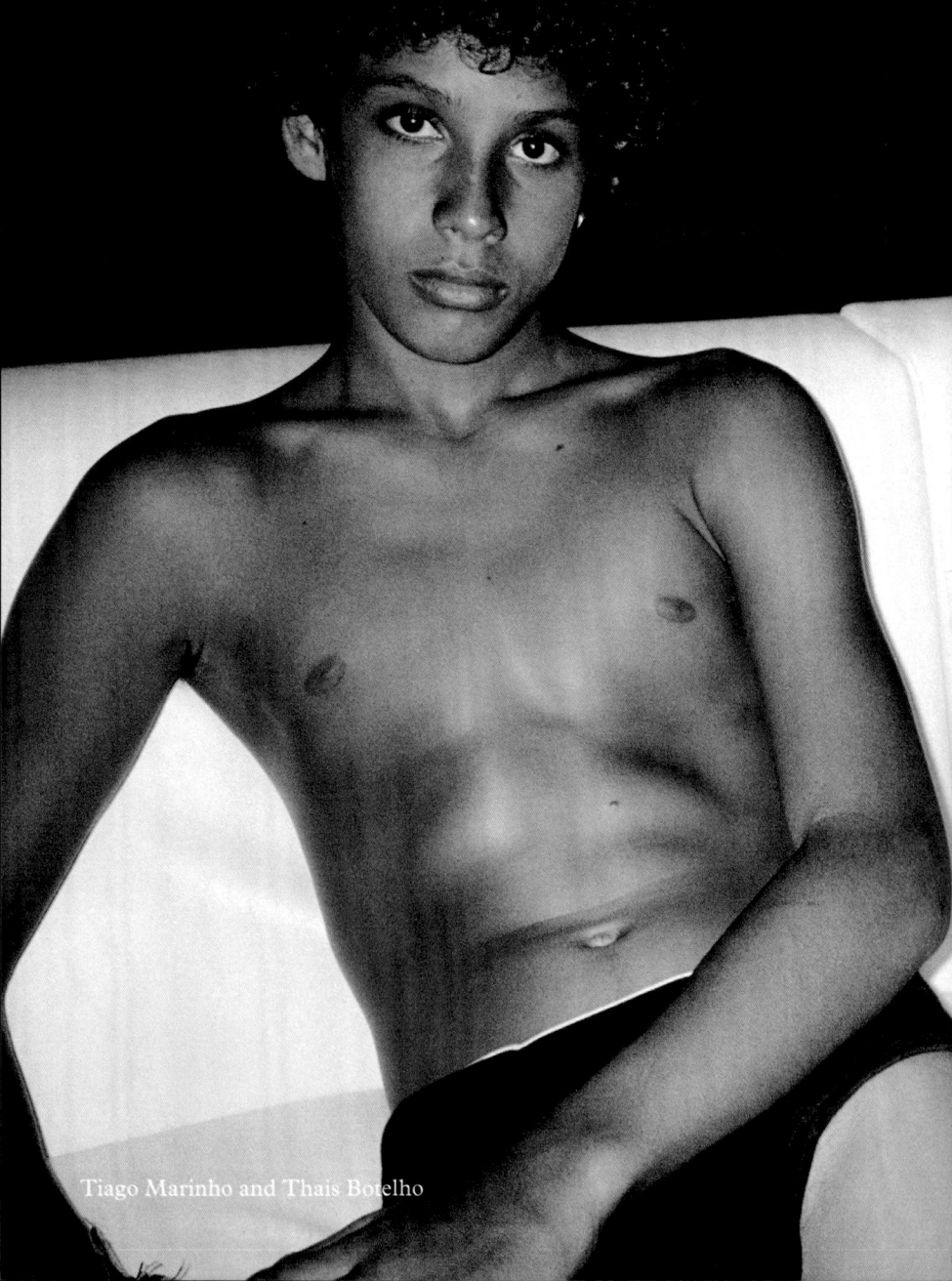

Tiago Marinho and Thais Botelho

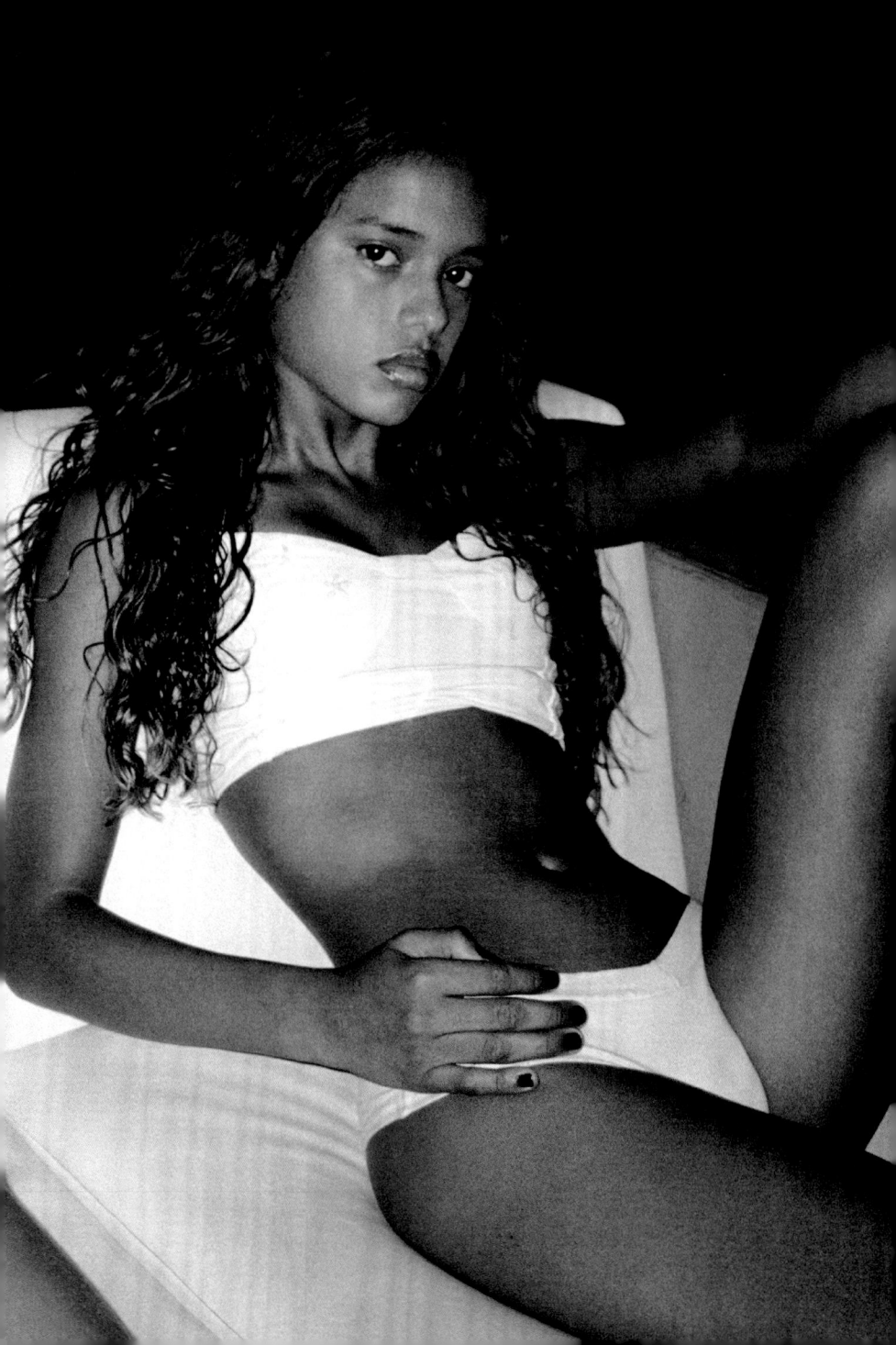

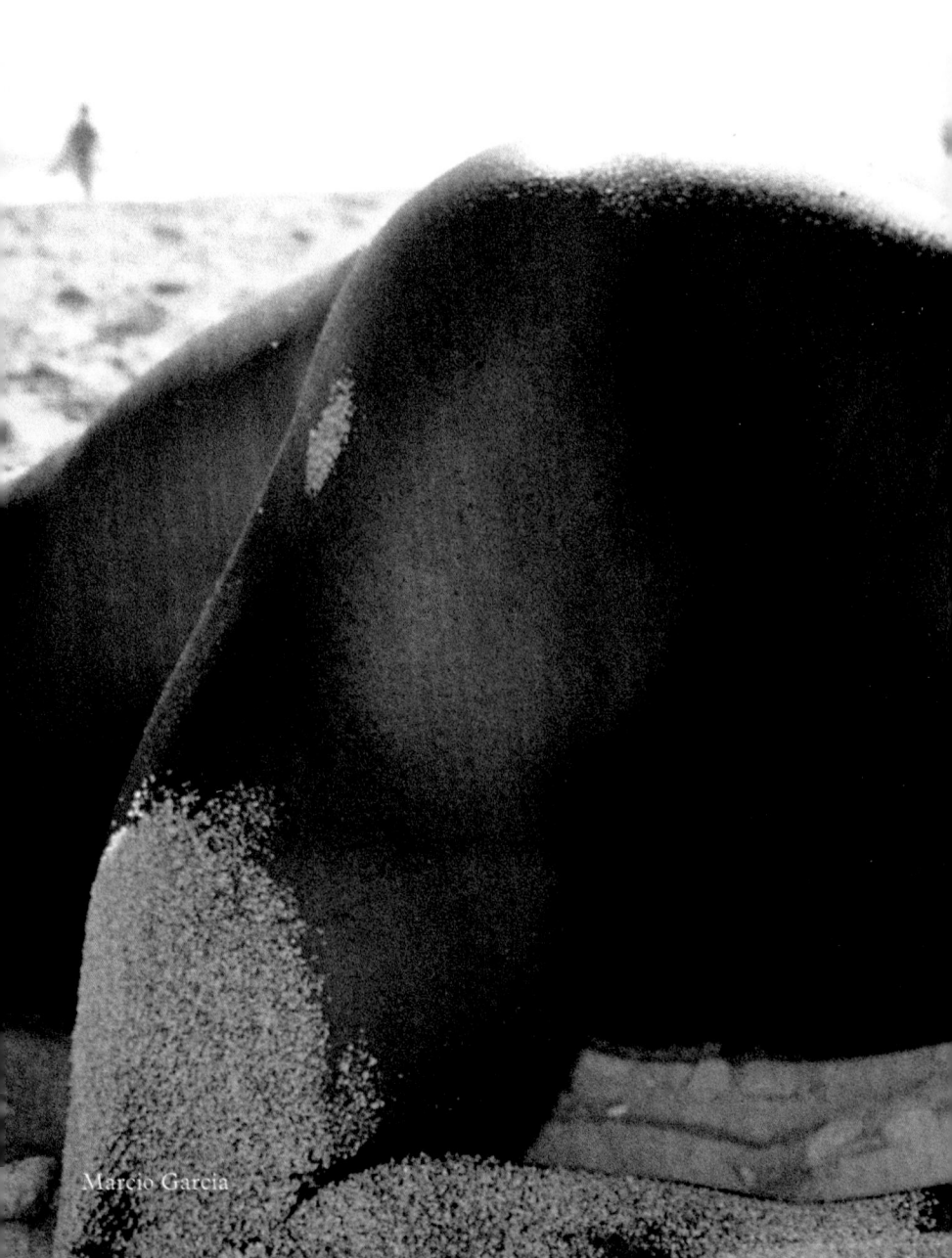

Marcio Garcia

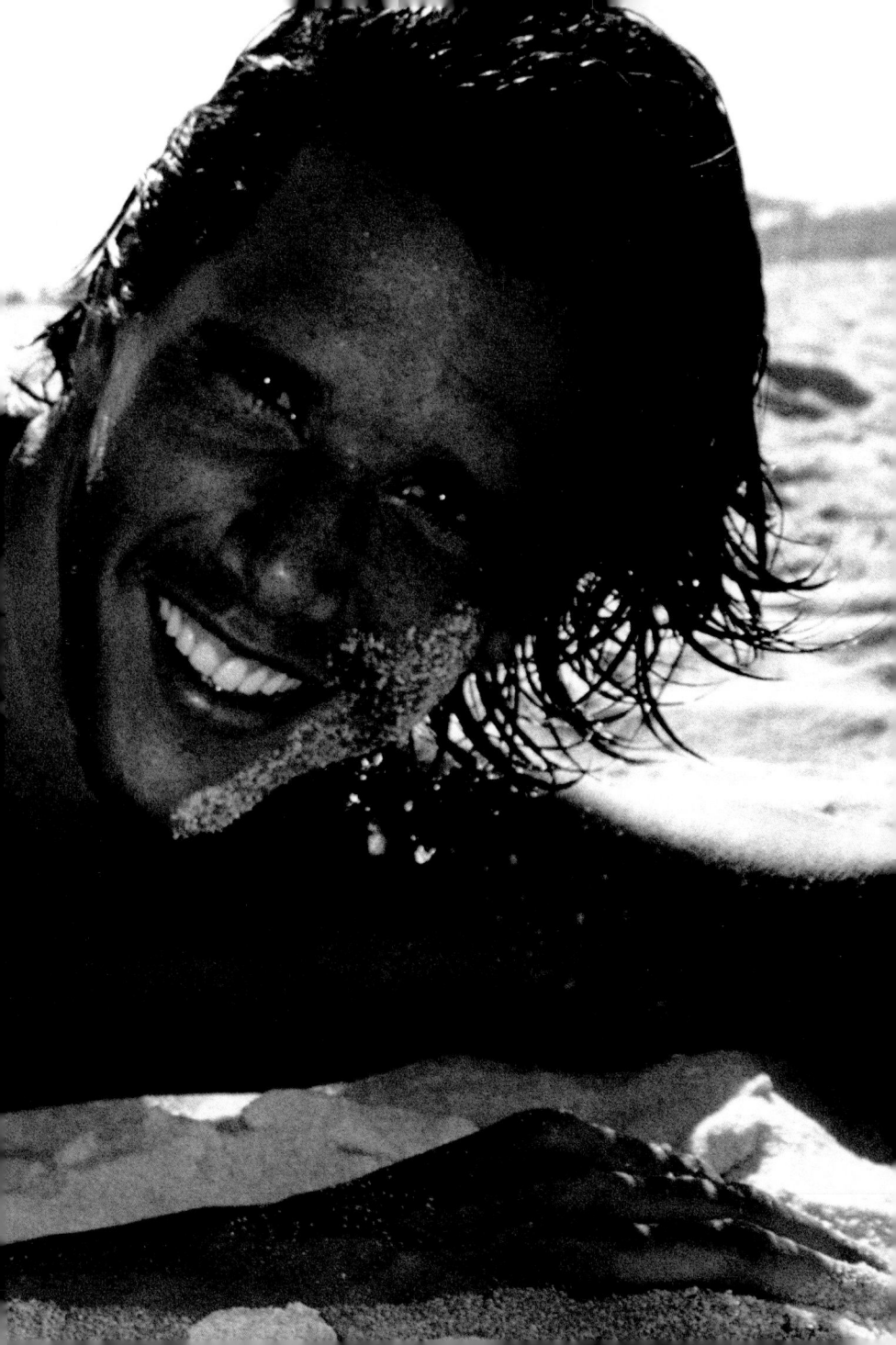

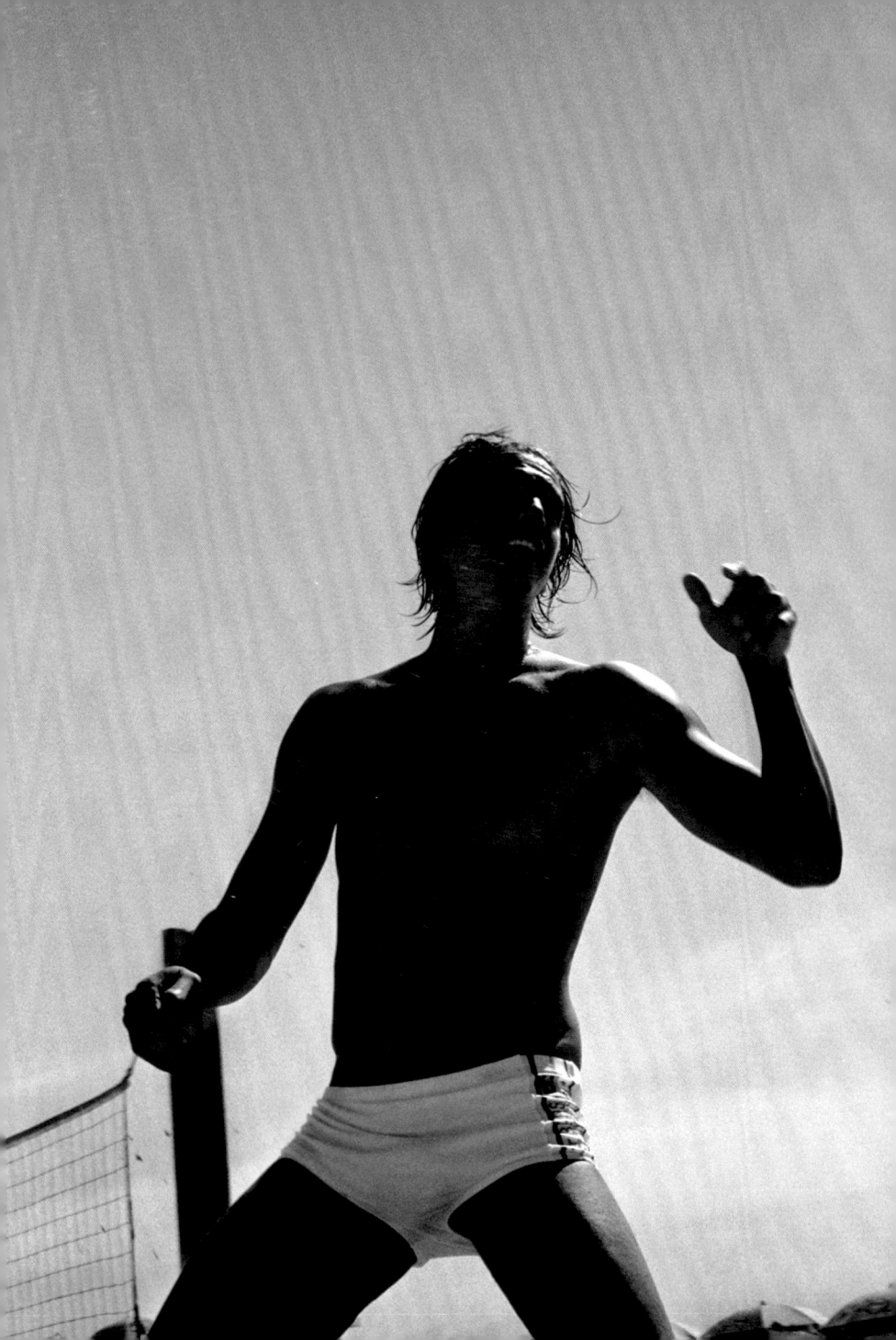

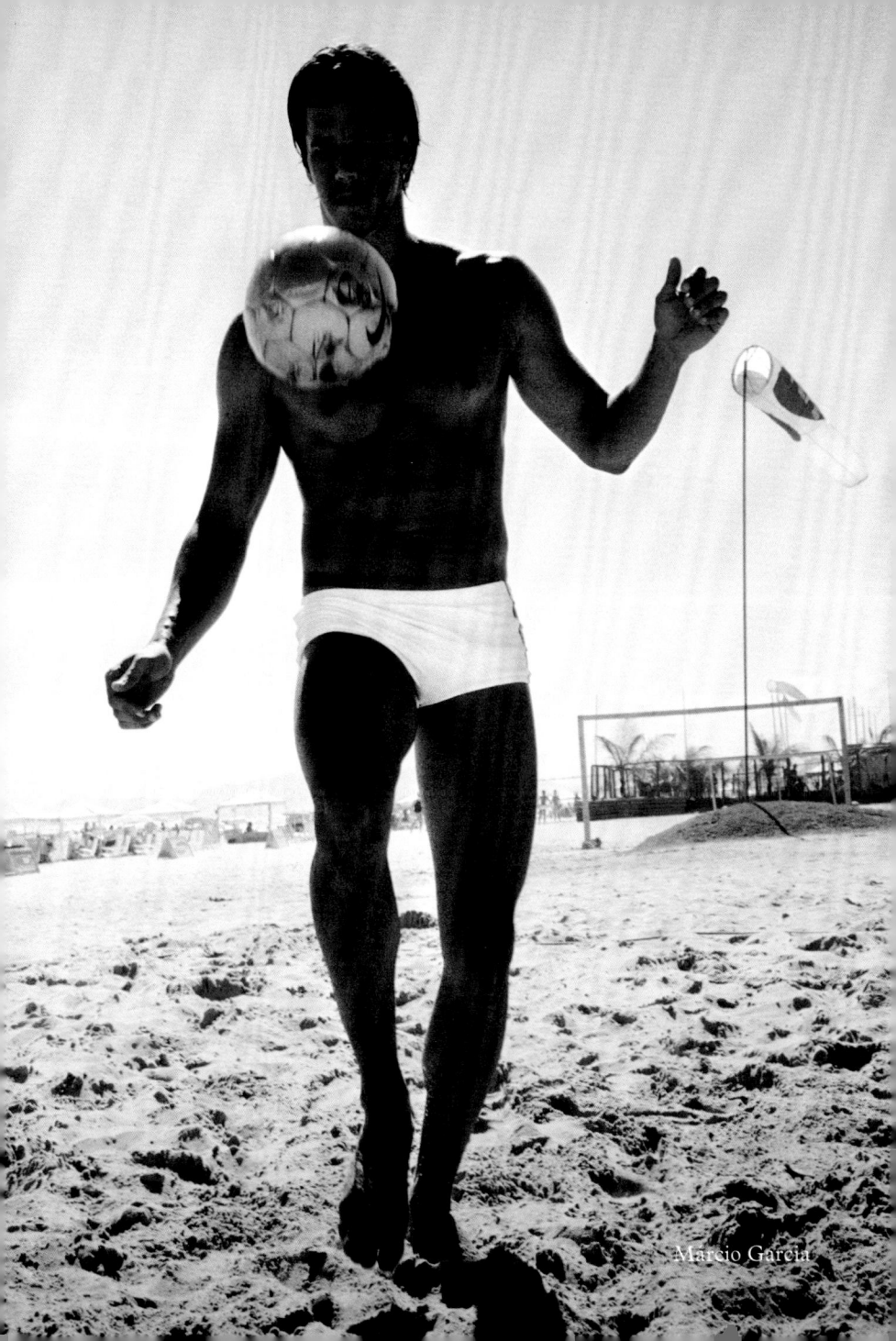

Marcio Garcia

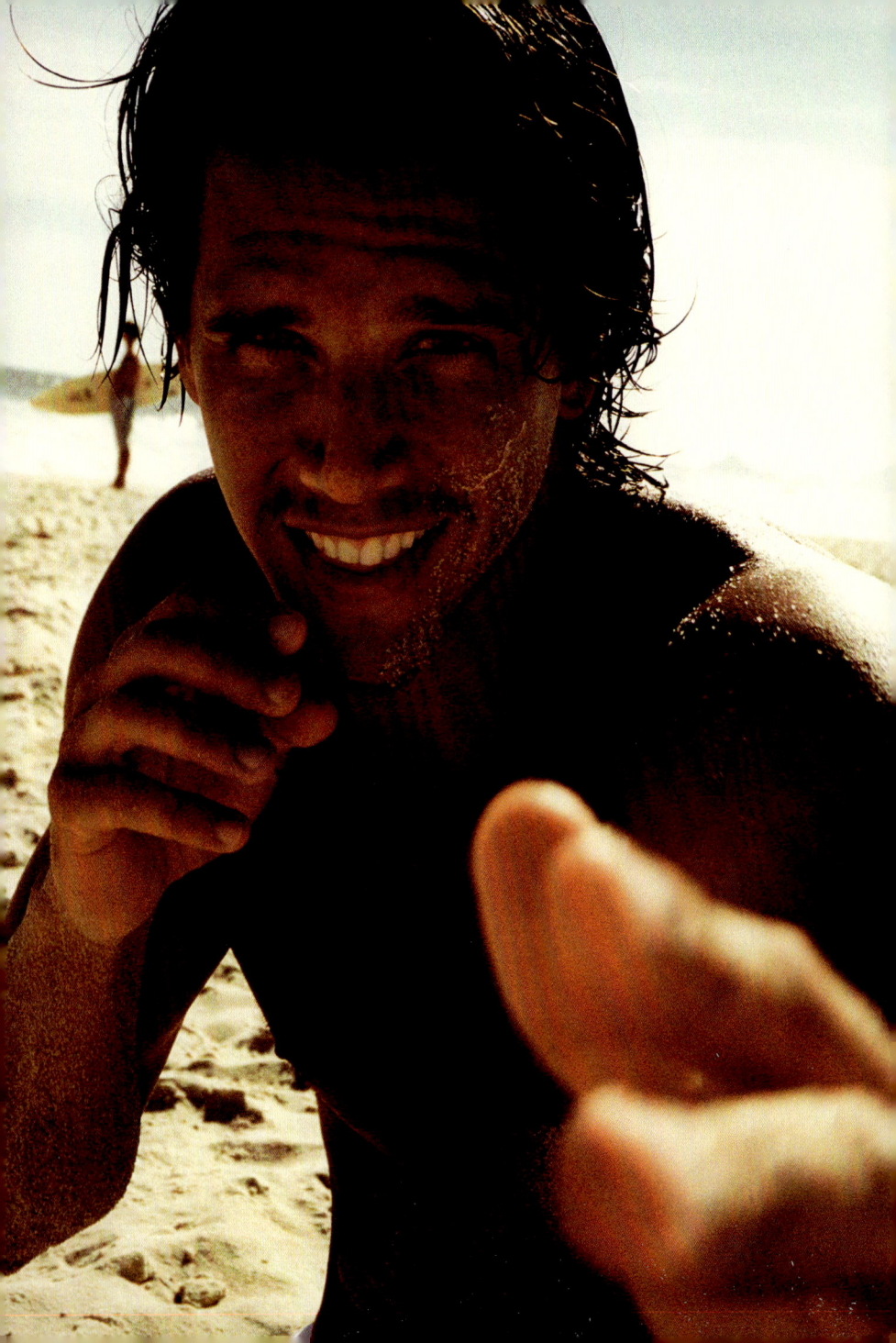

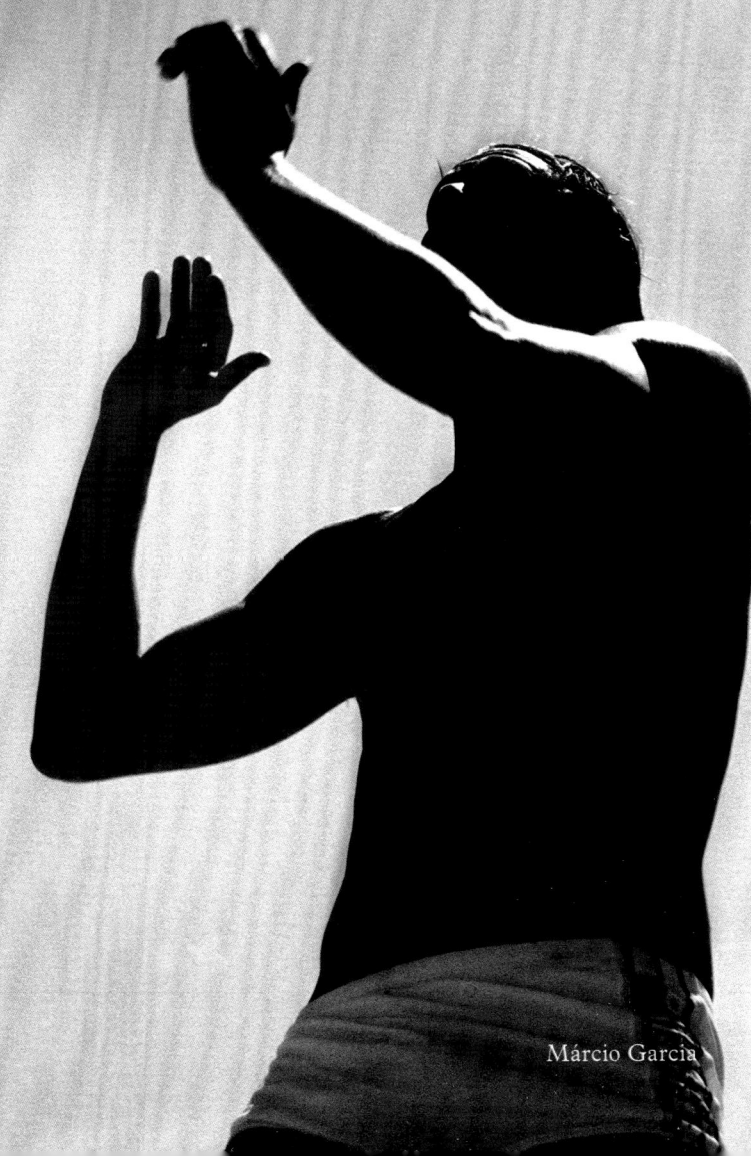

Márcio Garcia

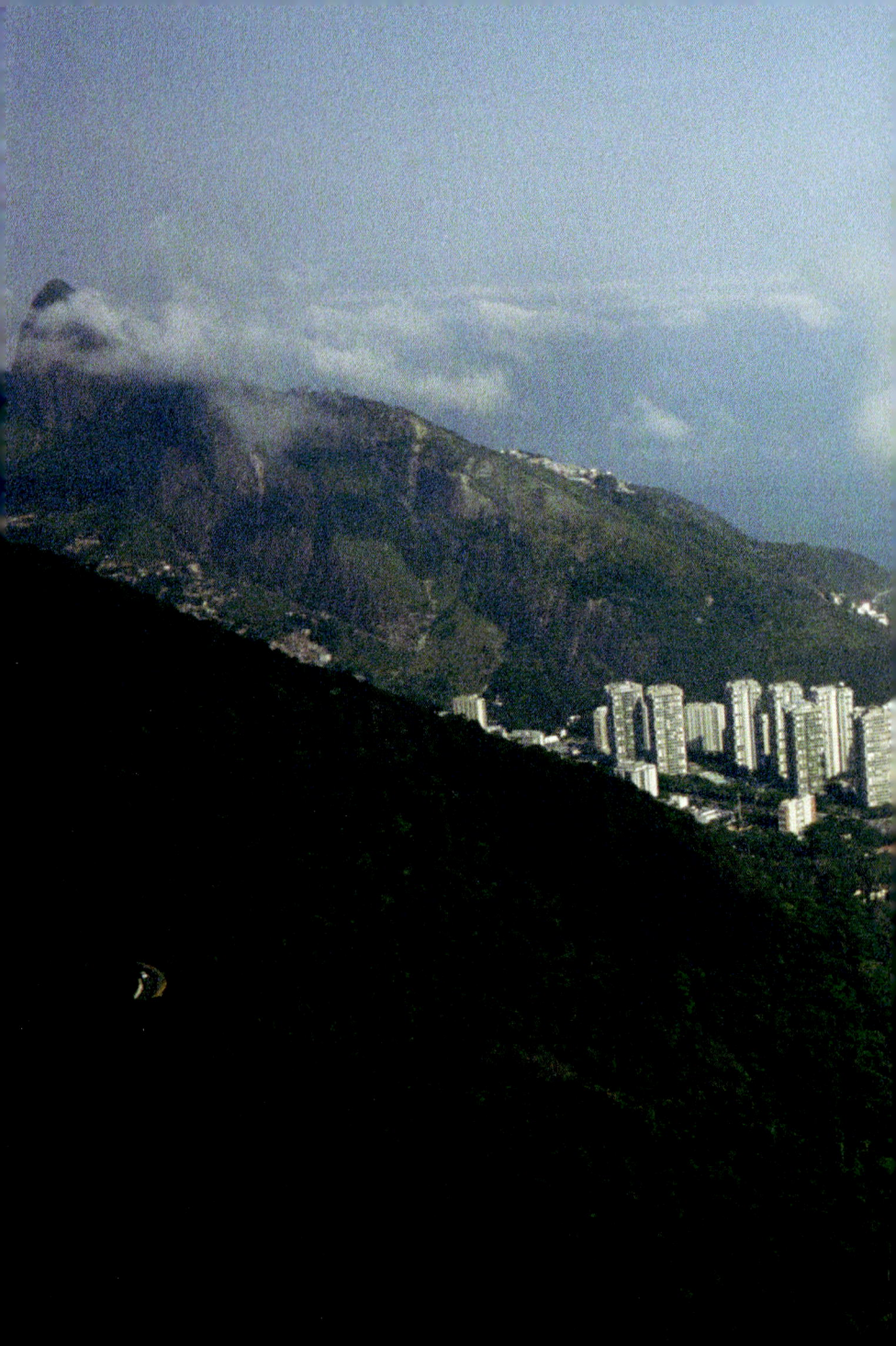

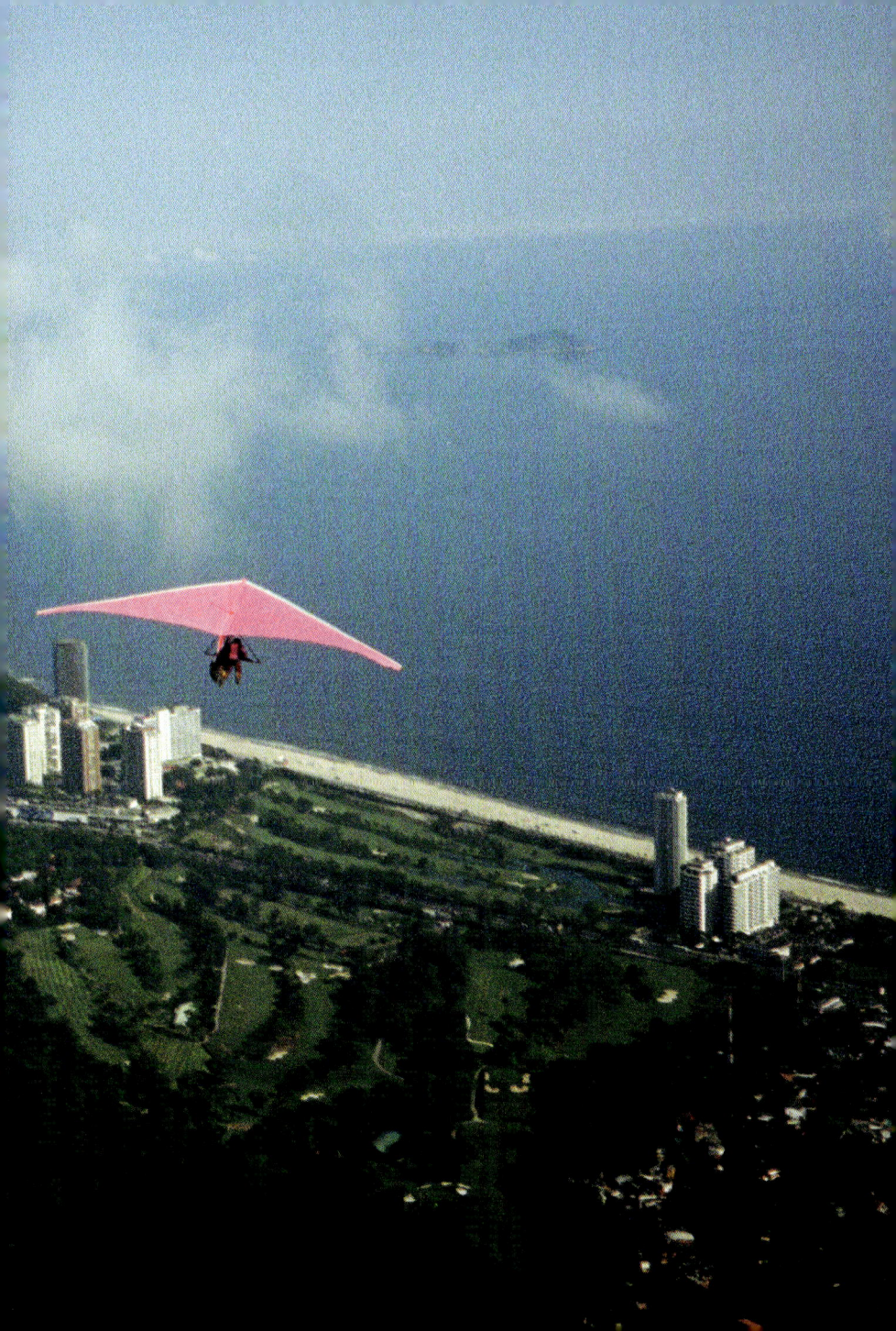

Márcio Garcia

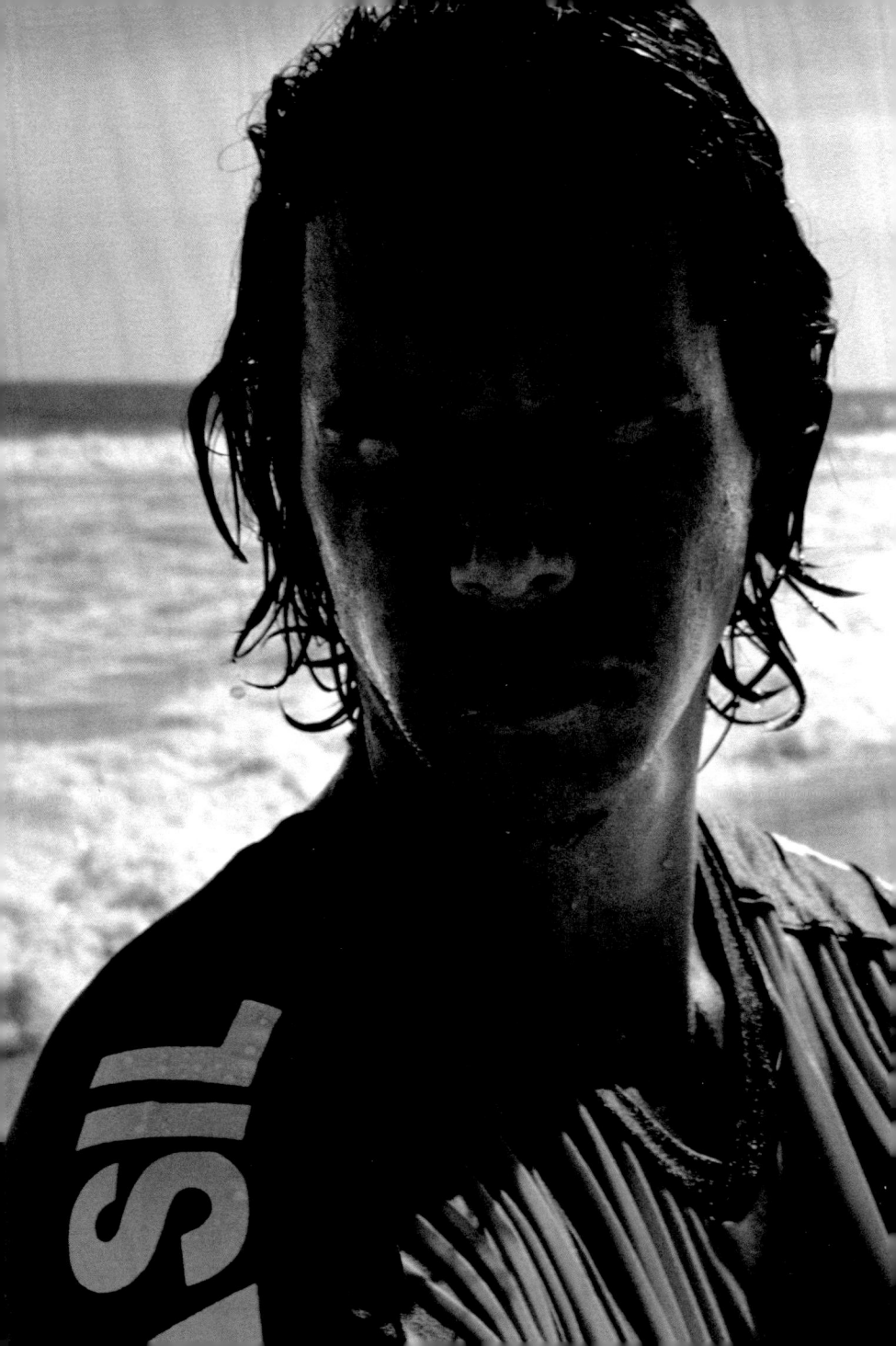

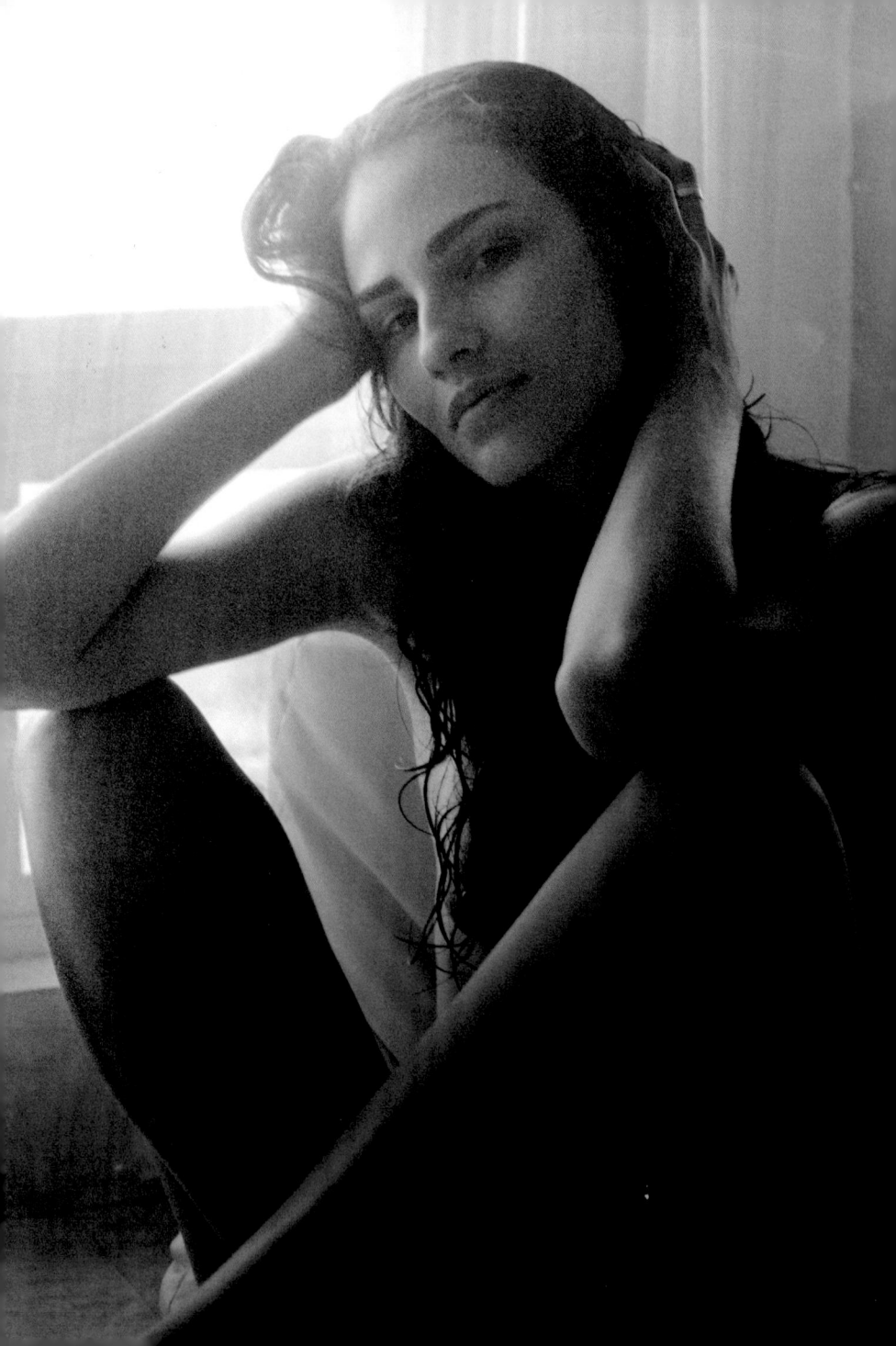

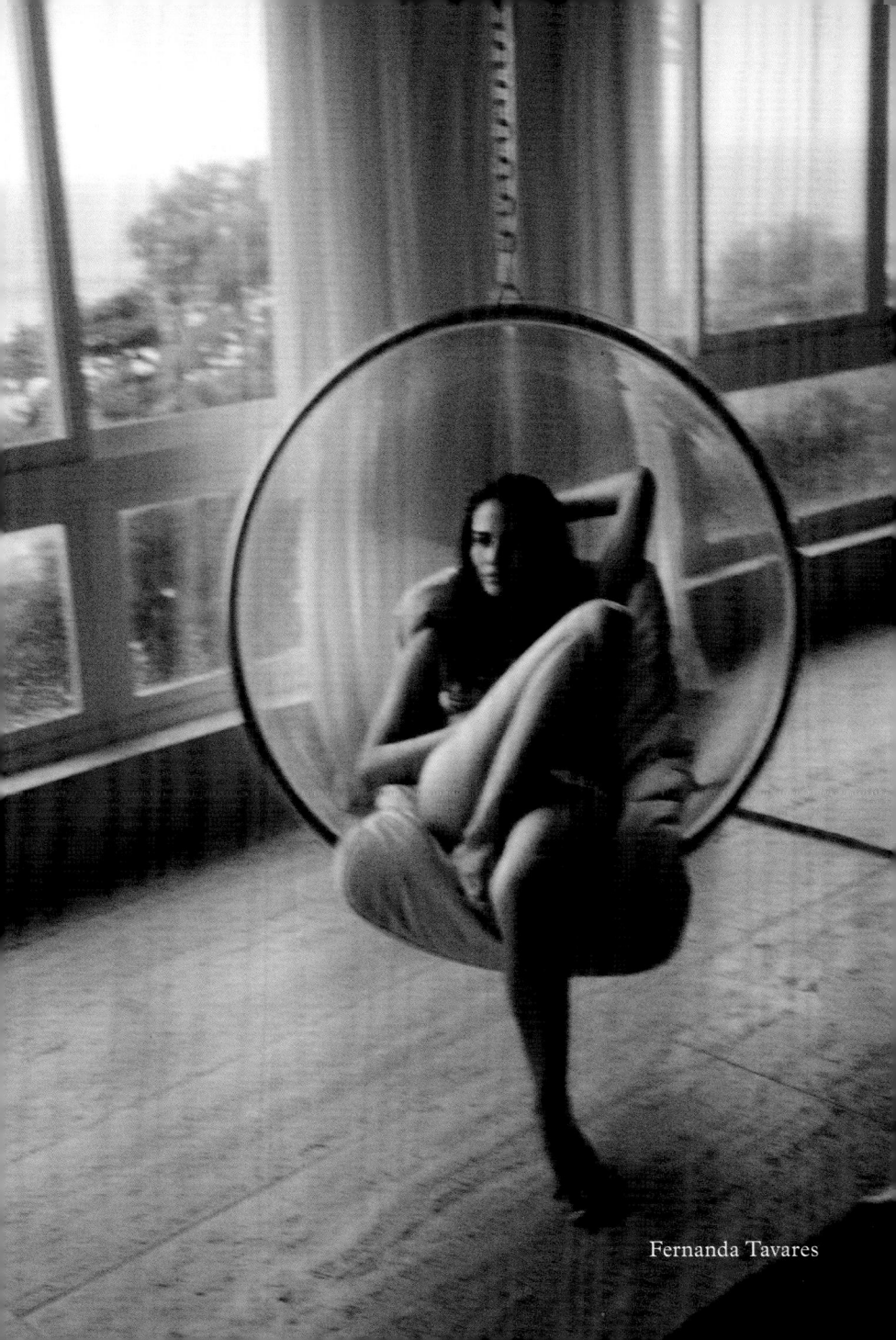

Fernanda Tavares

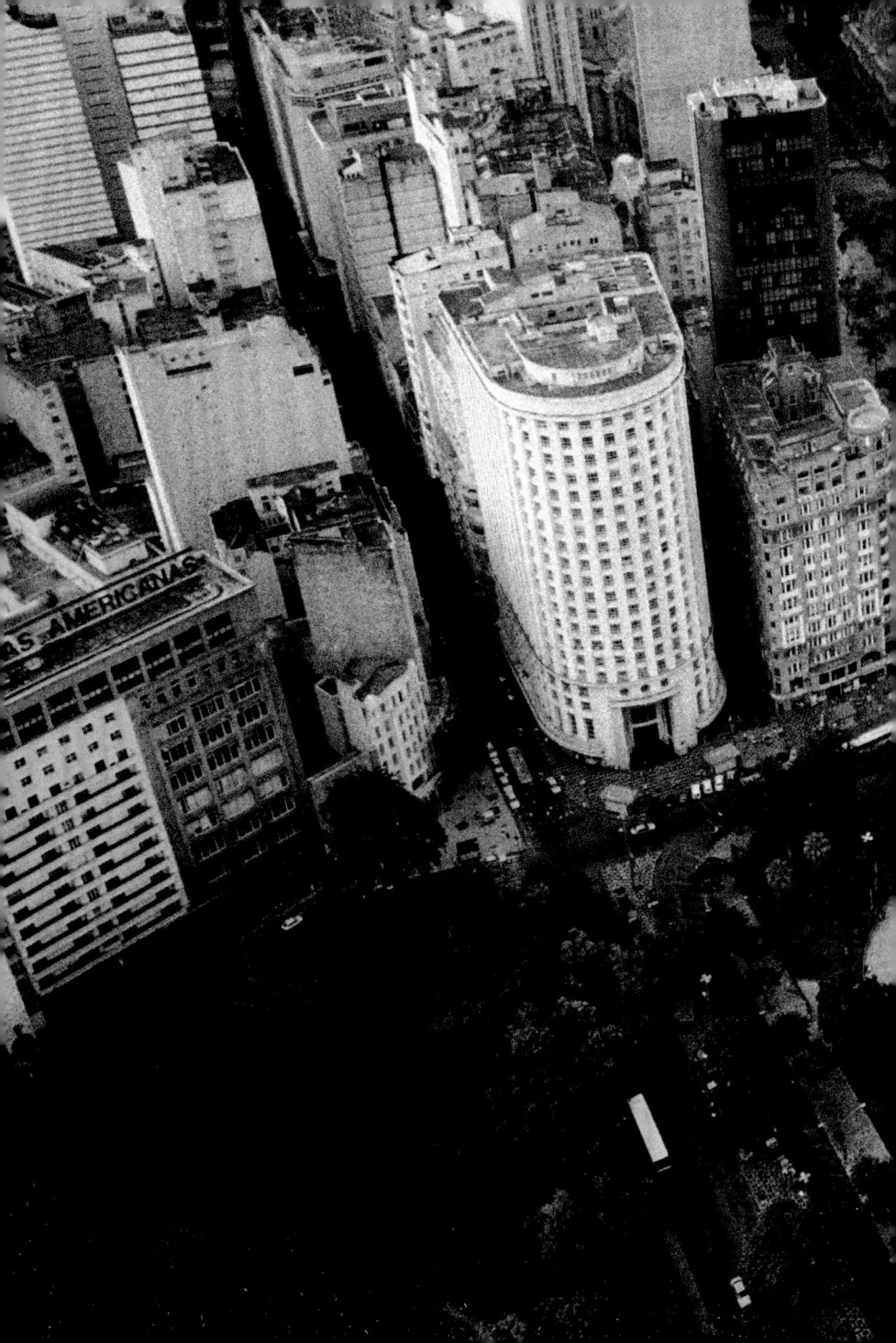

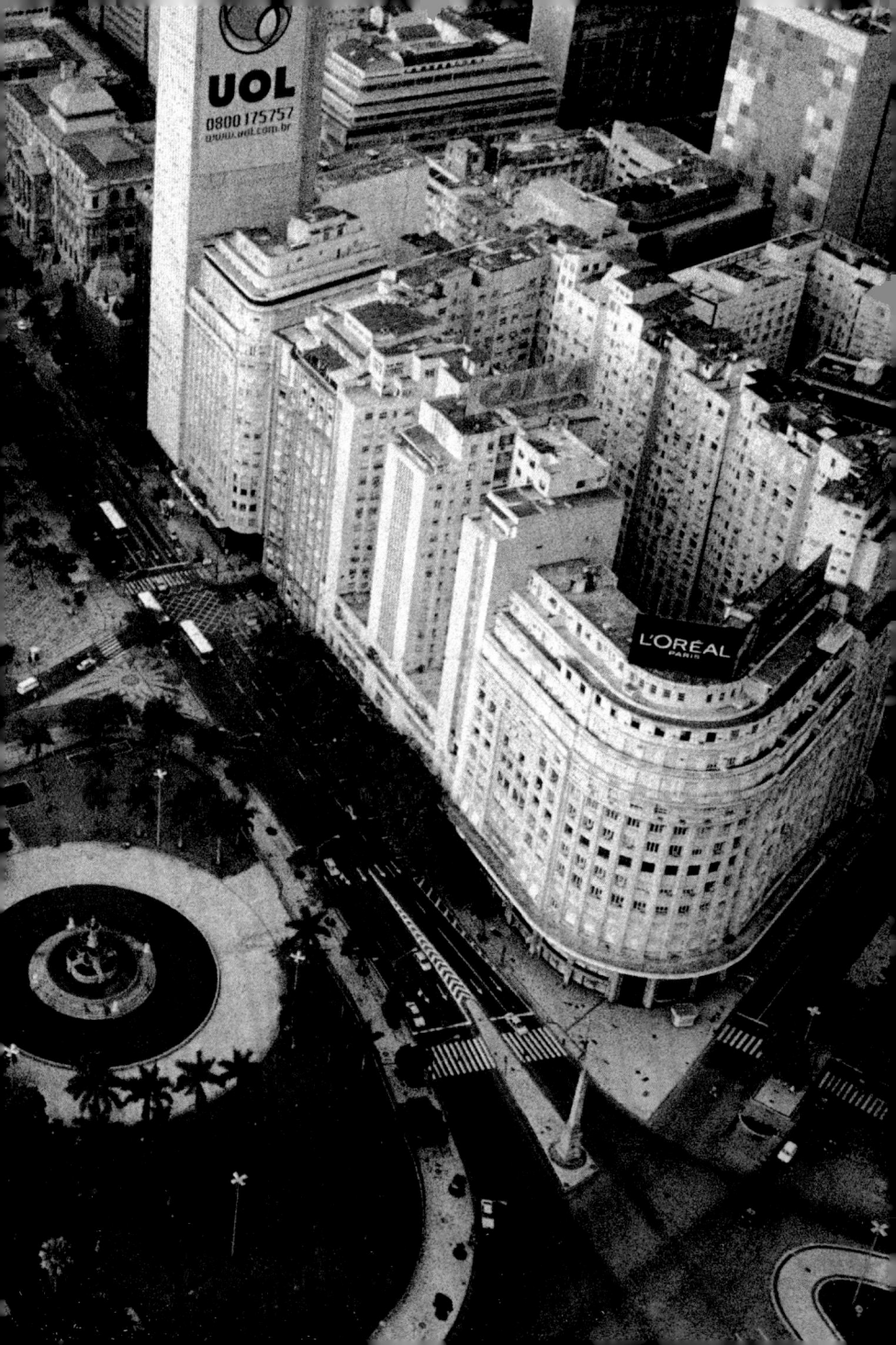

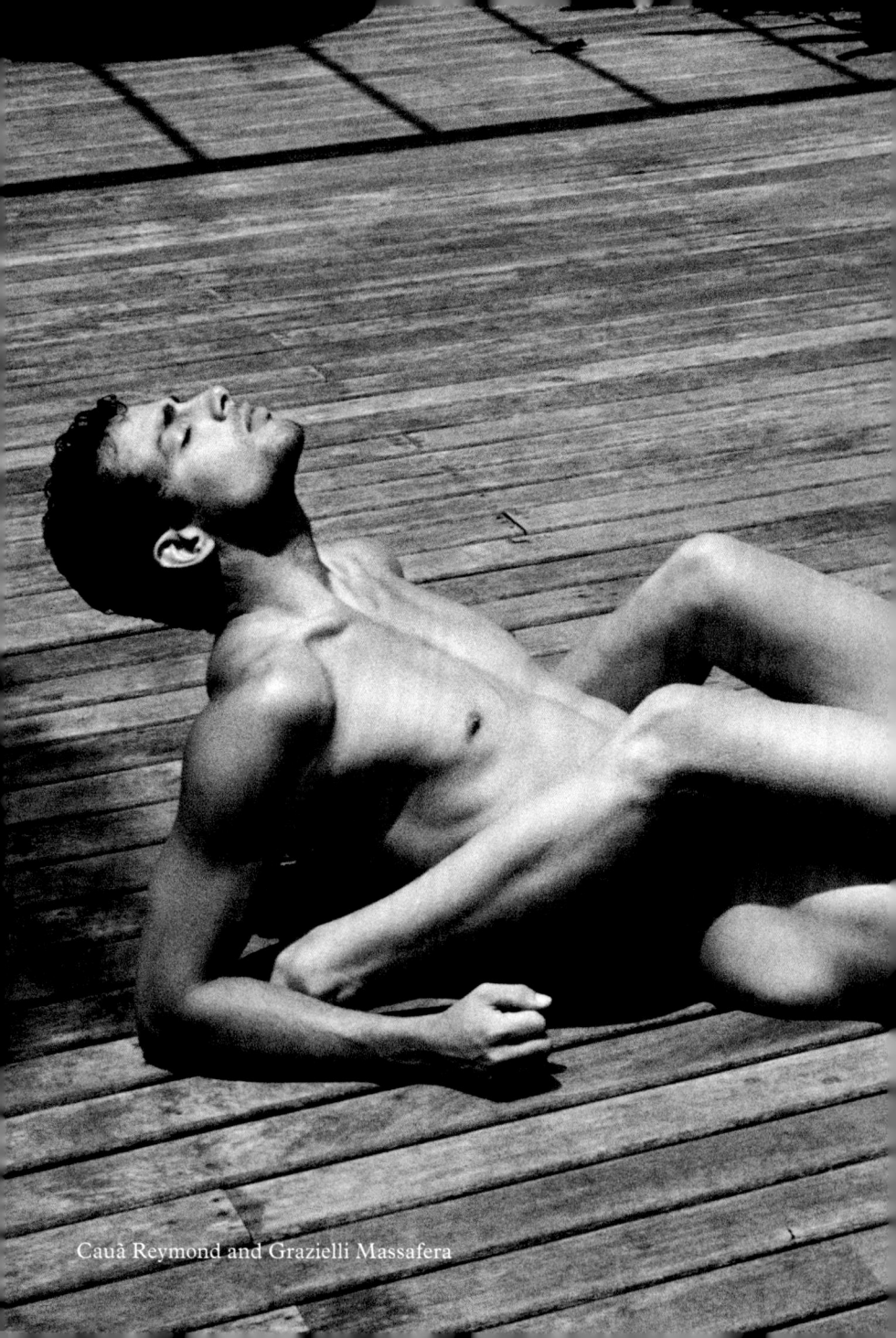

Cauã Reymond and Grazielli Massafera

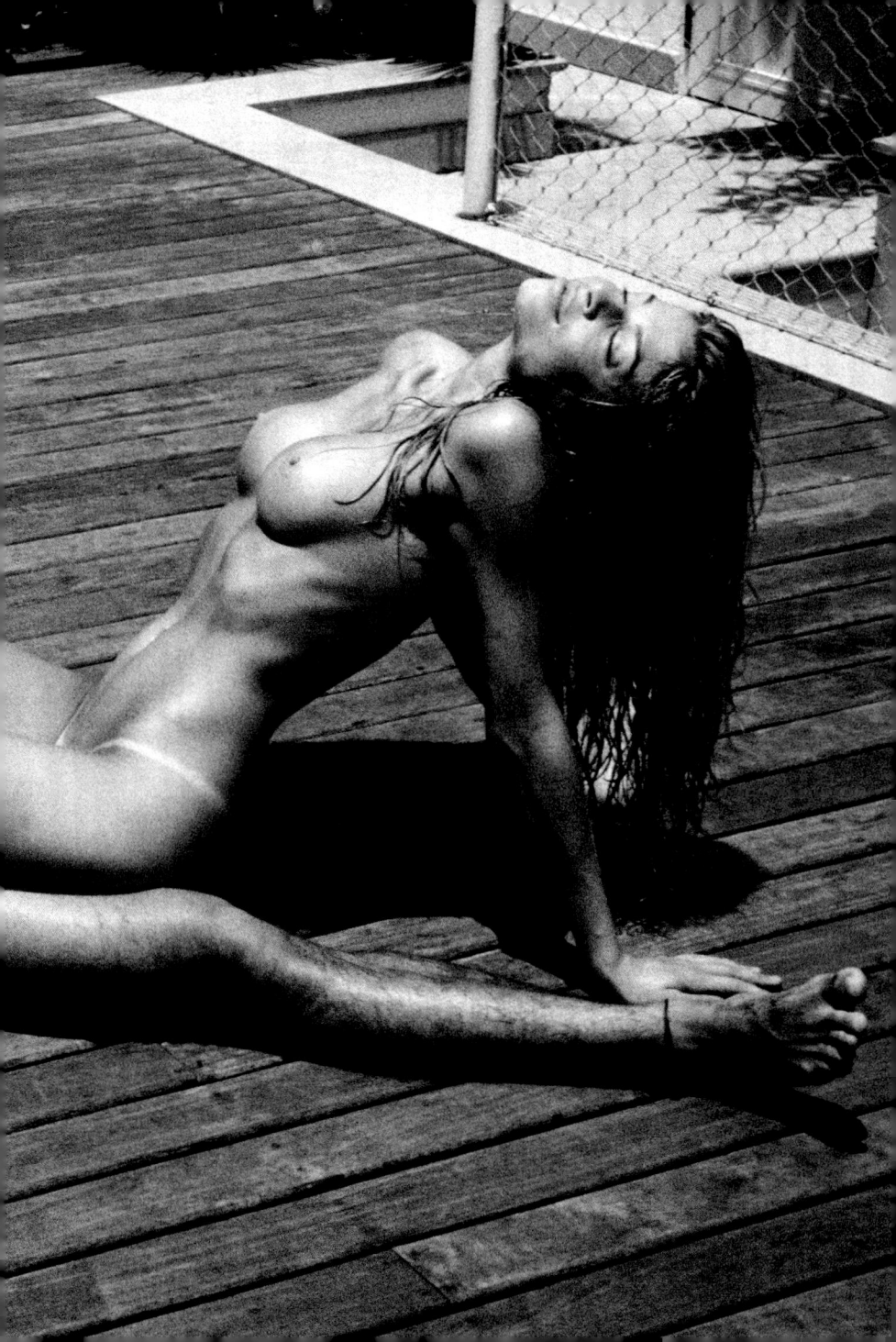

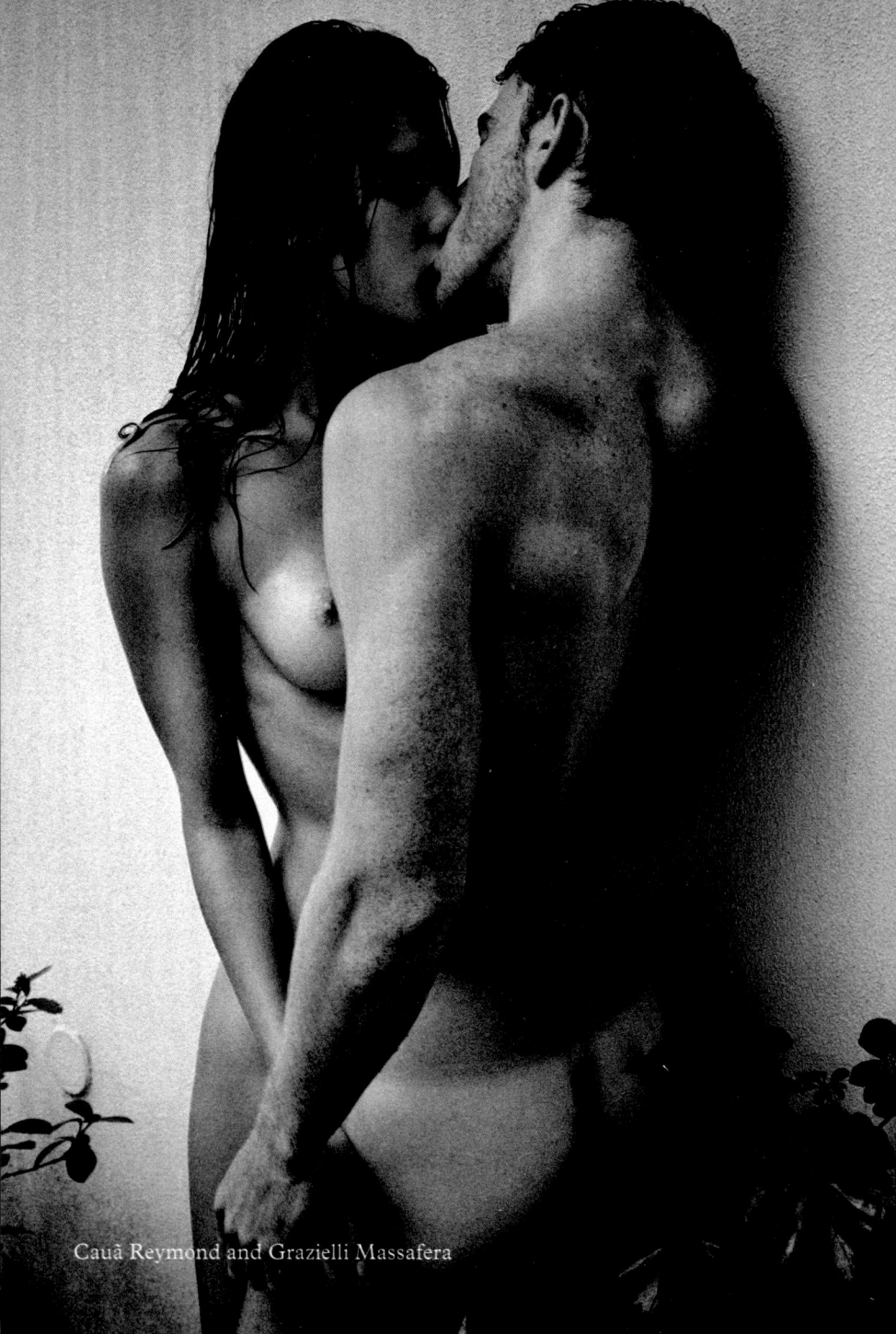

Cauã Reymond and Grazielli Massafera

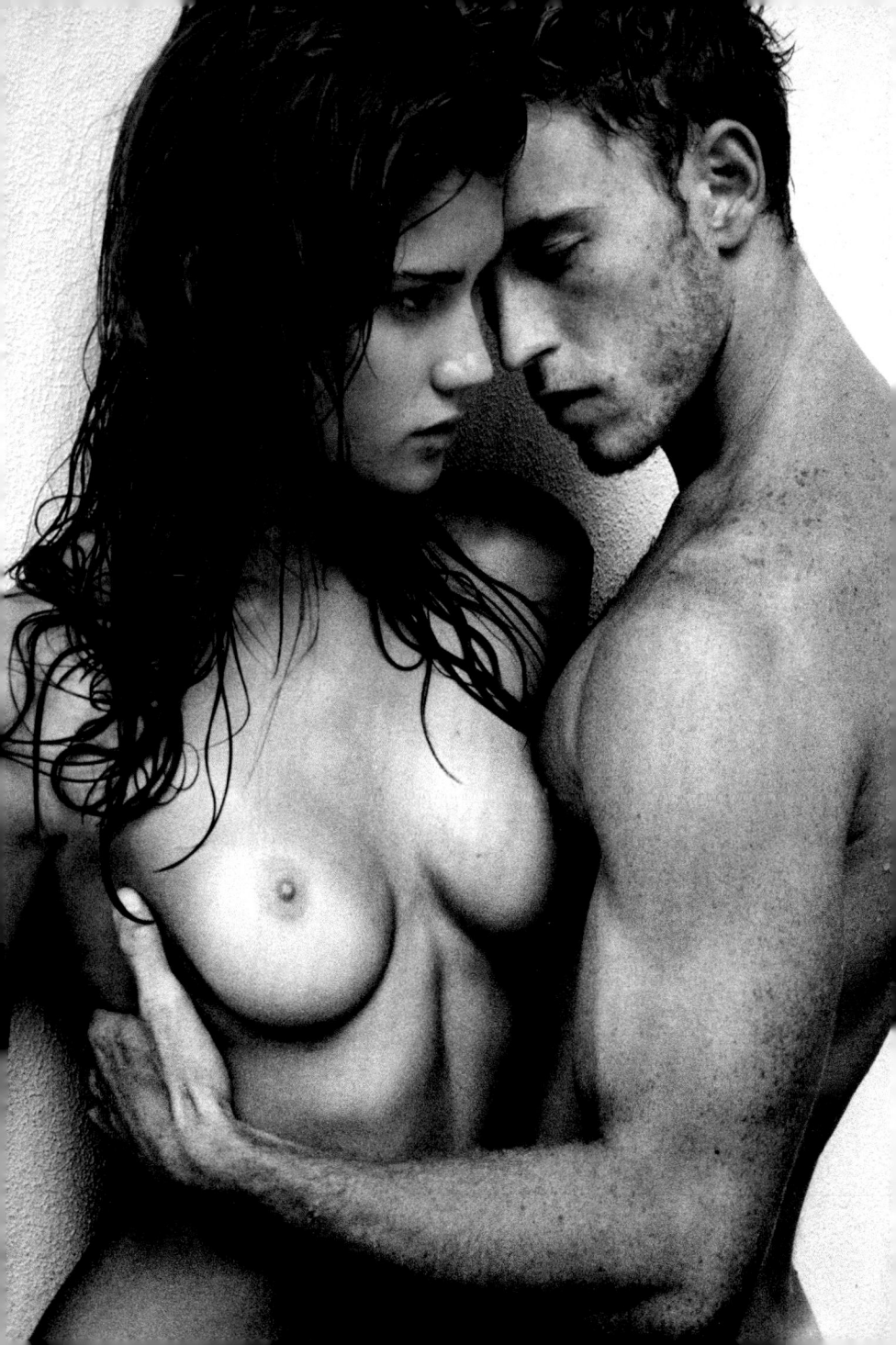

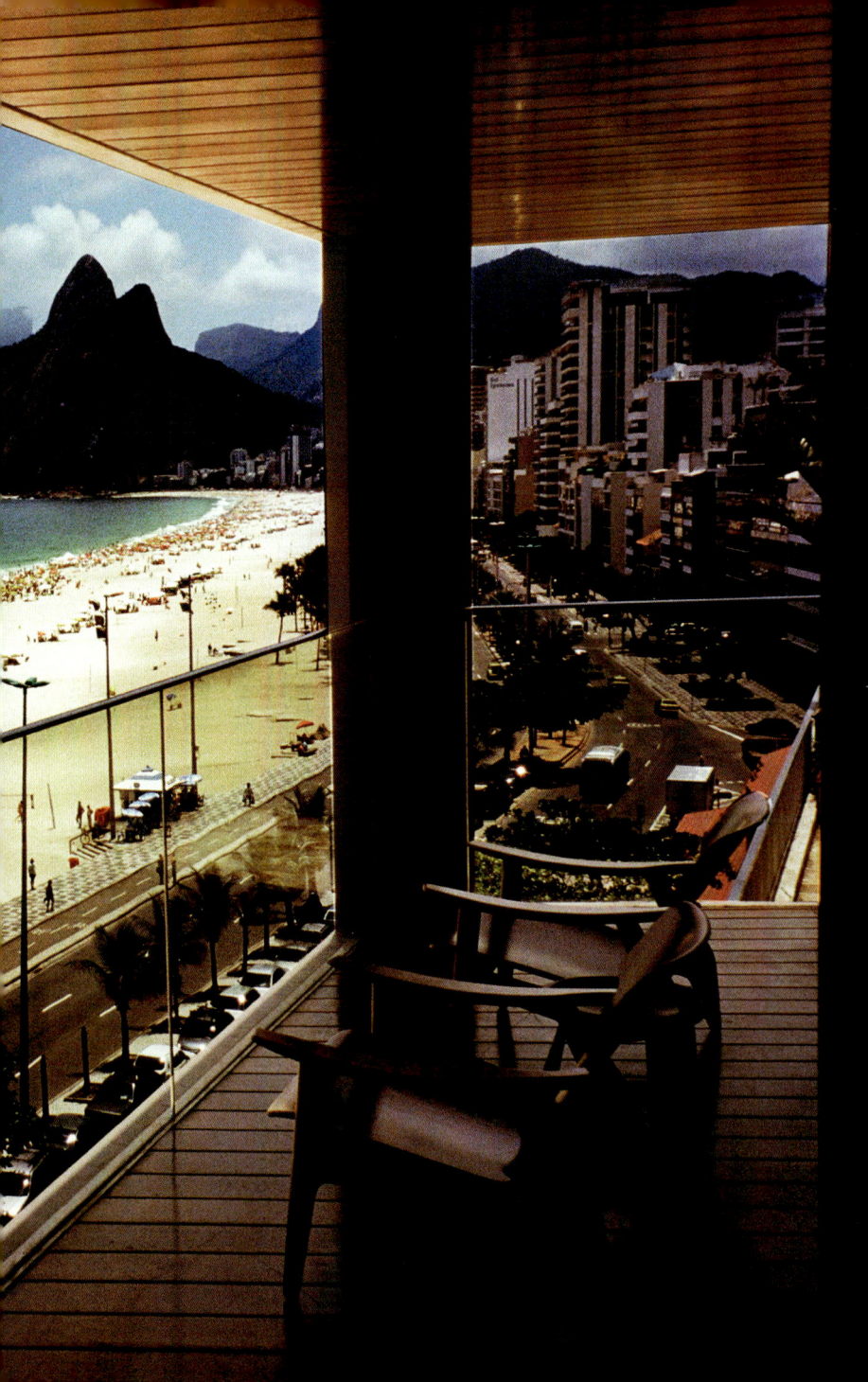

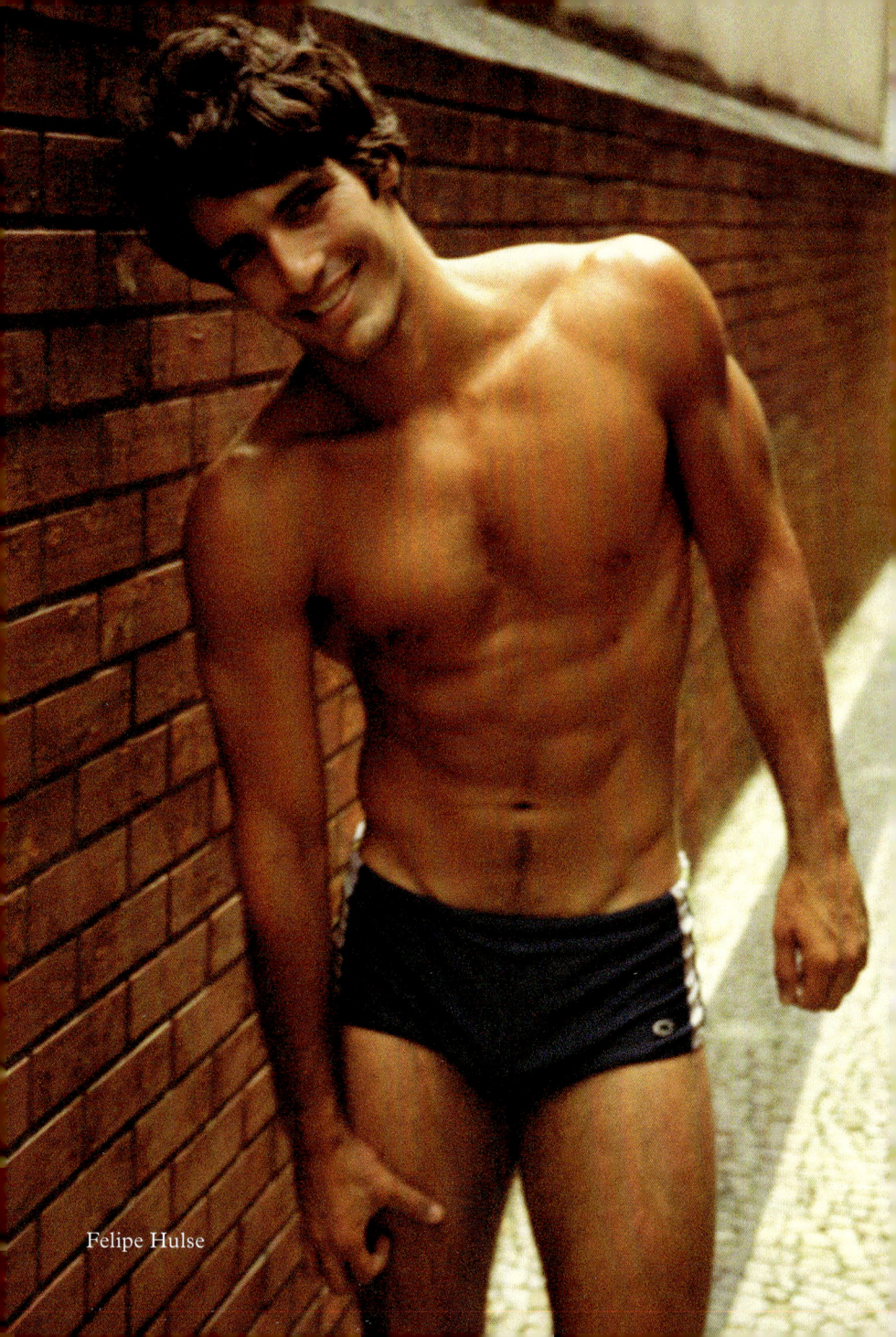

Felipe Hulse

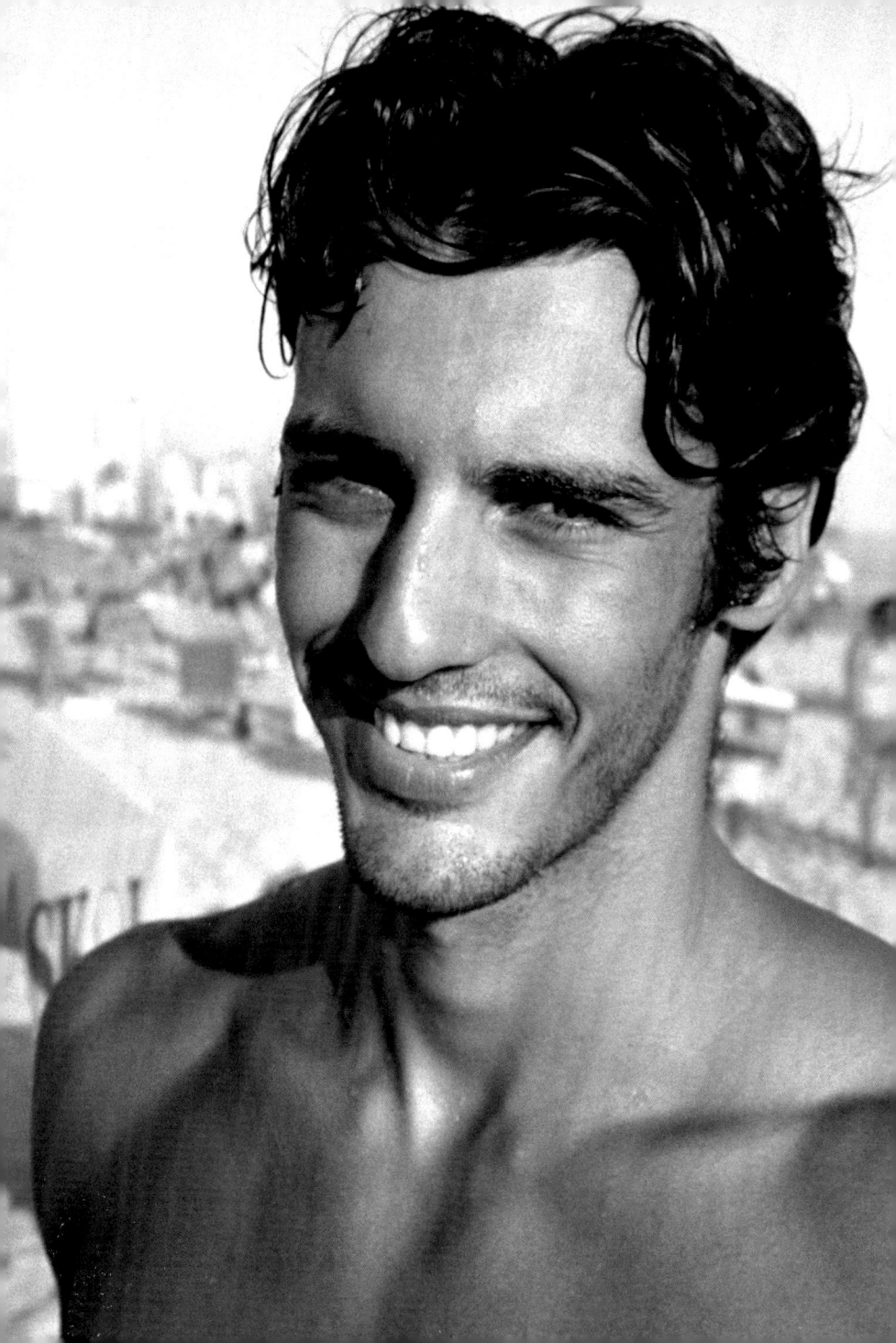

Isabeli Fontana

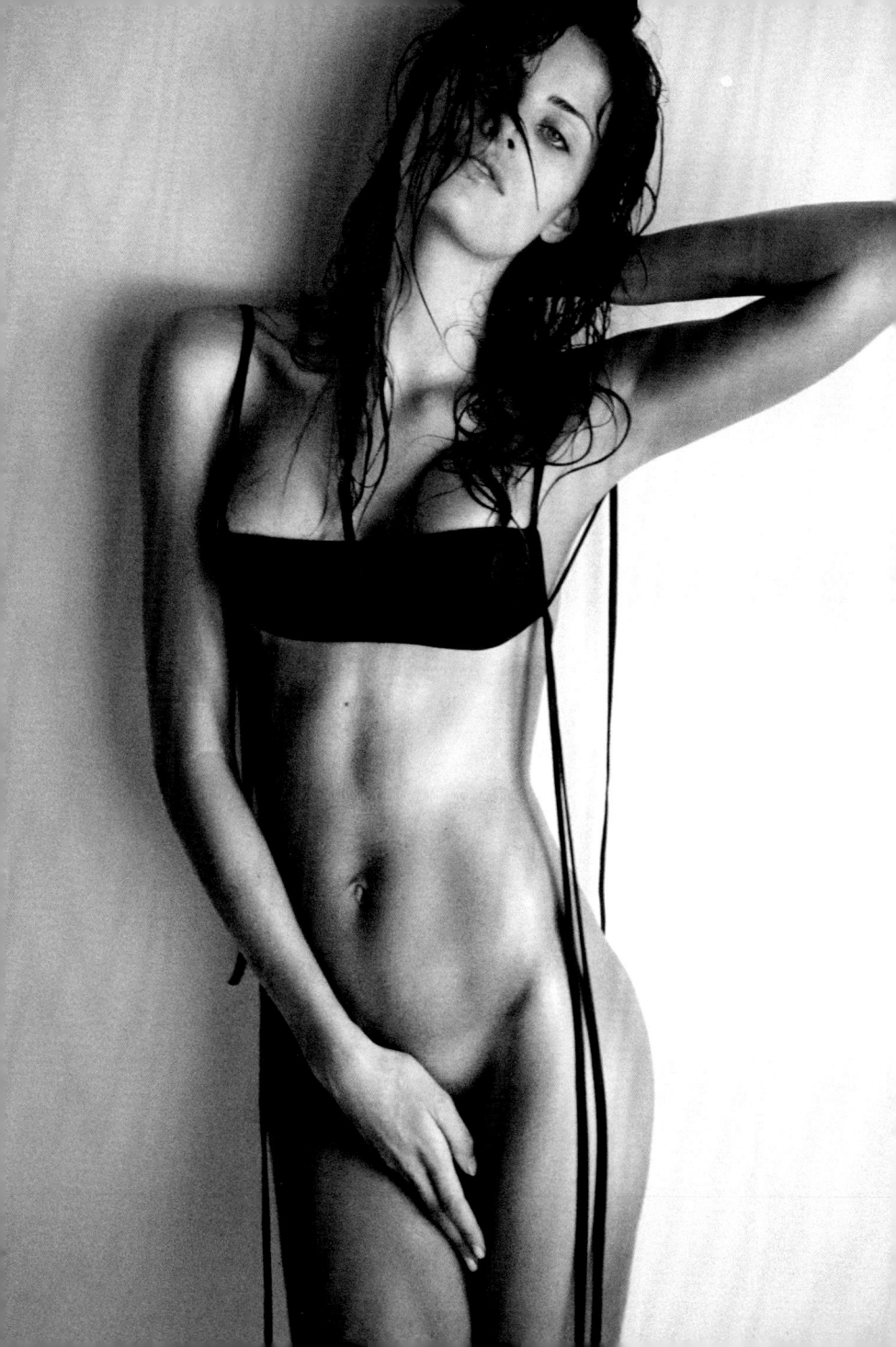

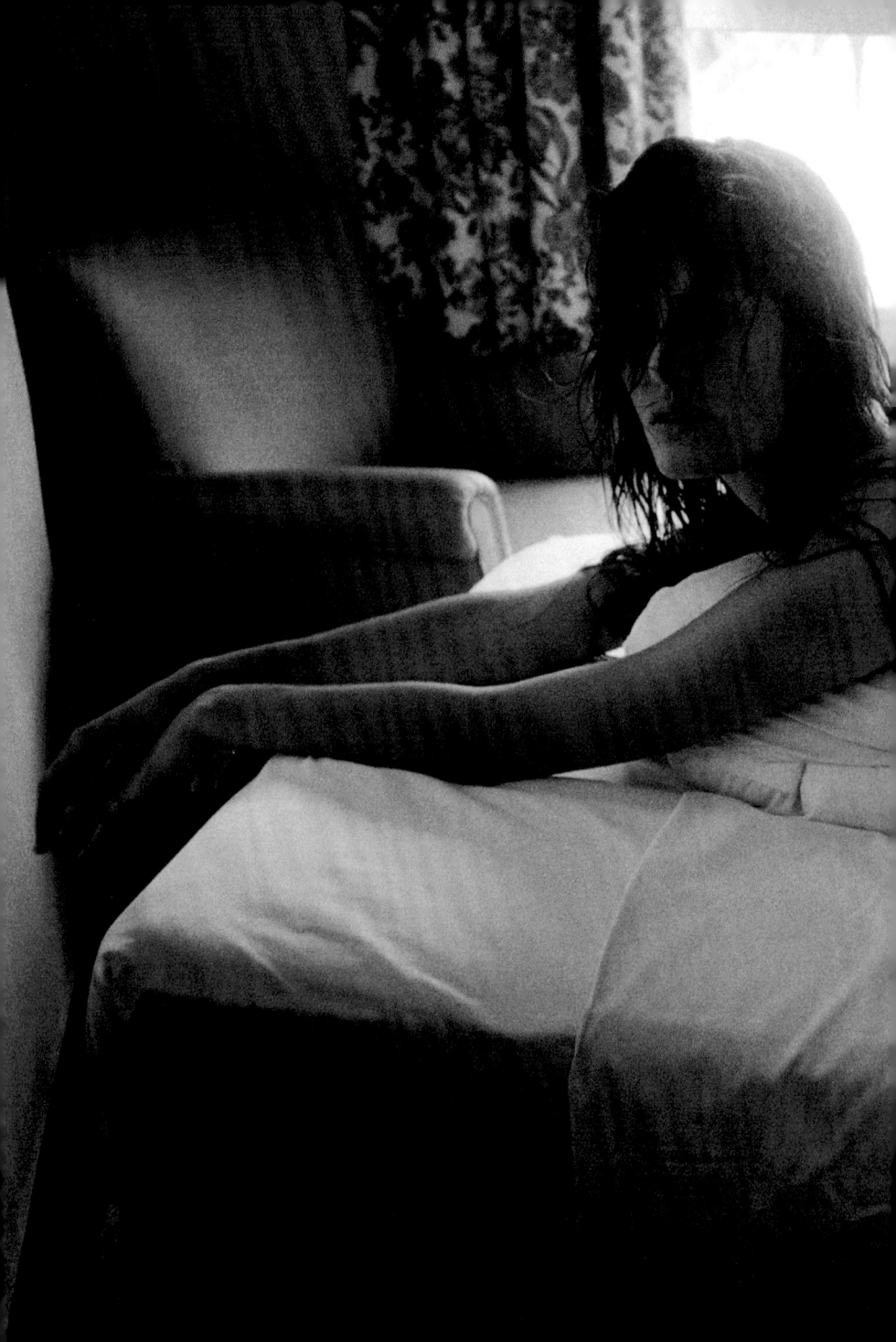

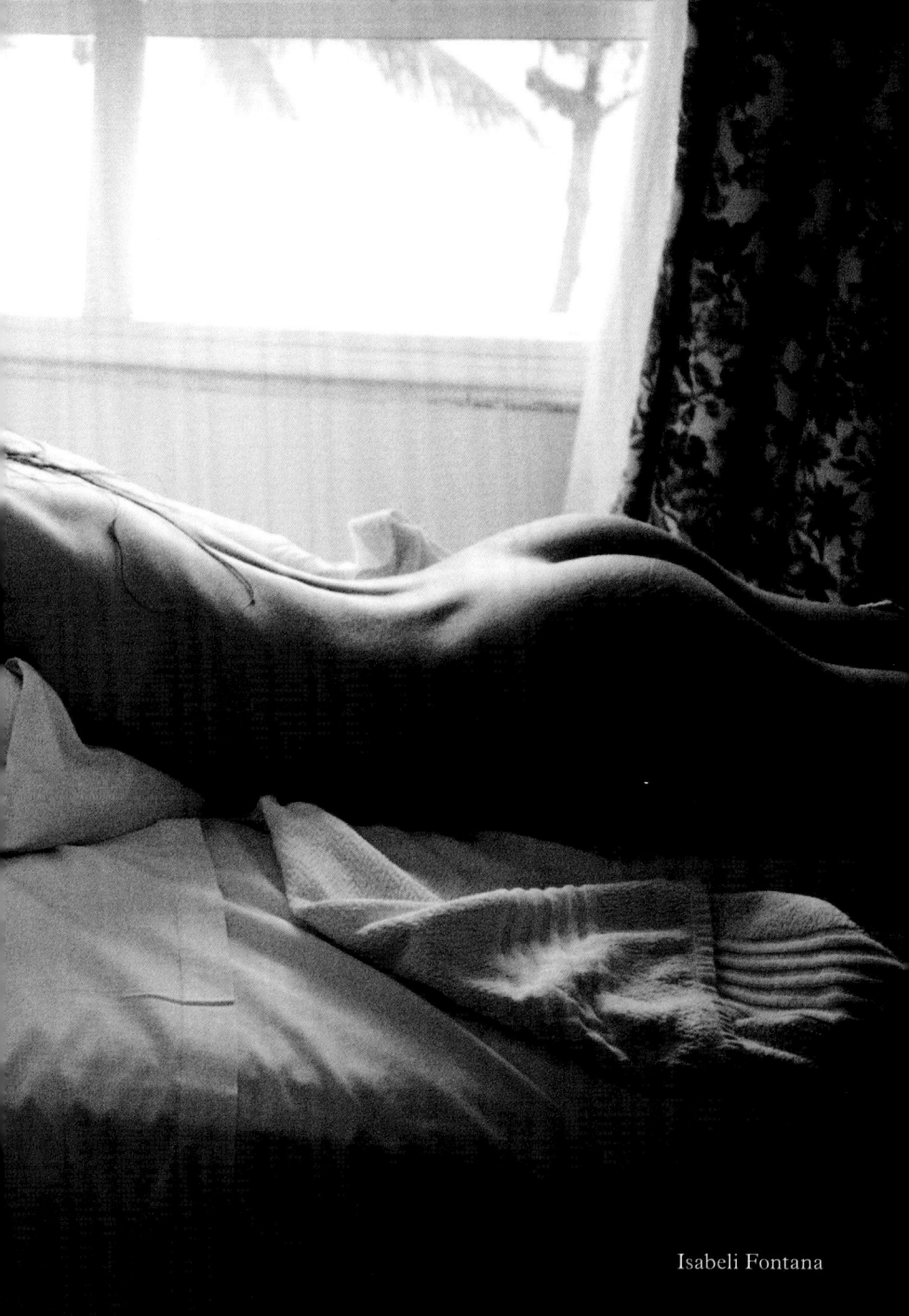

Isabeli Fontana

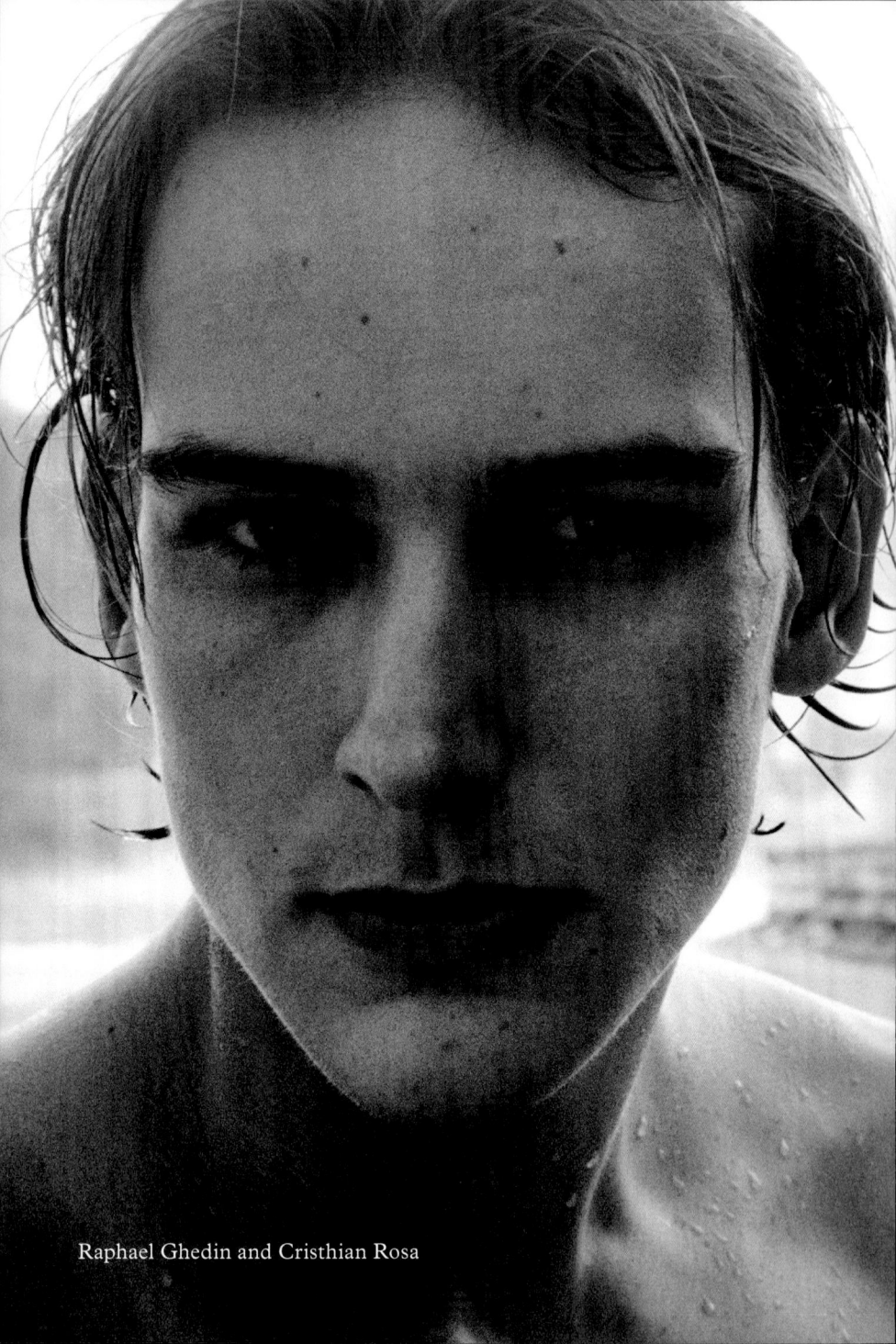

Raphael Ghedin and Cristhian Rosa

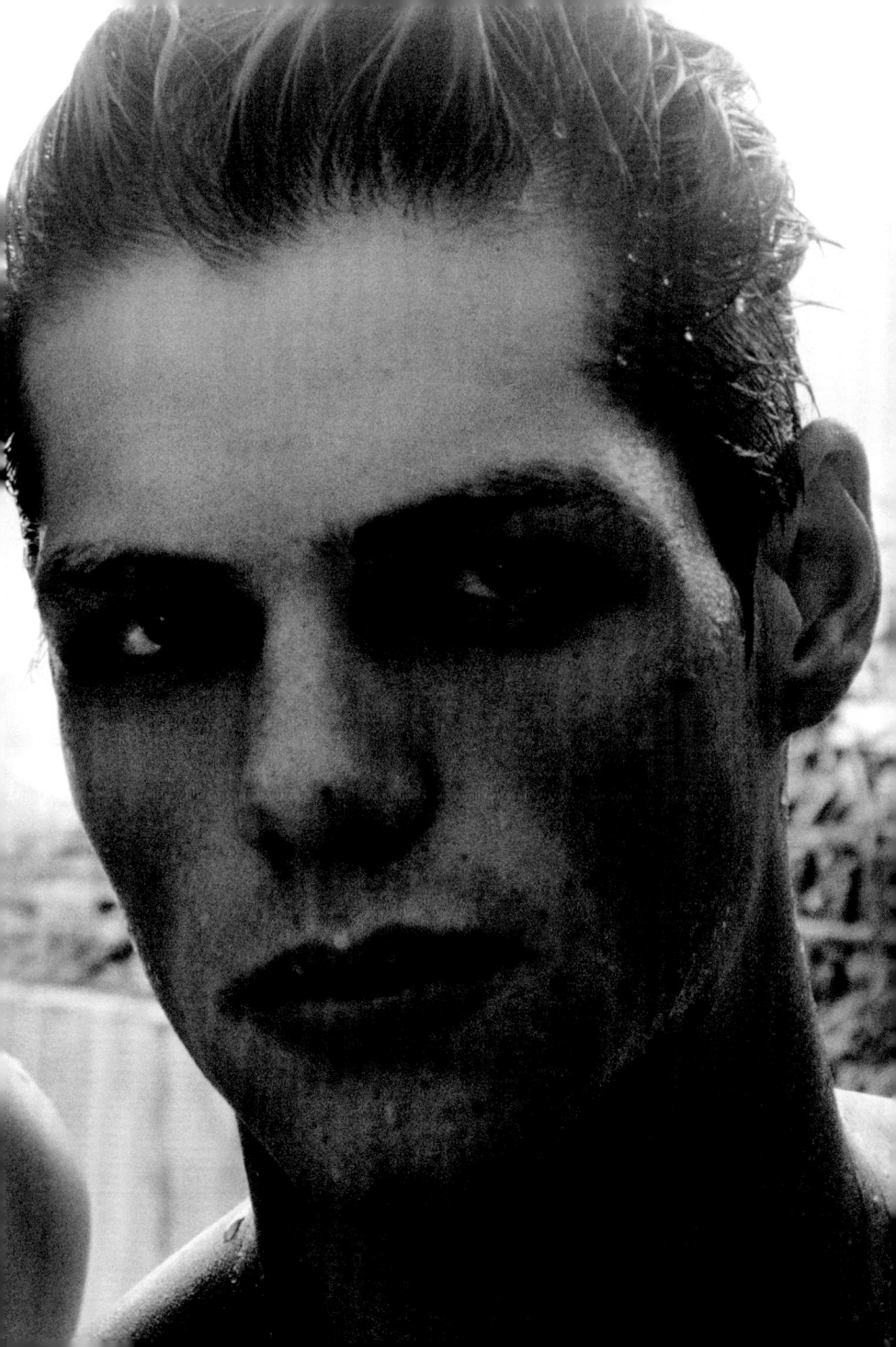

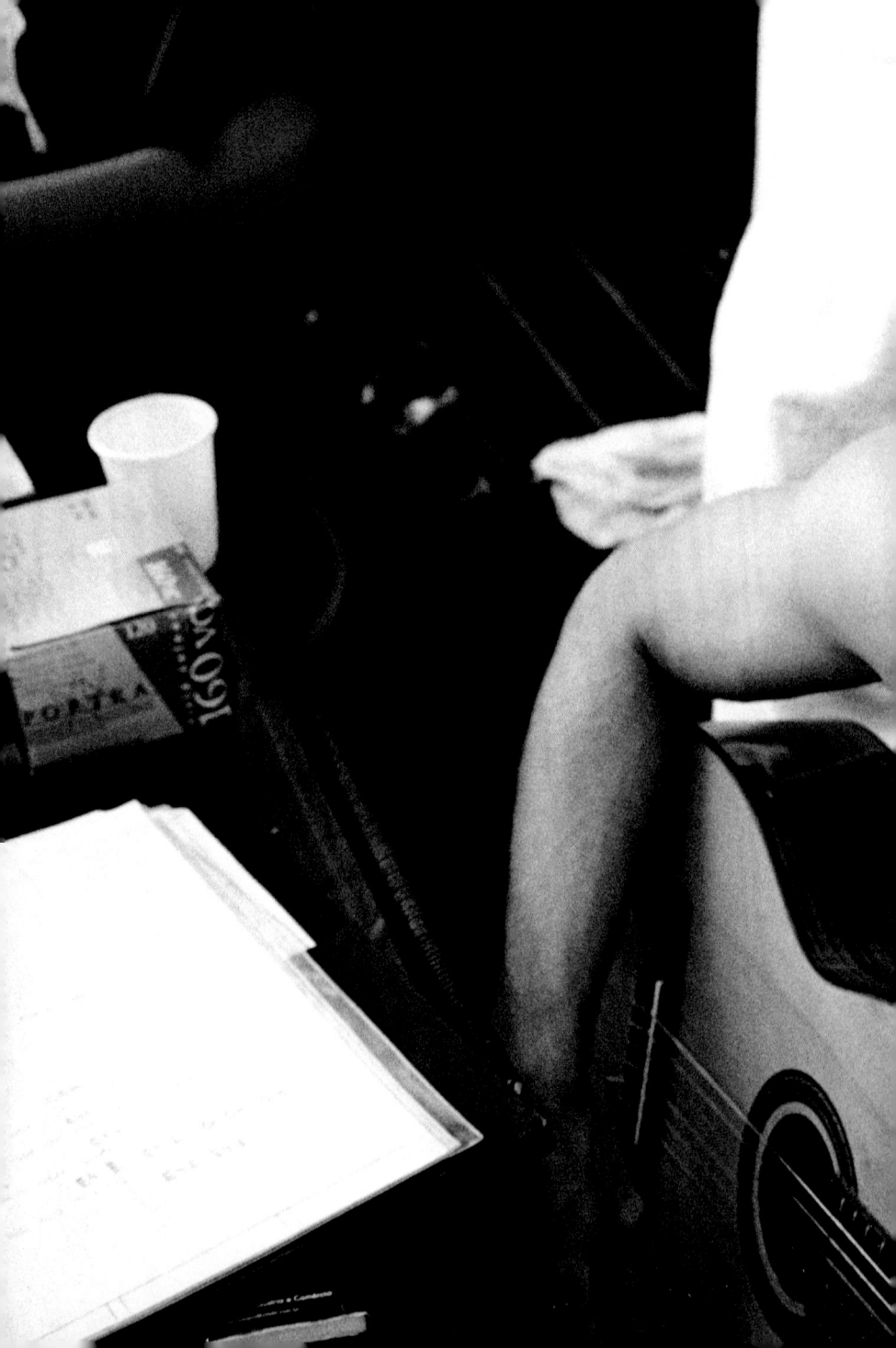

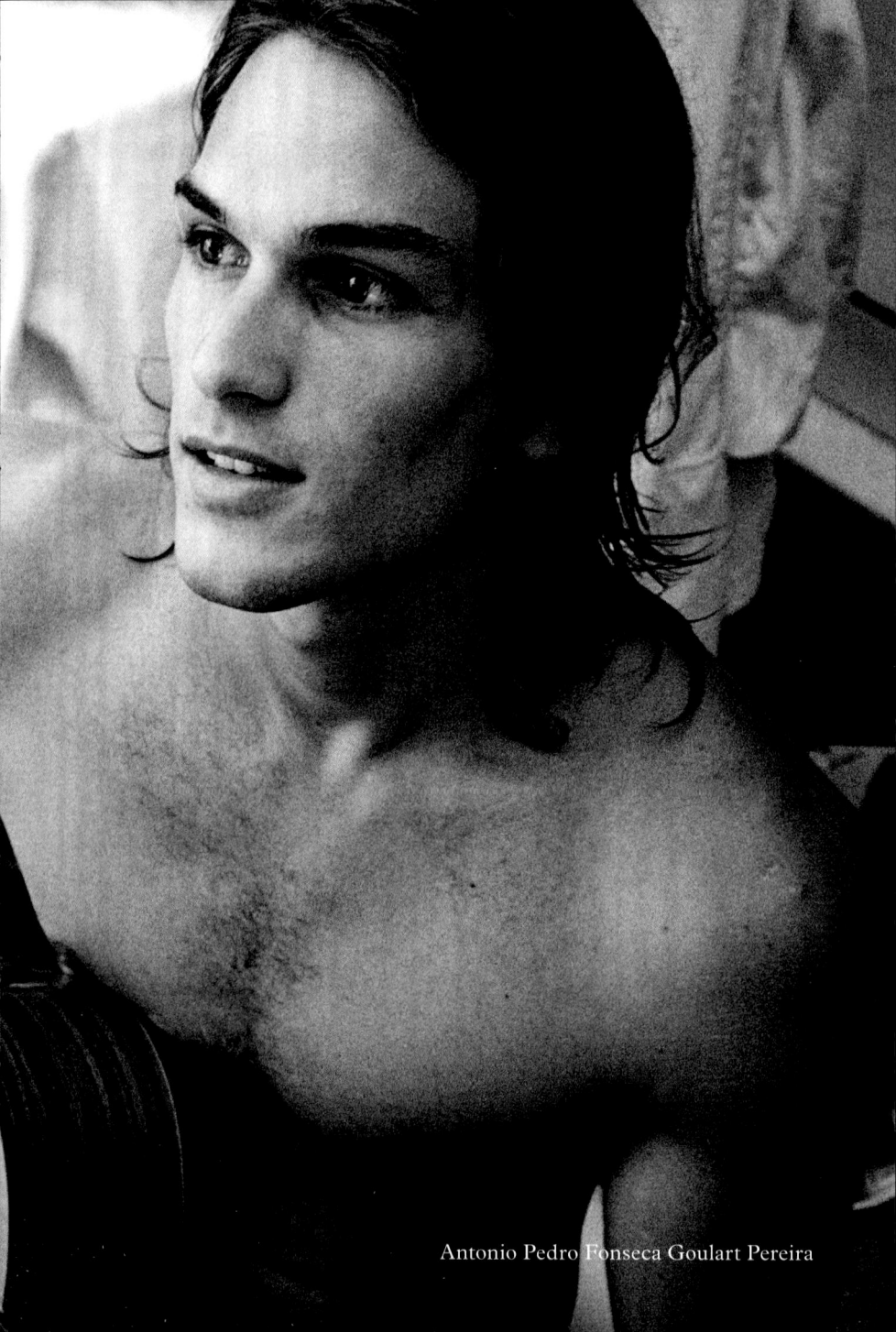

Antonio Pedro Fonseca Goulart Pereira

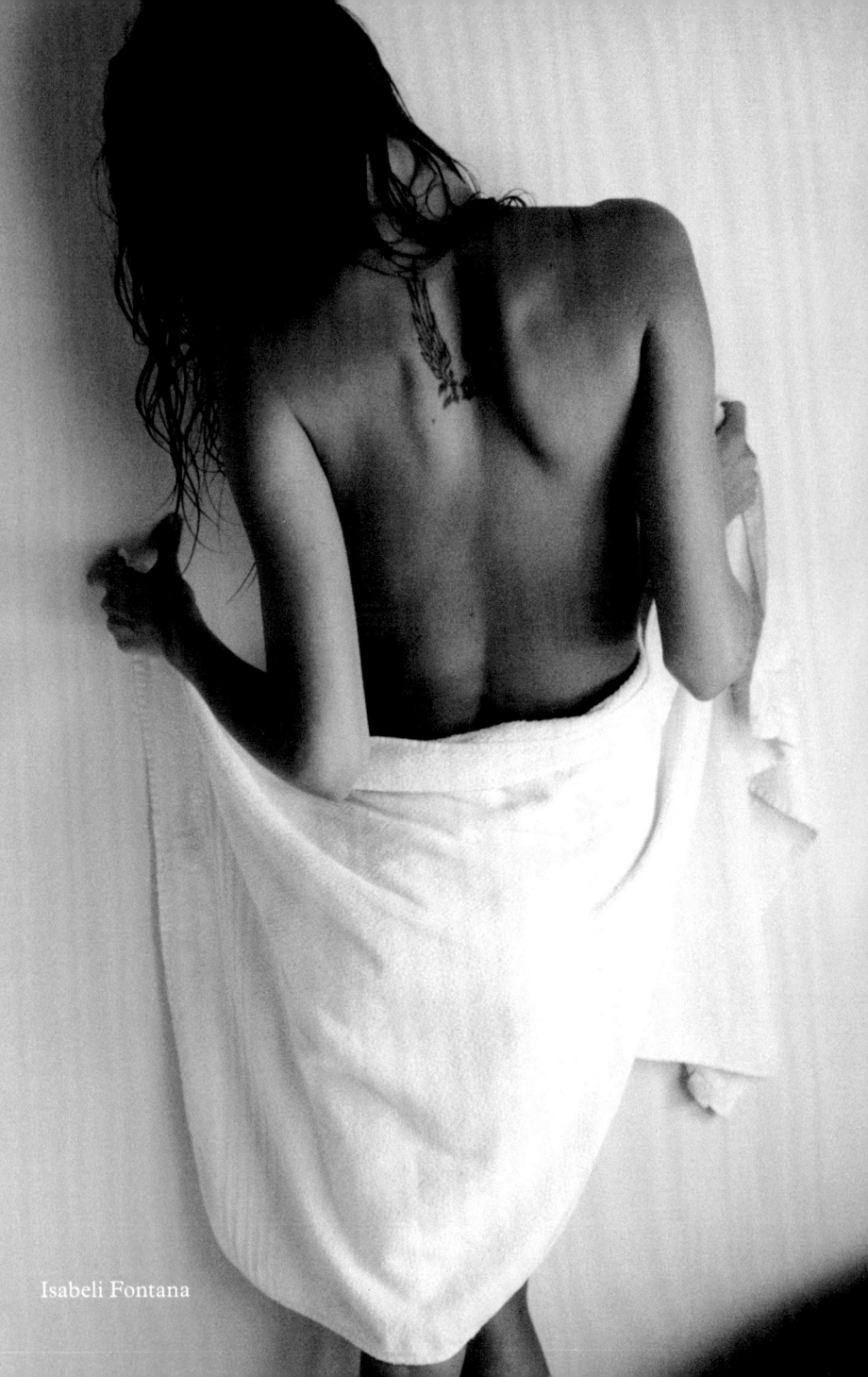

Isabeli Fontana

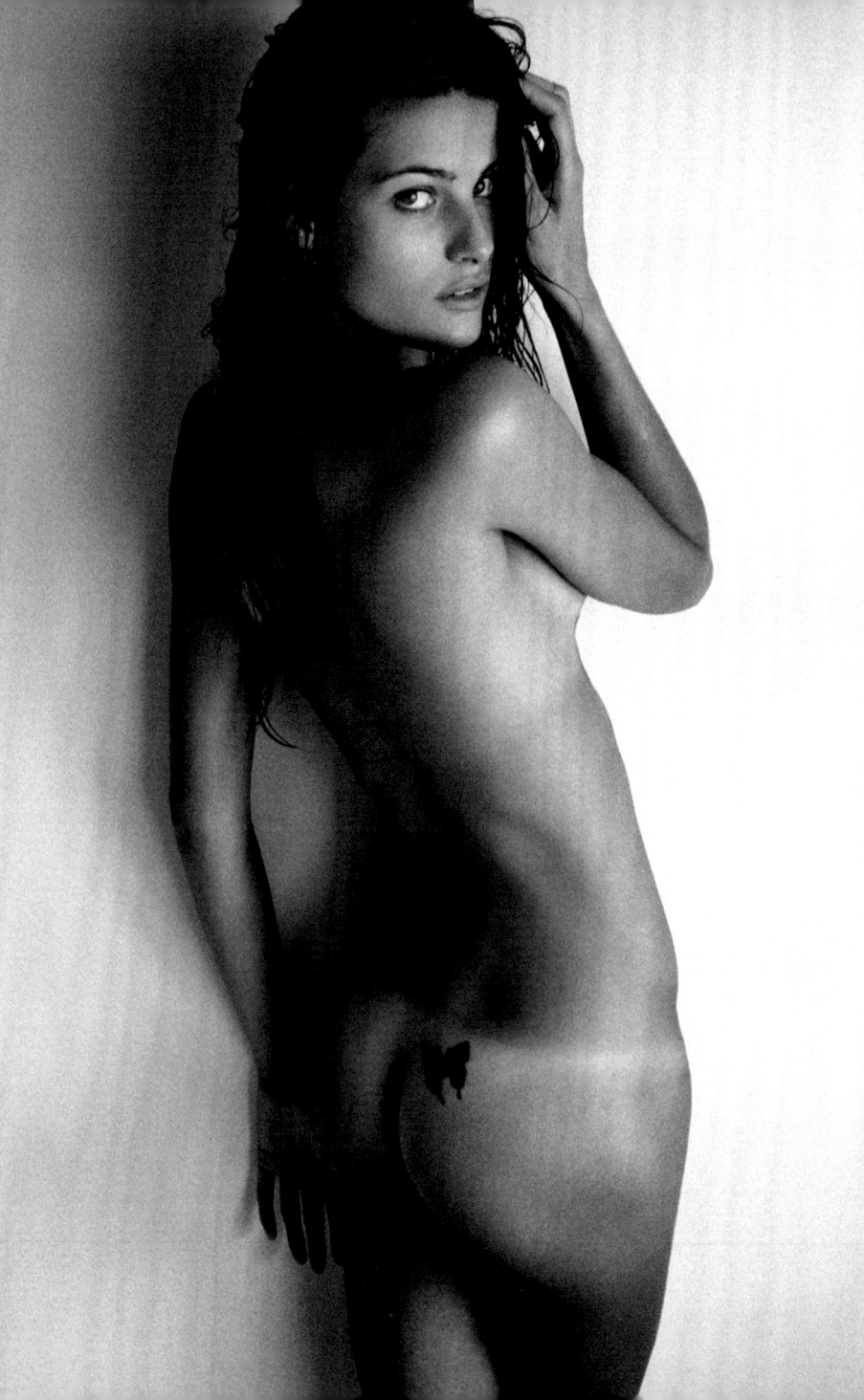

Isabeli Fontana

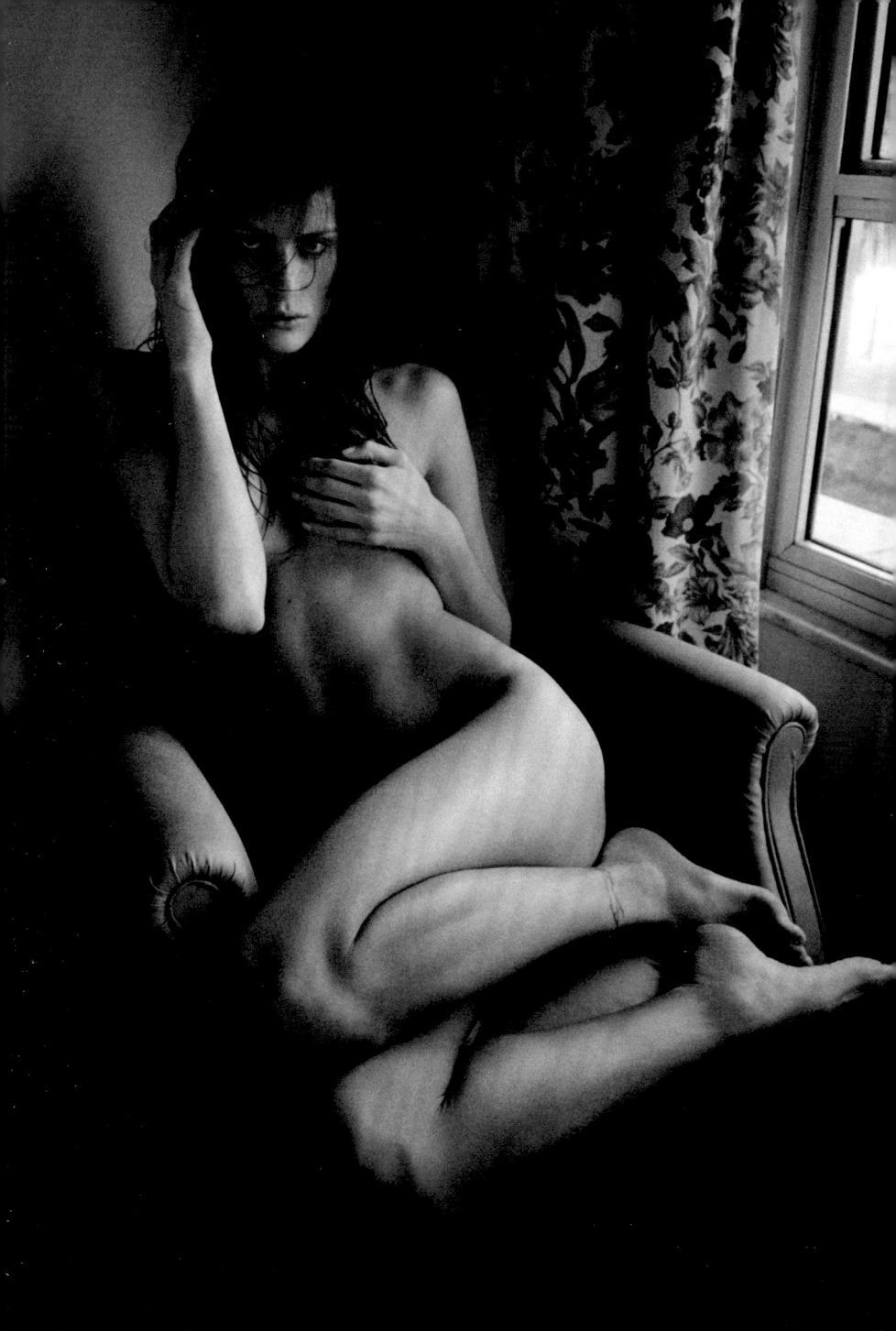

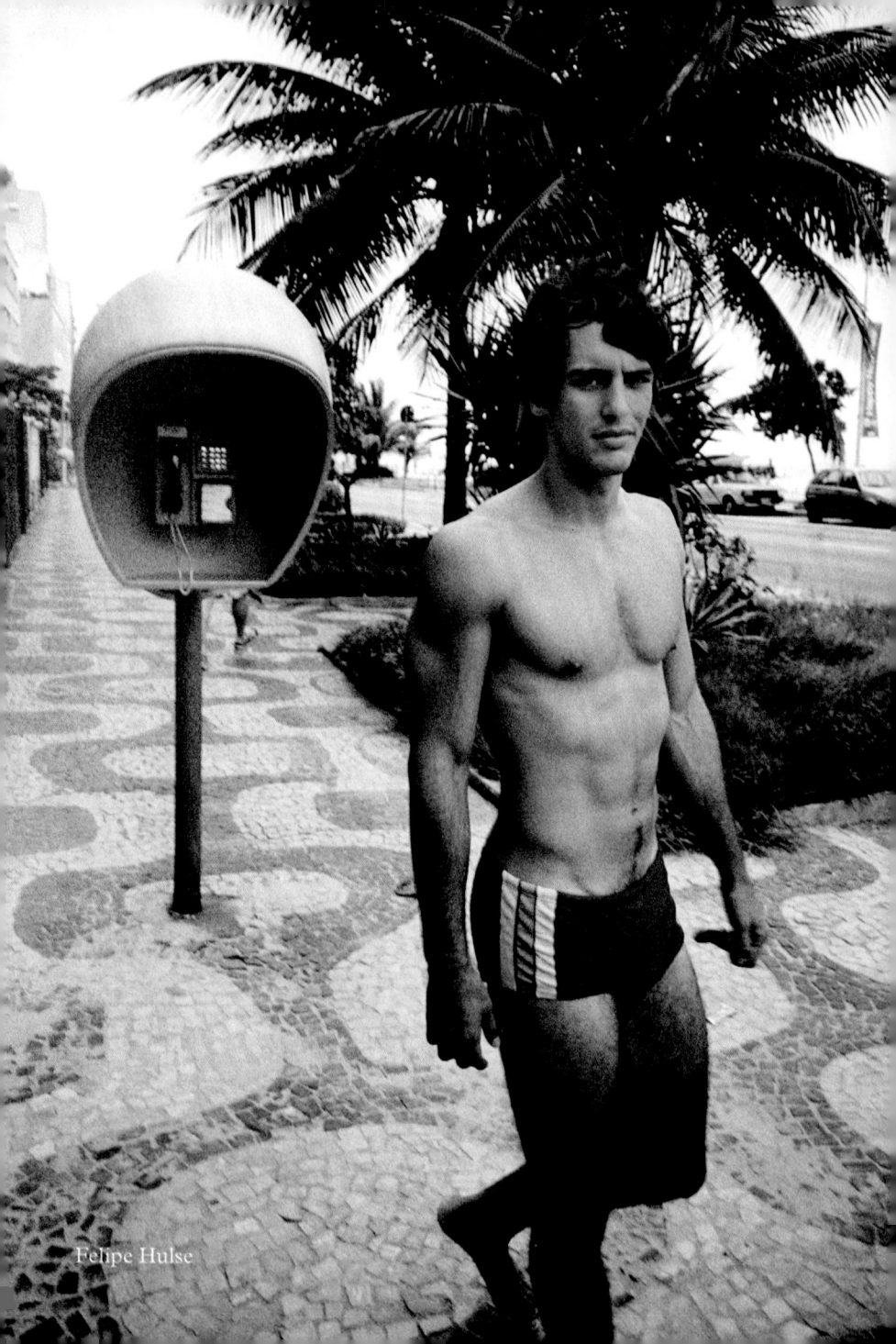

Felipe Hulse

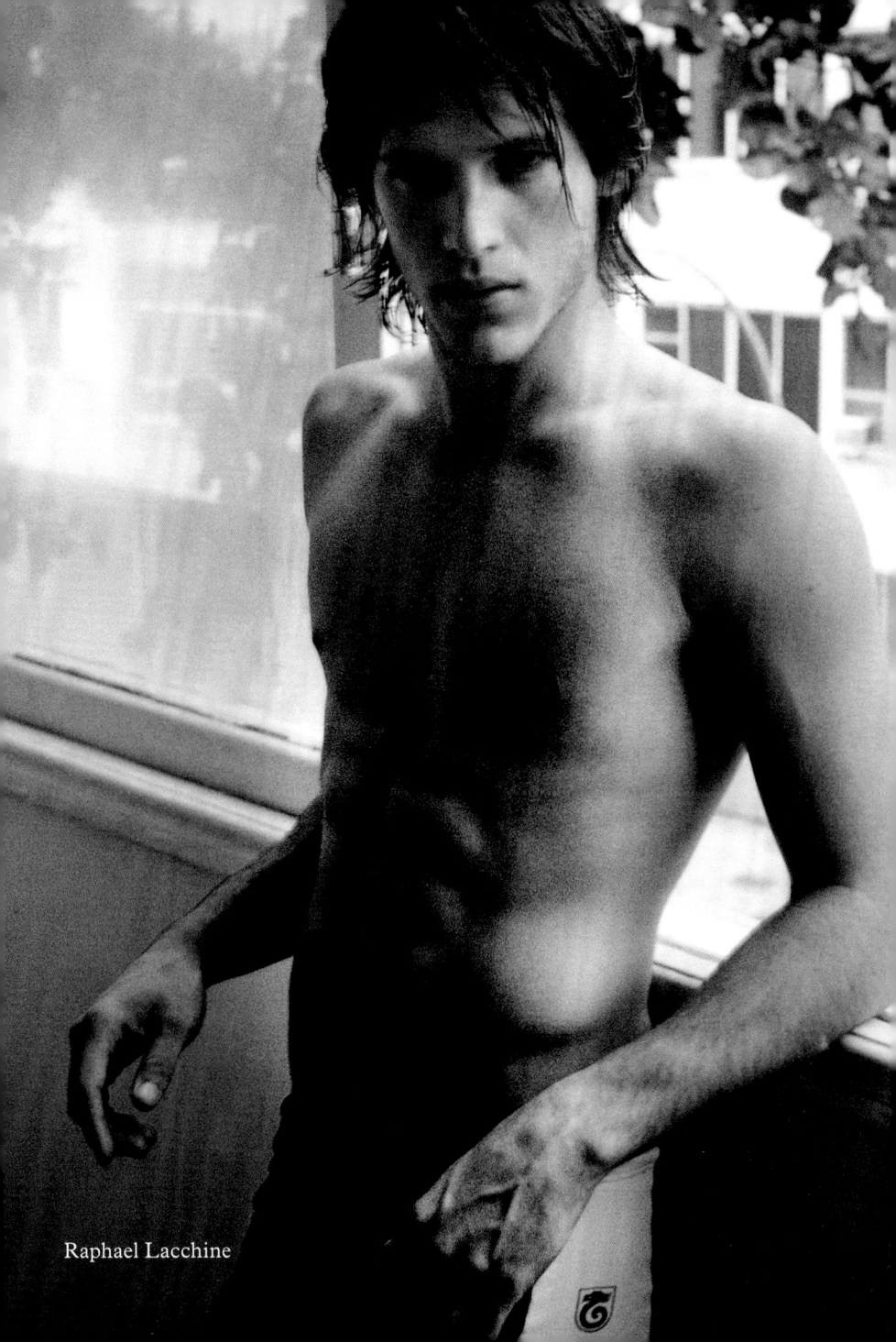

Raphael Lacchine

Raphael Lacchine

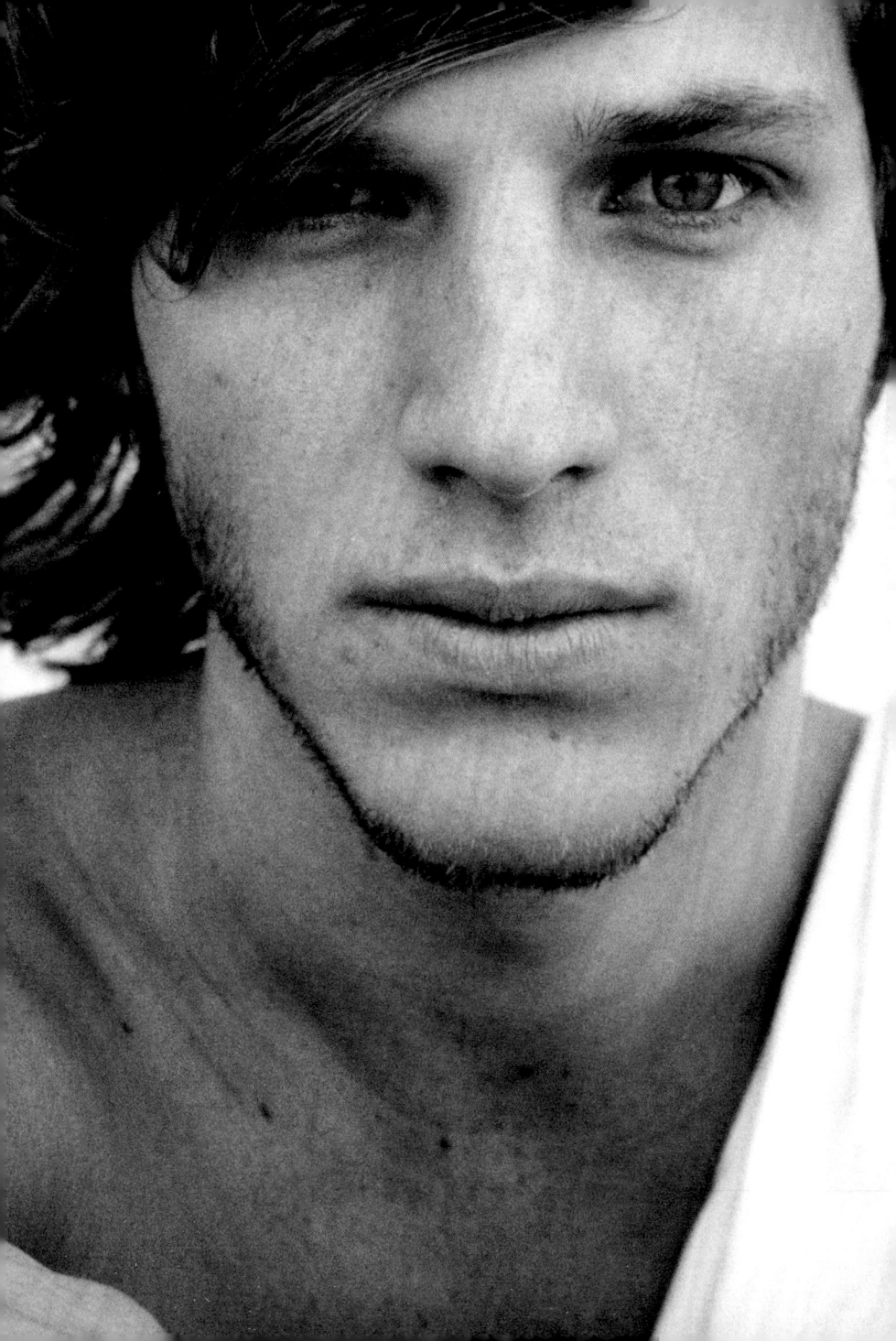

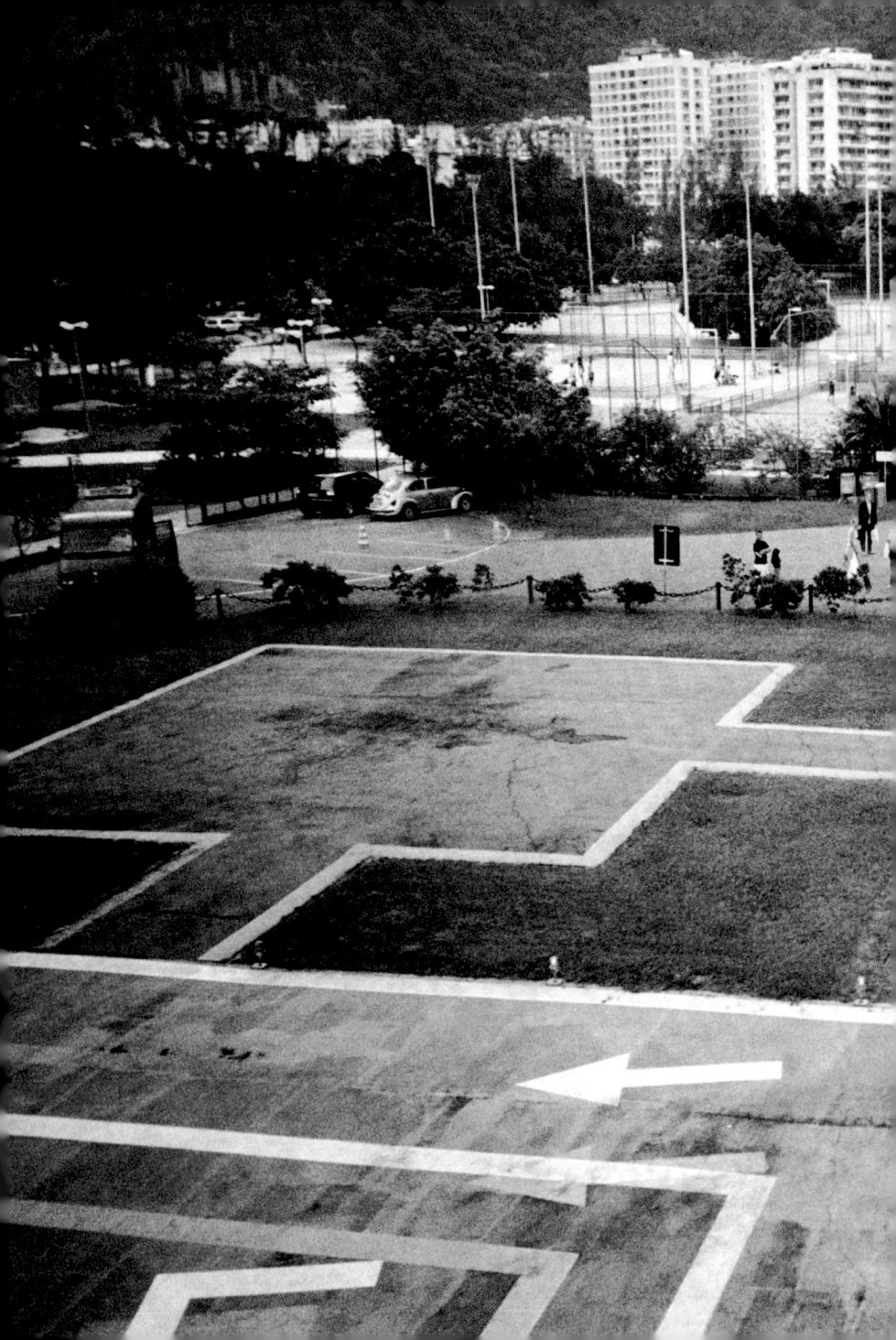

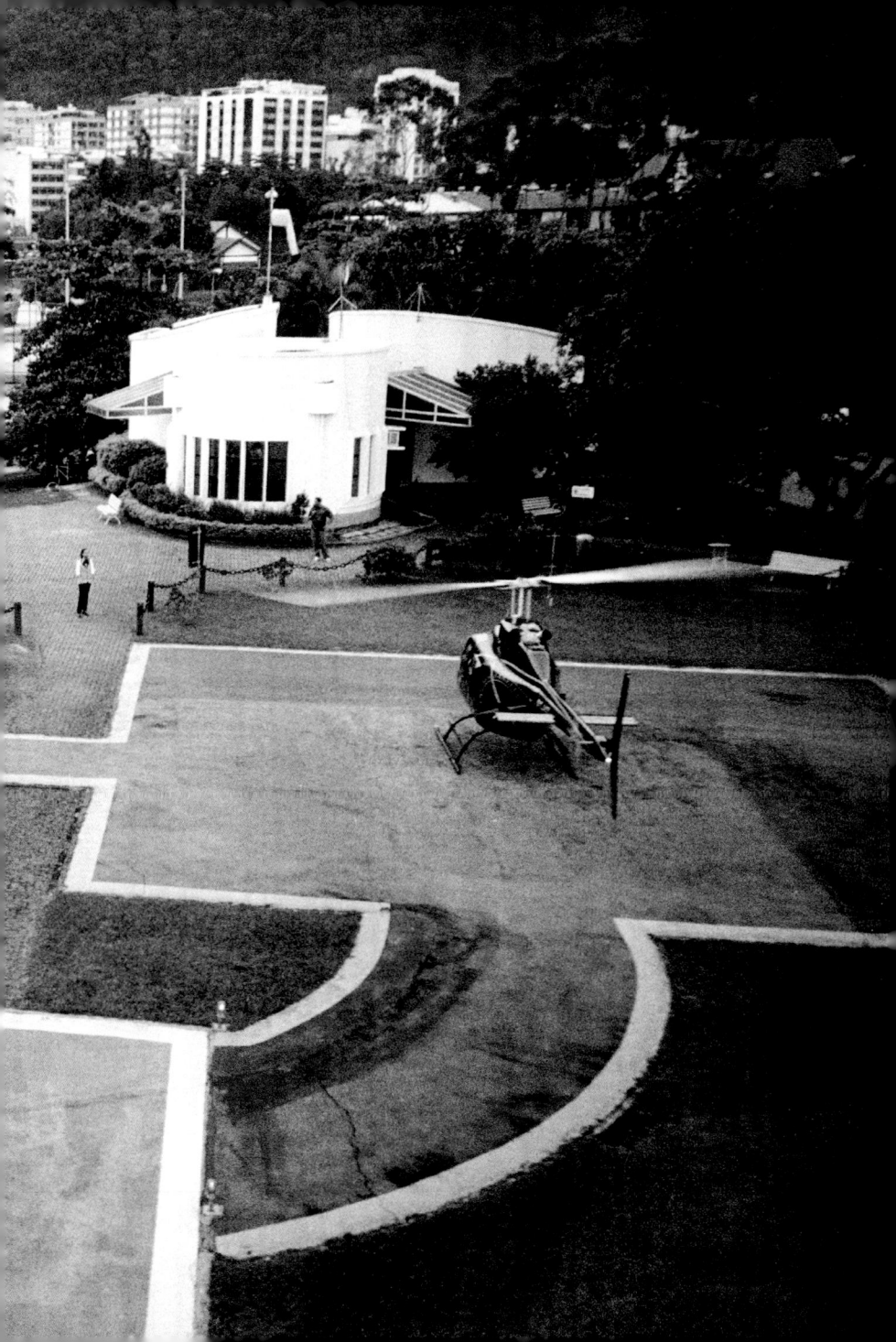

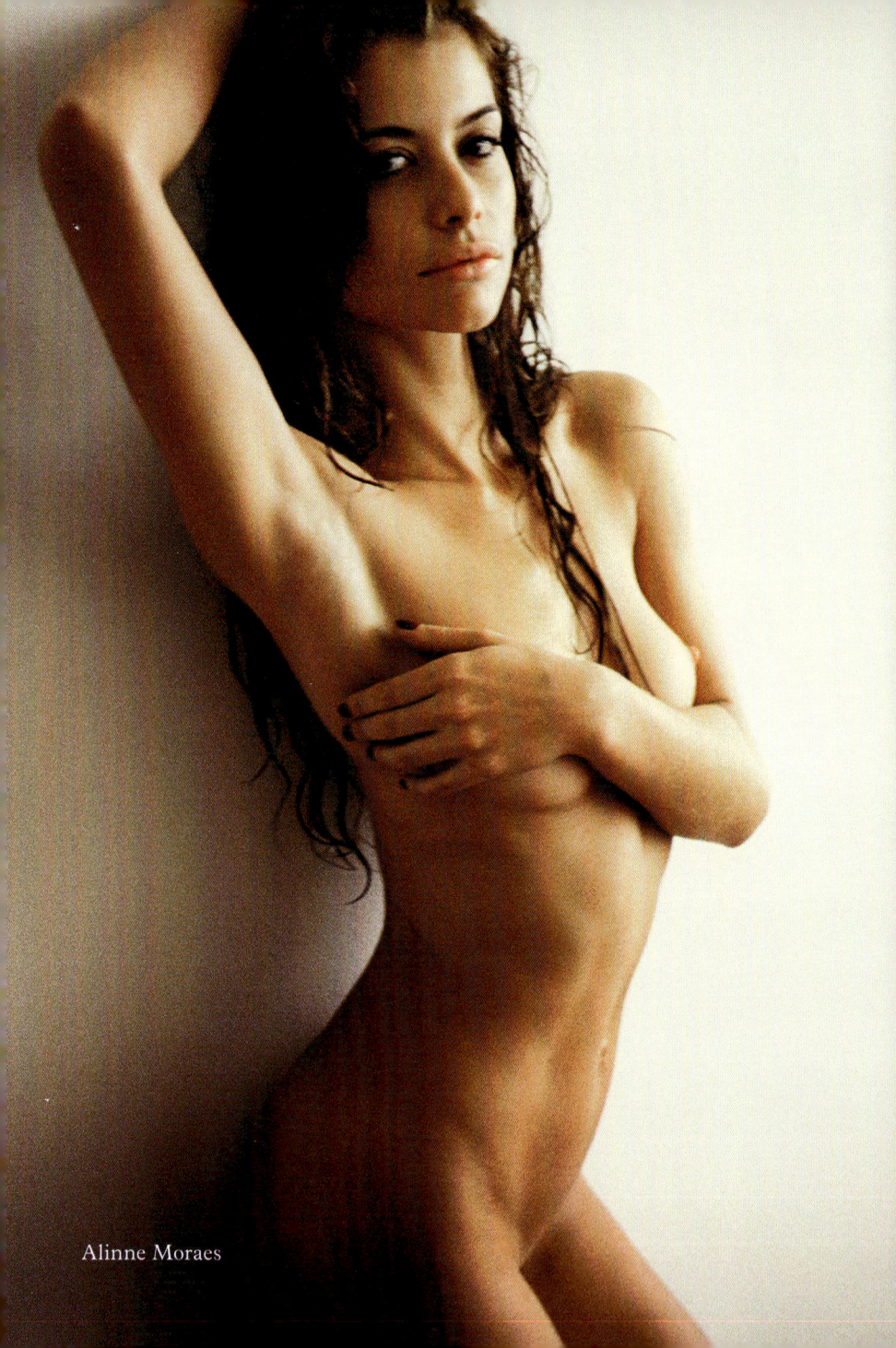

Alinne Moraes

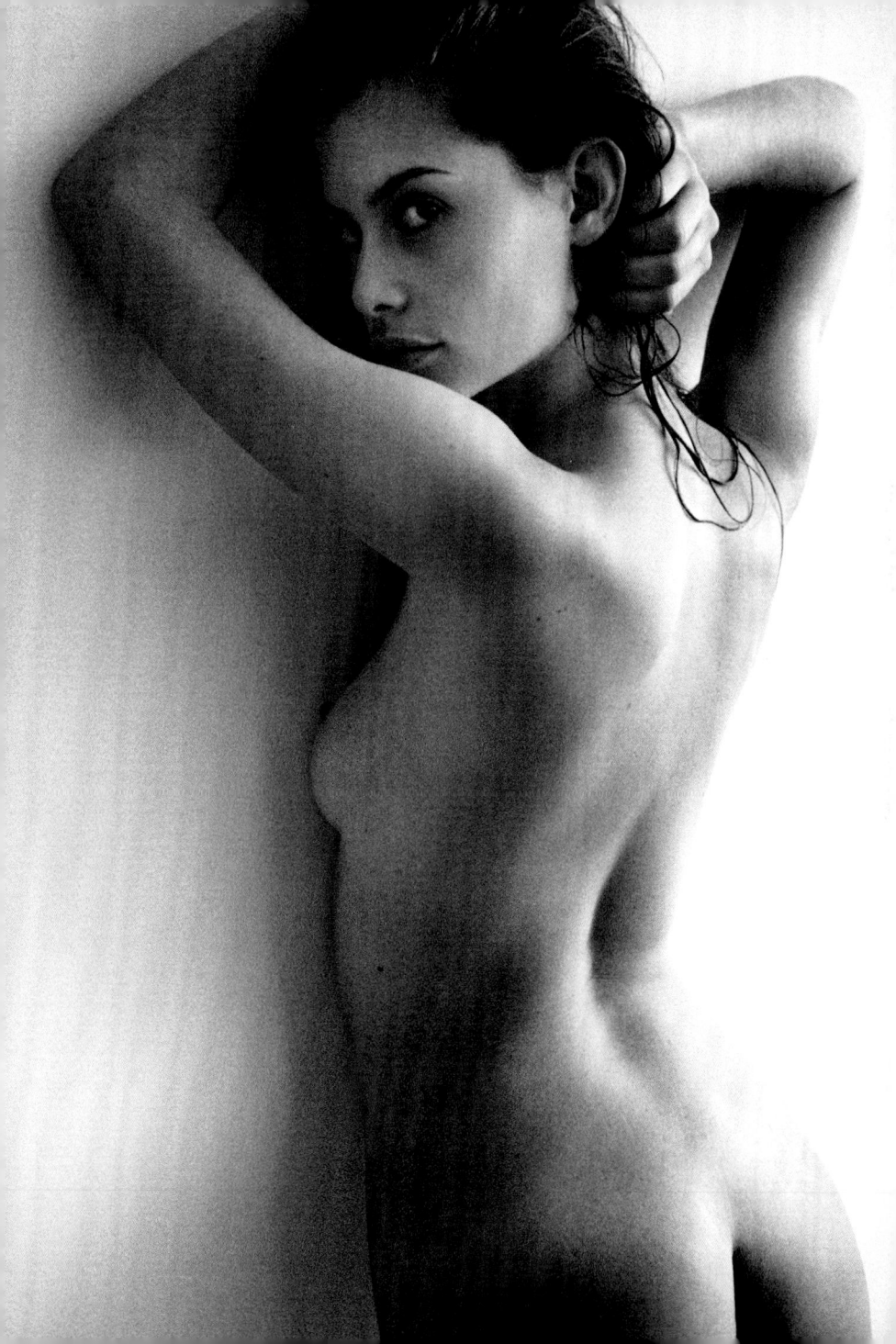

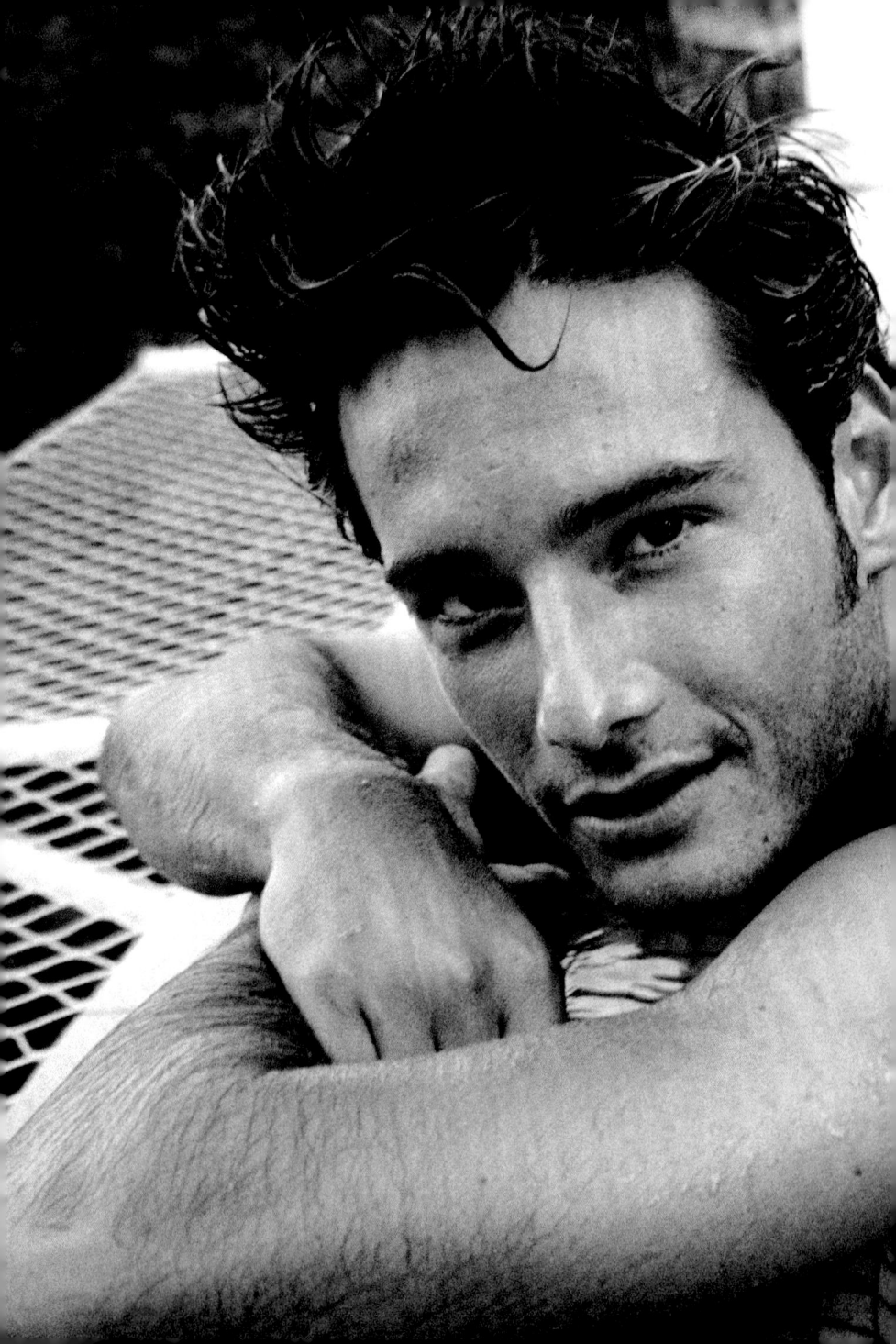

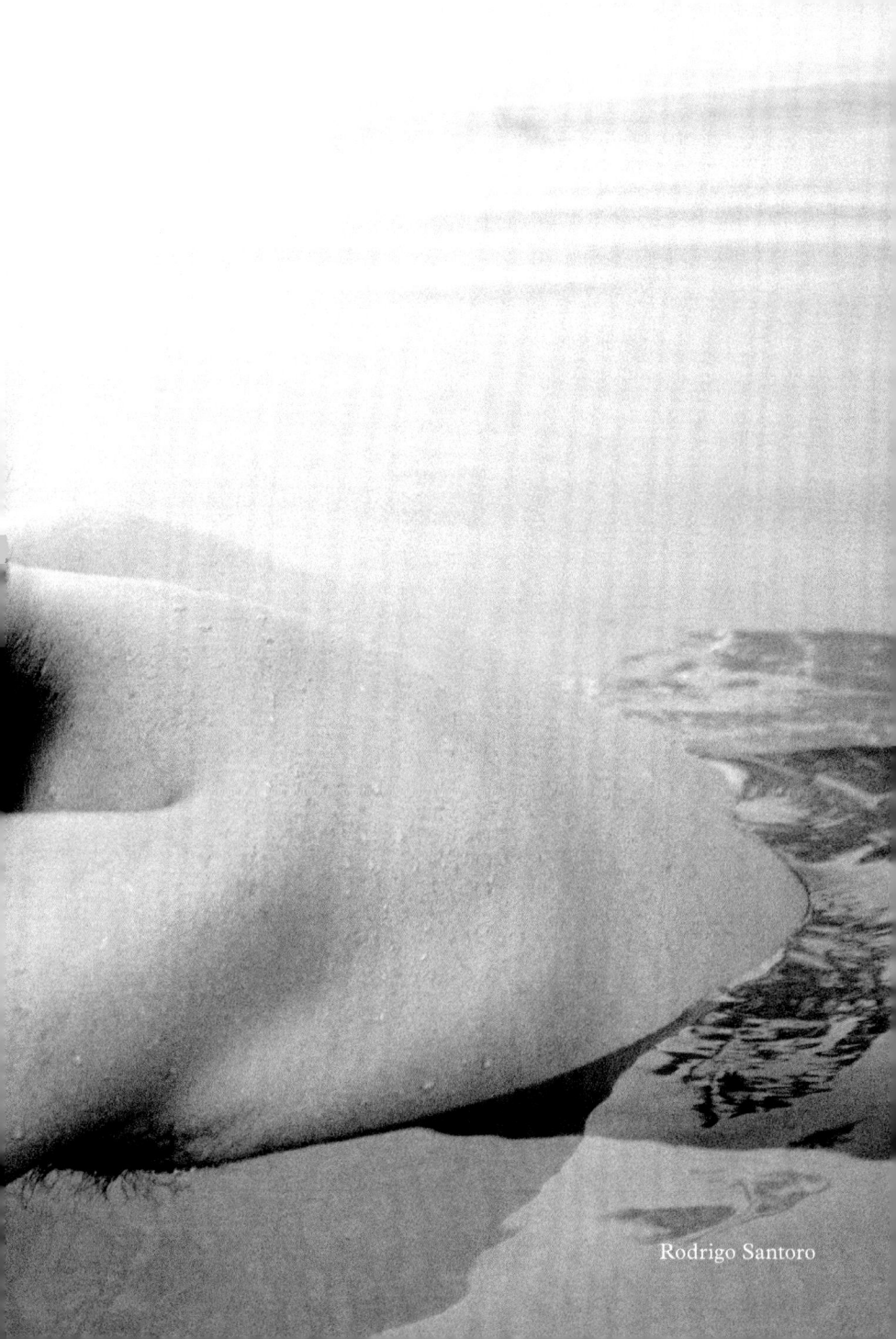

Rodrigo Santoro

Daniella Sarahyba

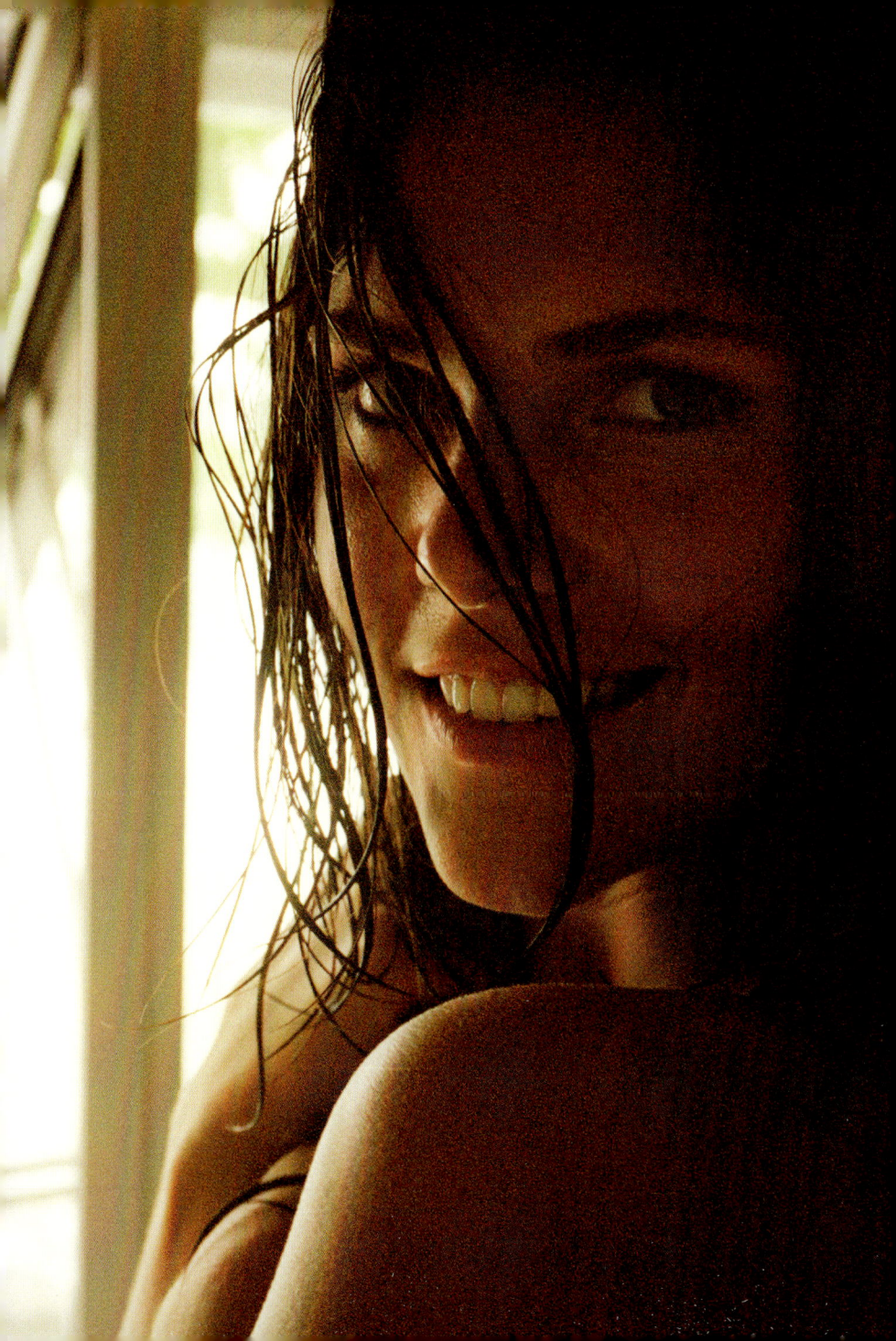

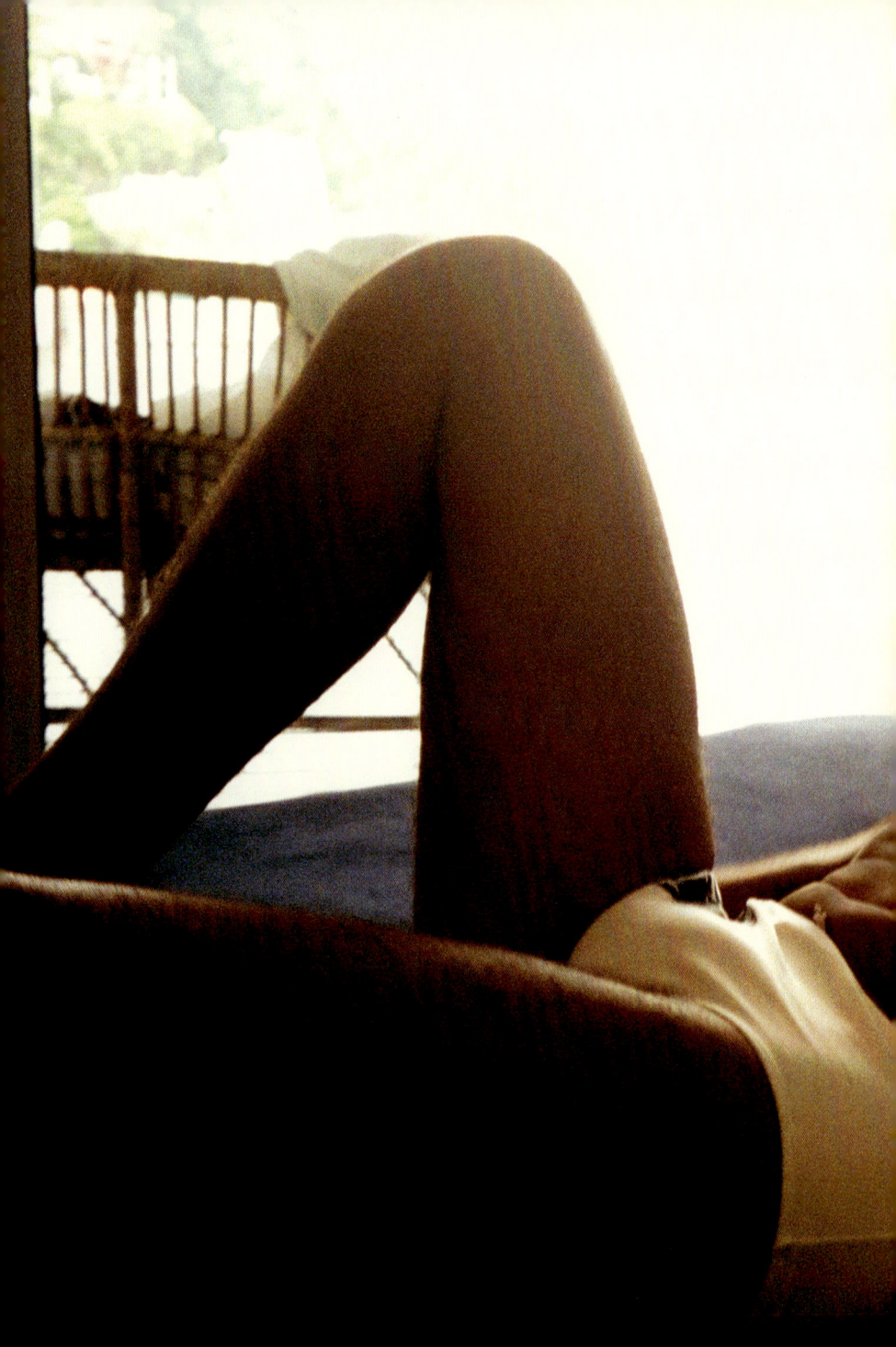

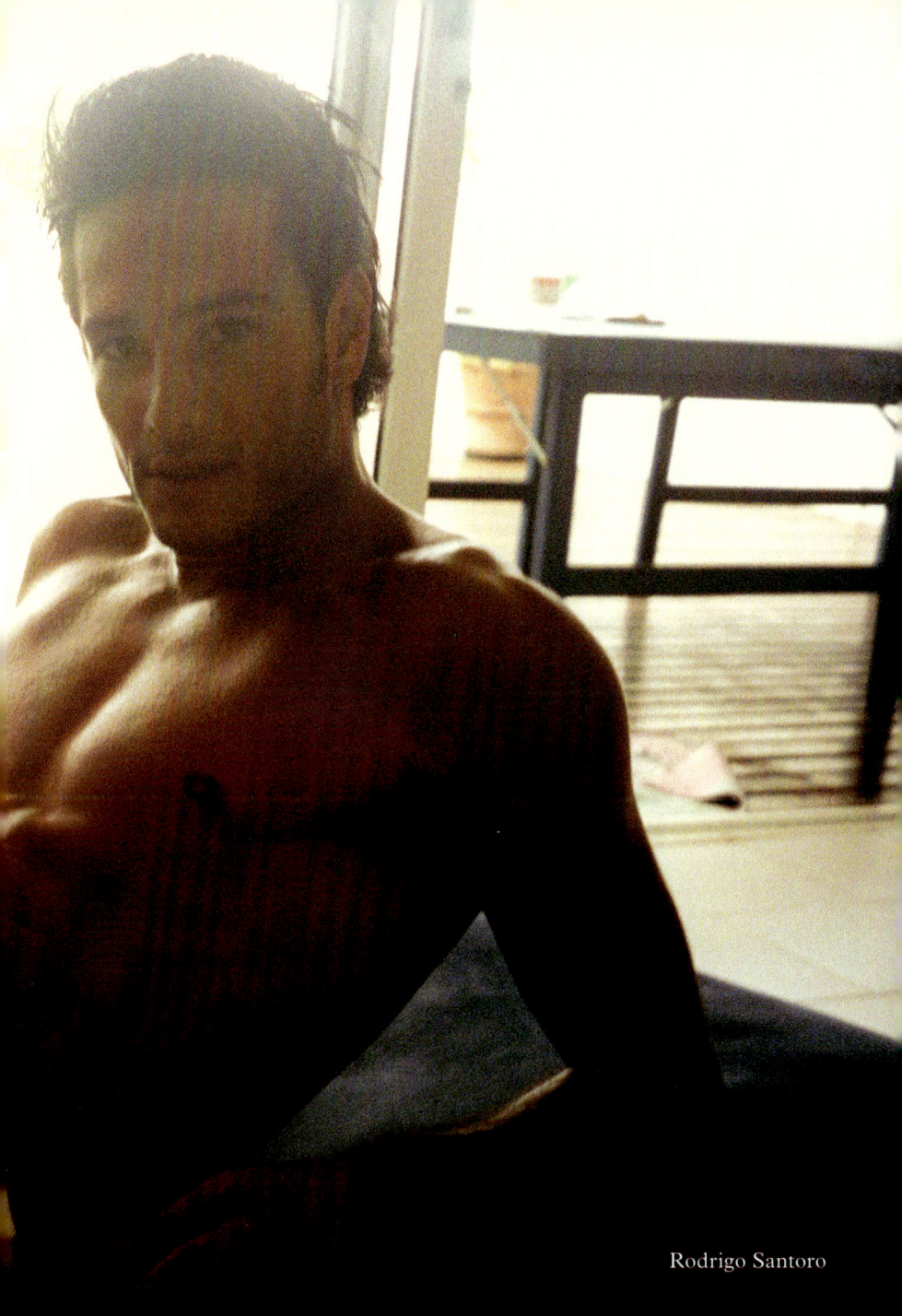

Rodrigo Santoro

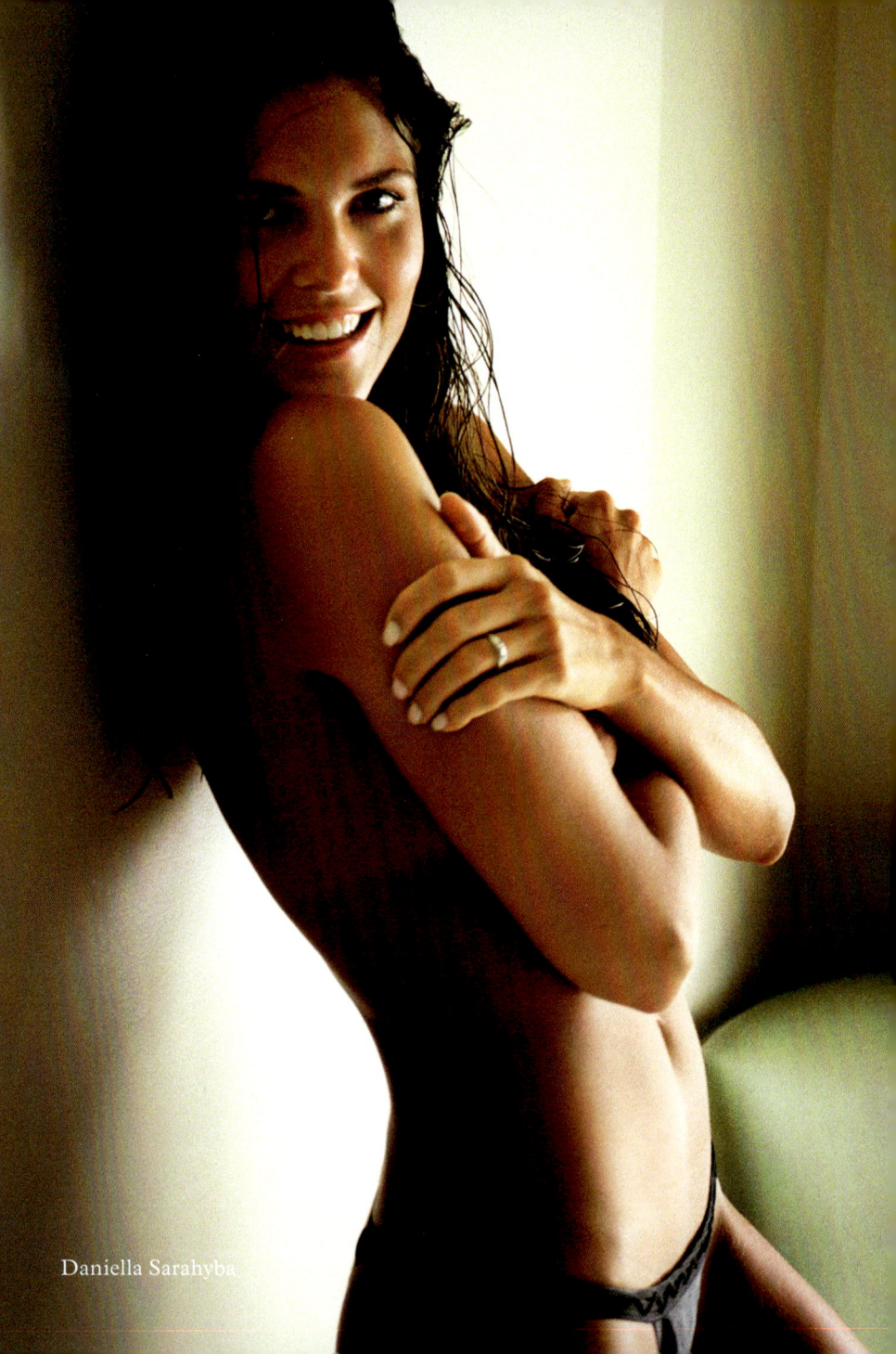

Daniella Sarahyba

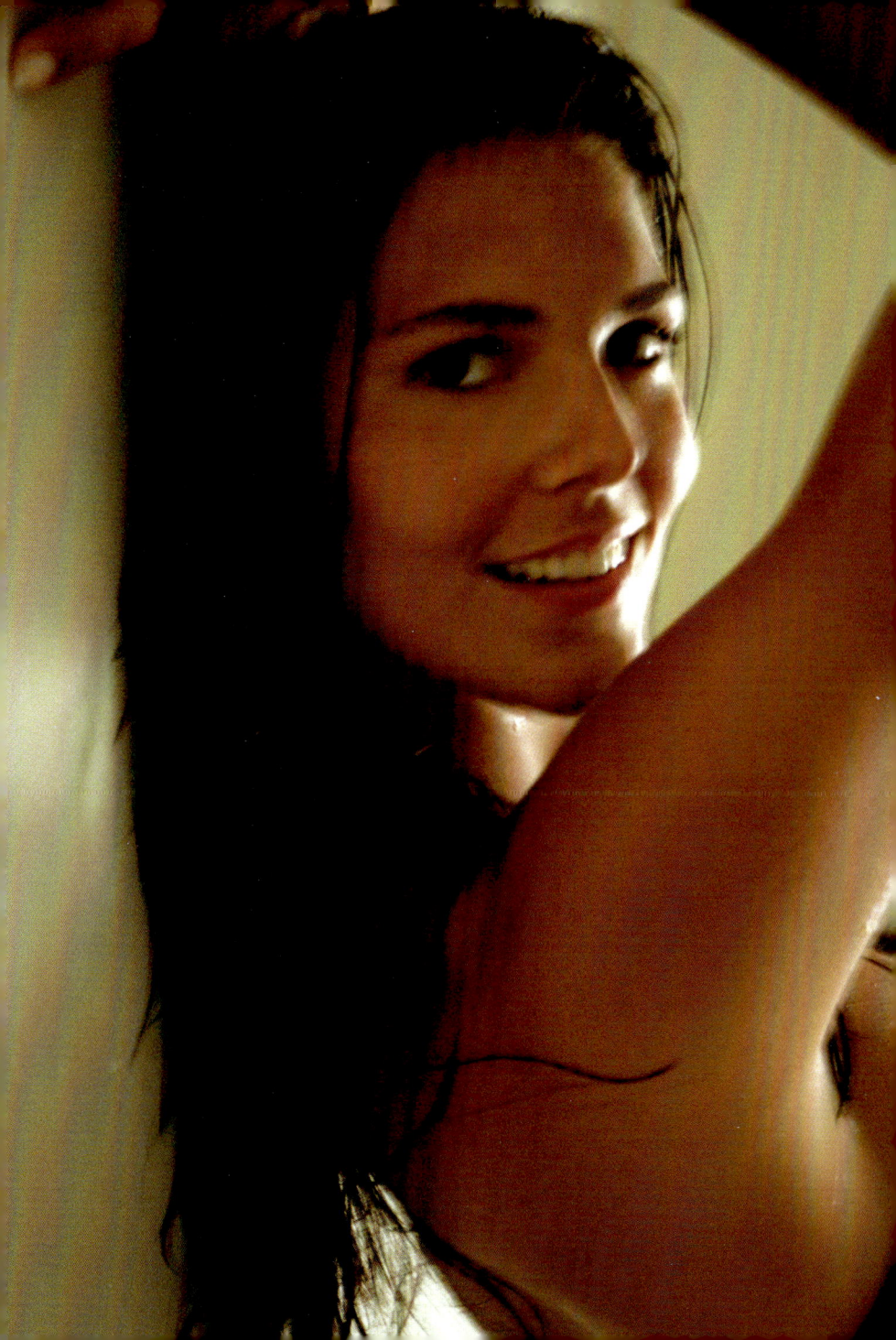

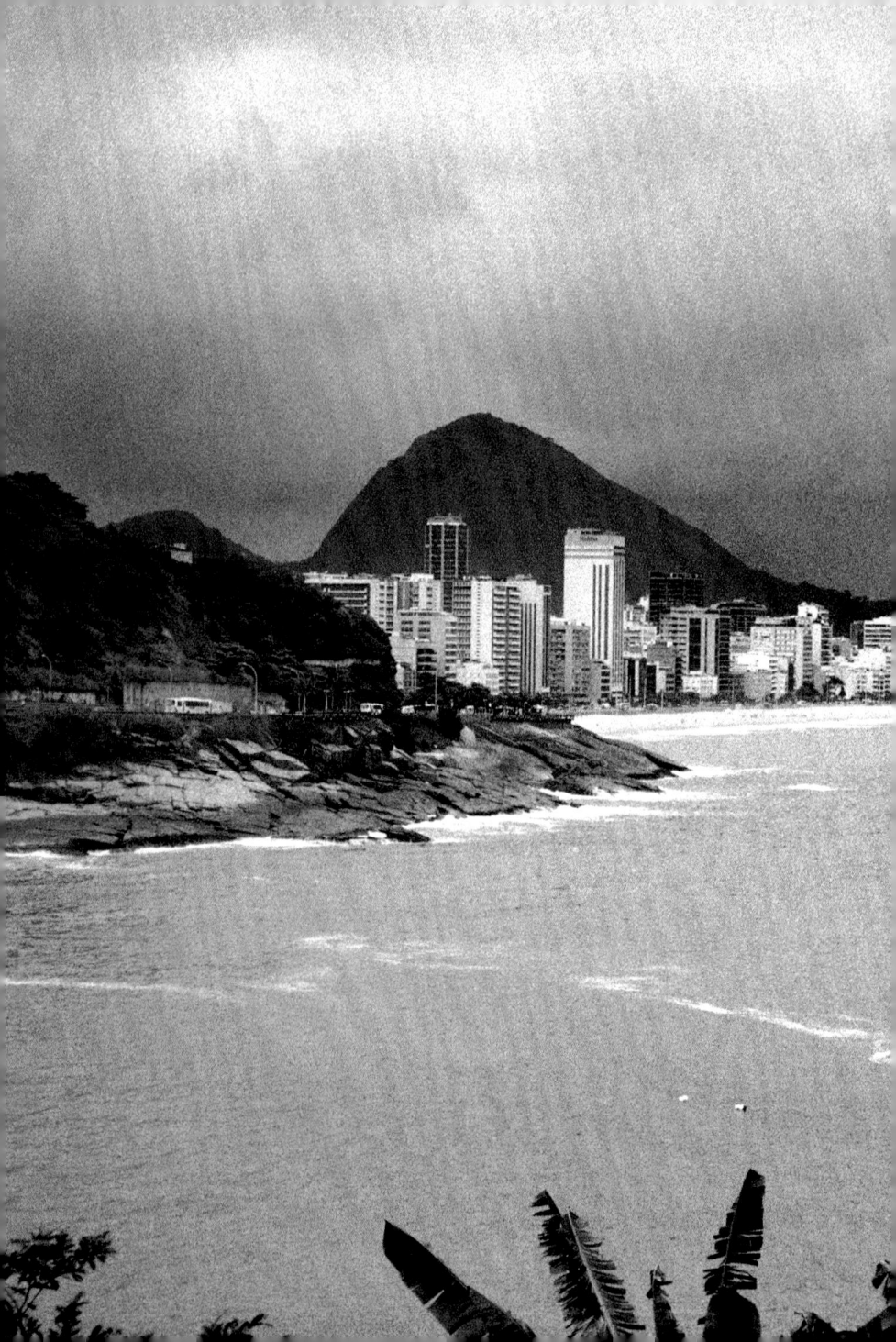

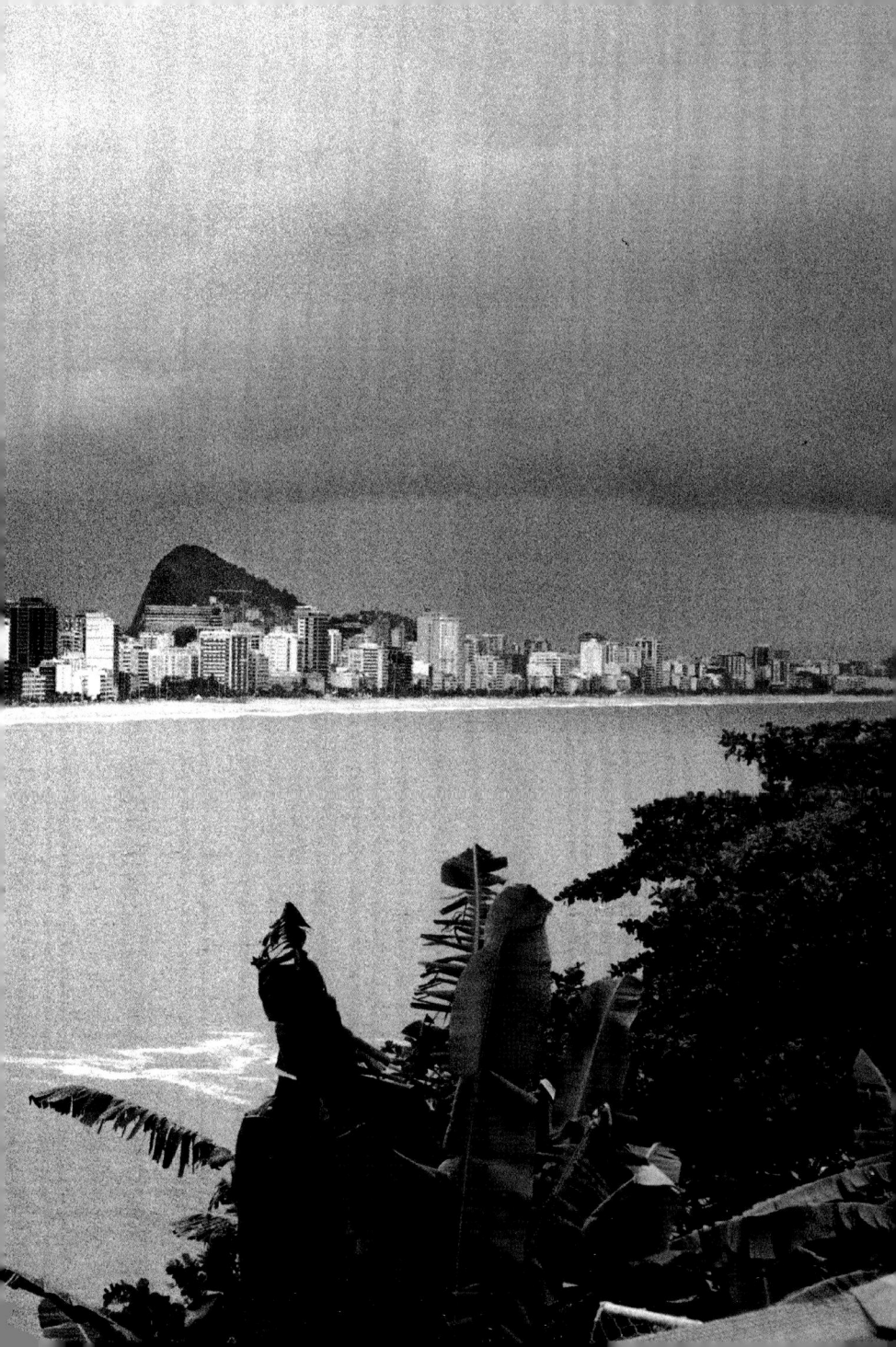

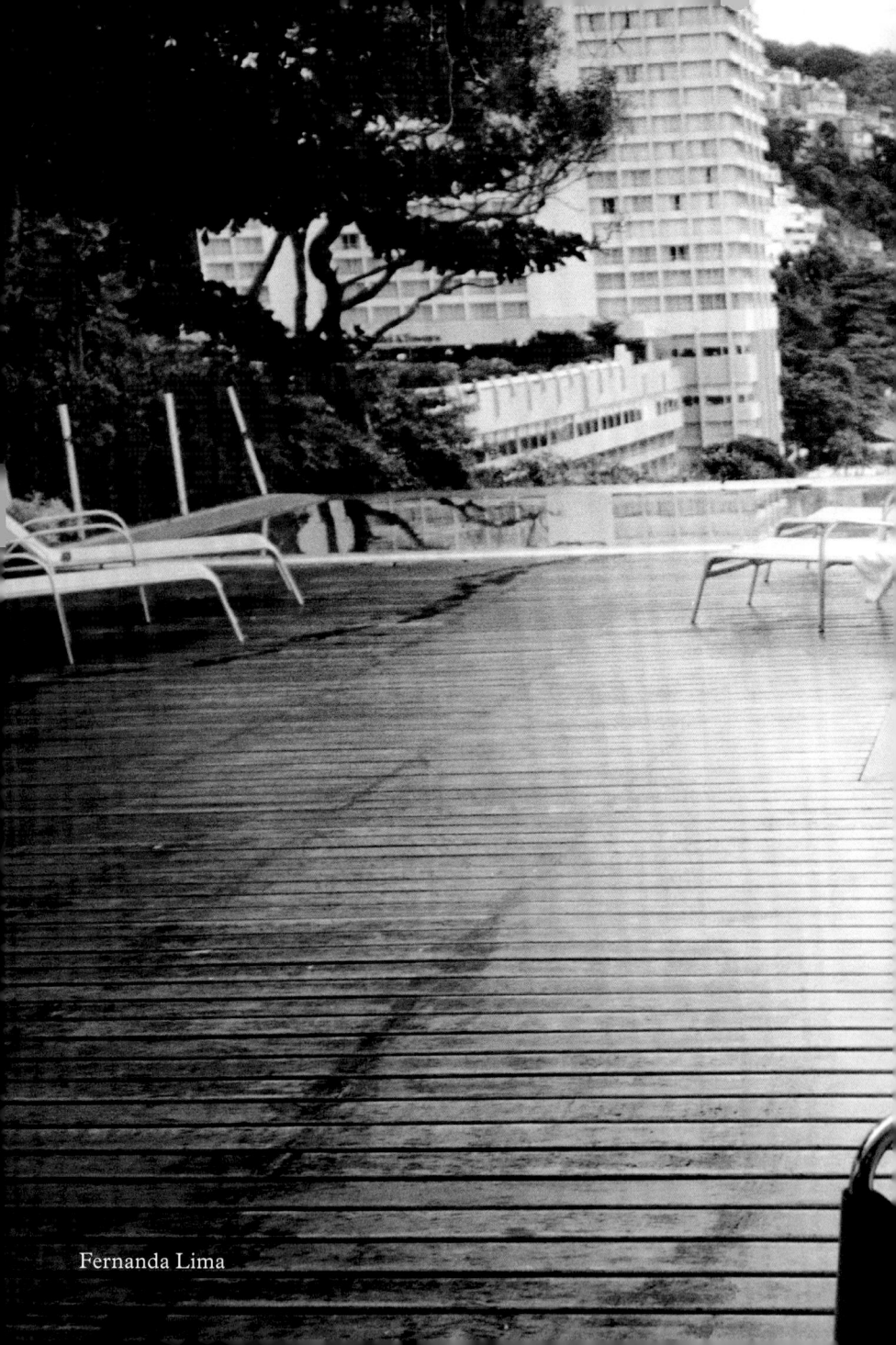
Fernanda Lima

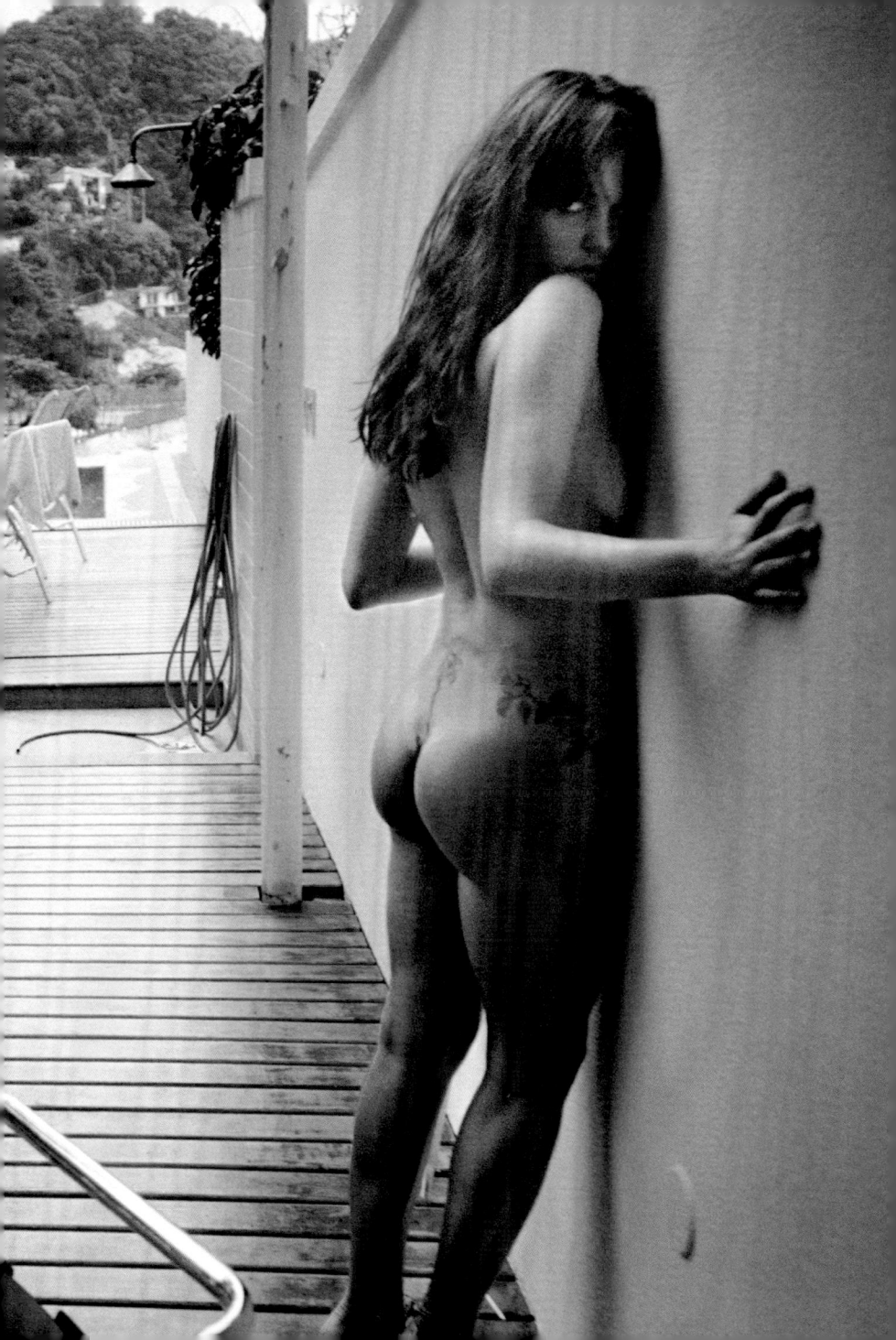

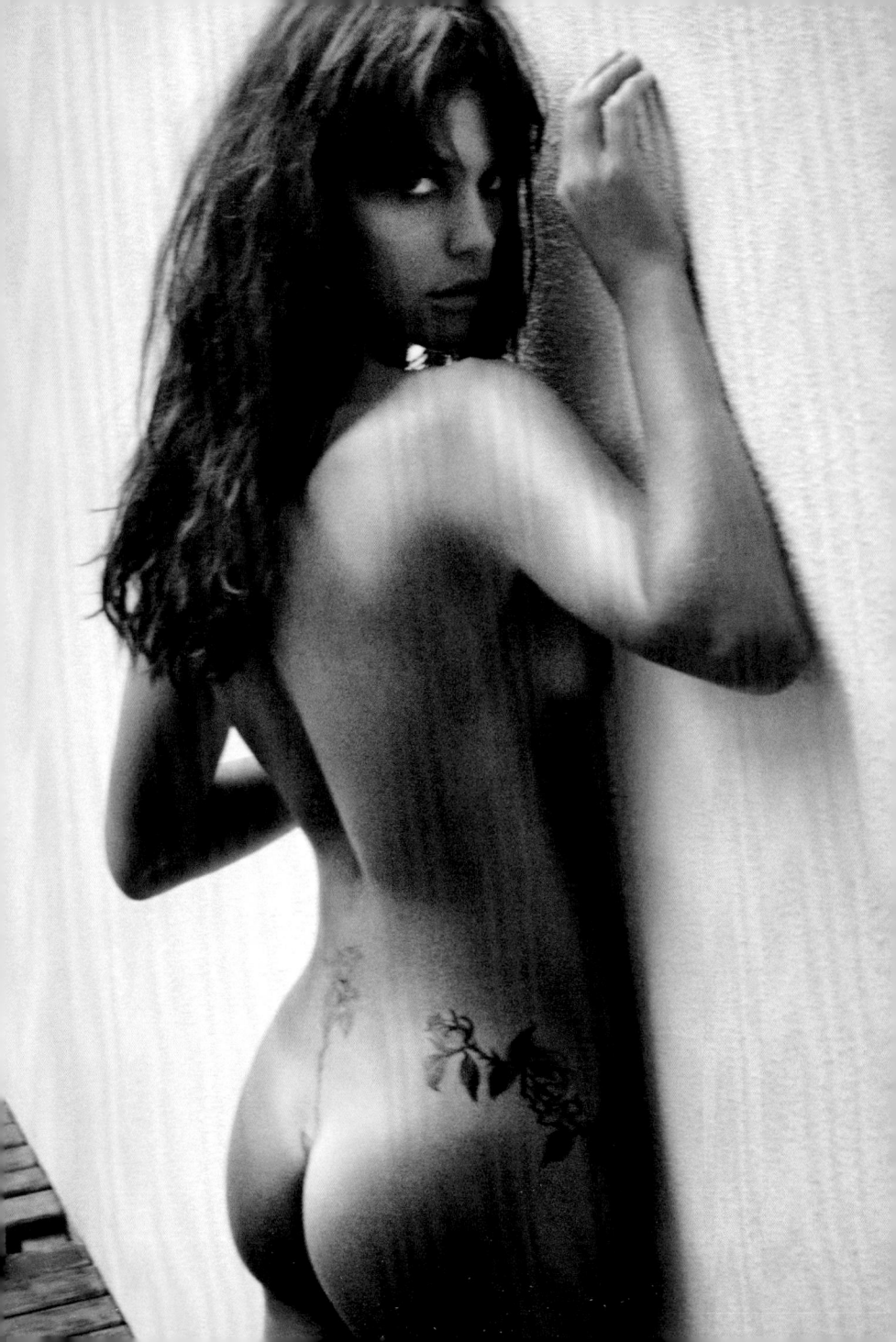

Fernanda Lima

Fernanda Lima

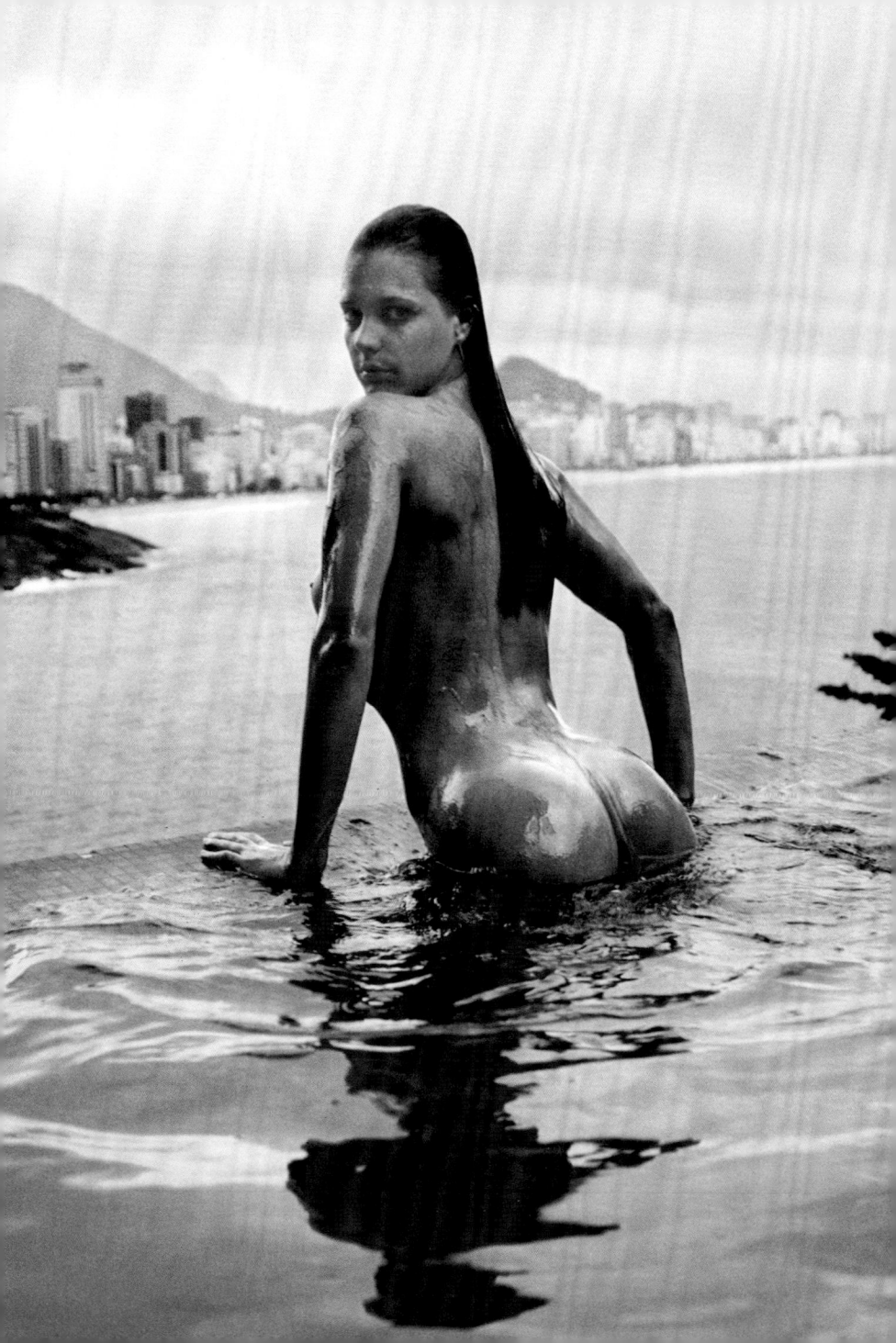

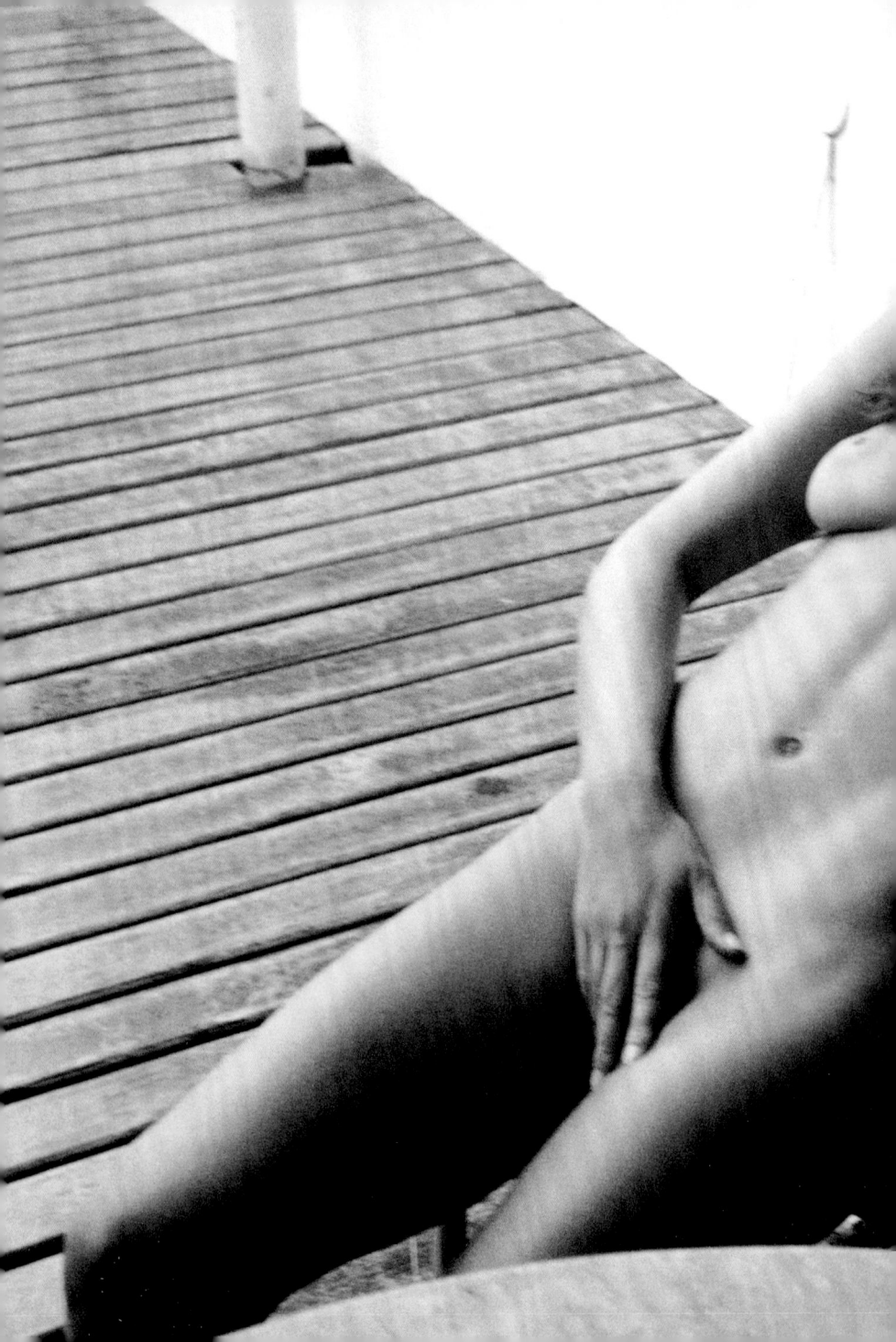

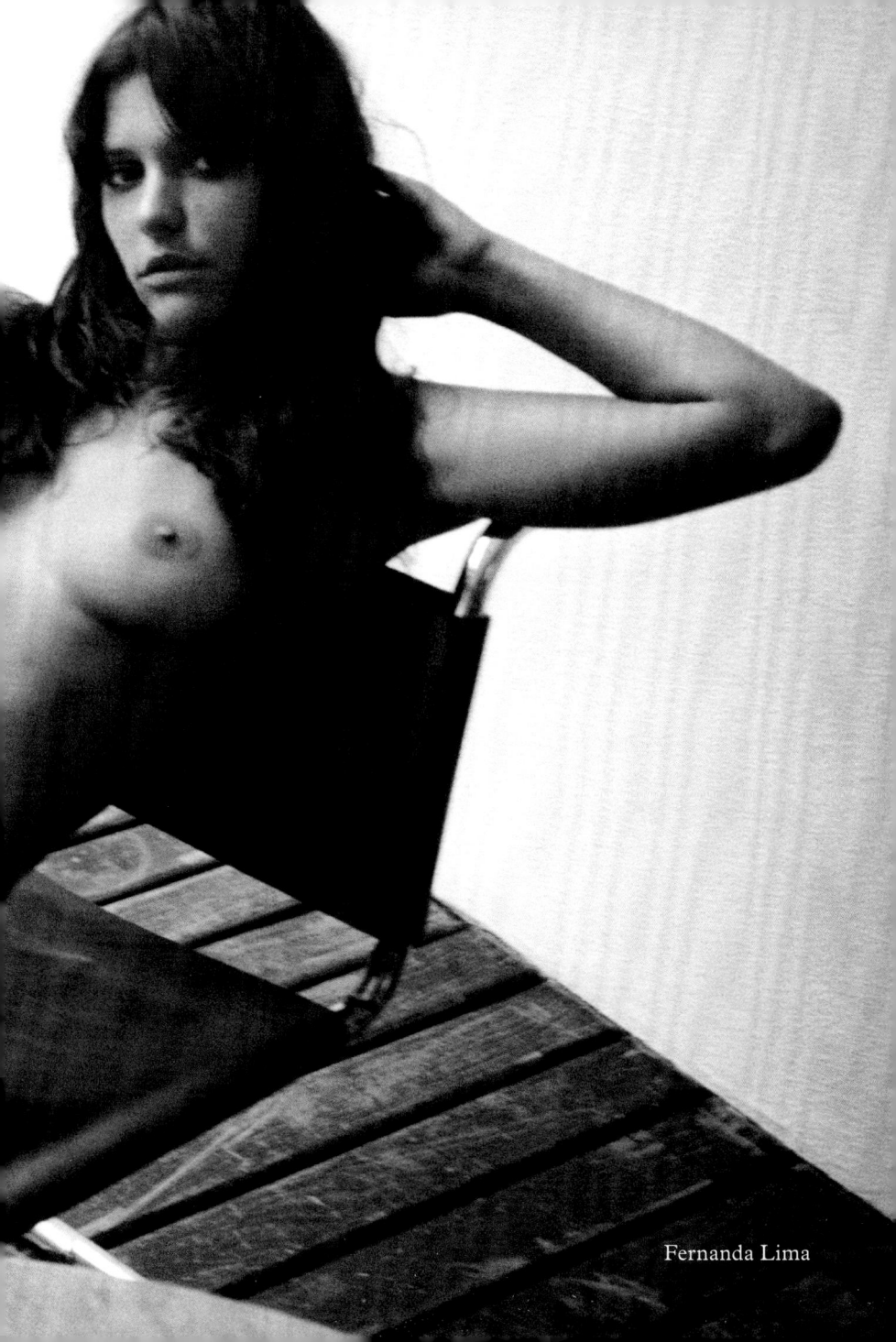

Fernanda Lima

Fernanda Lima

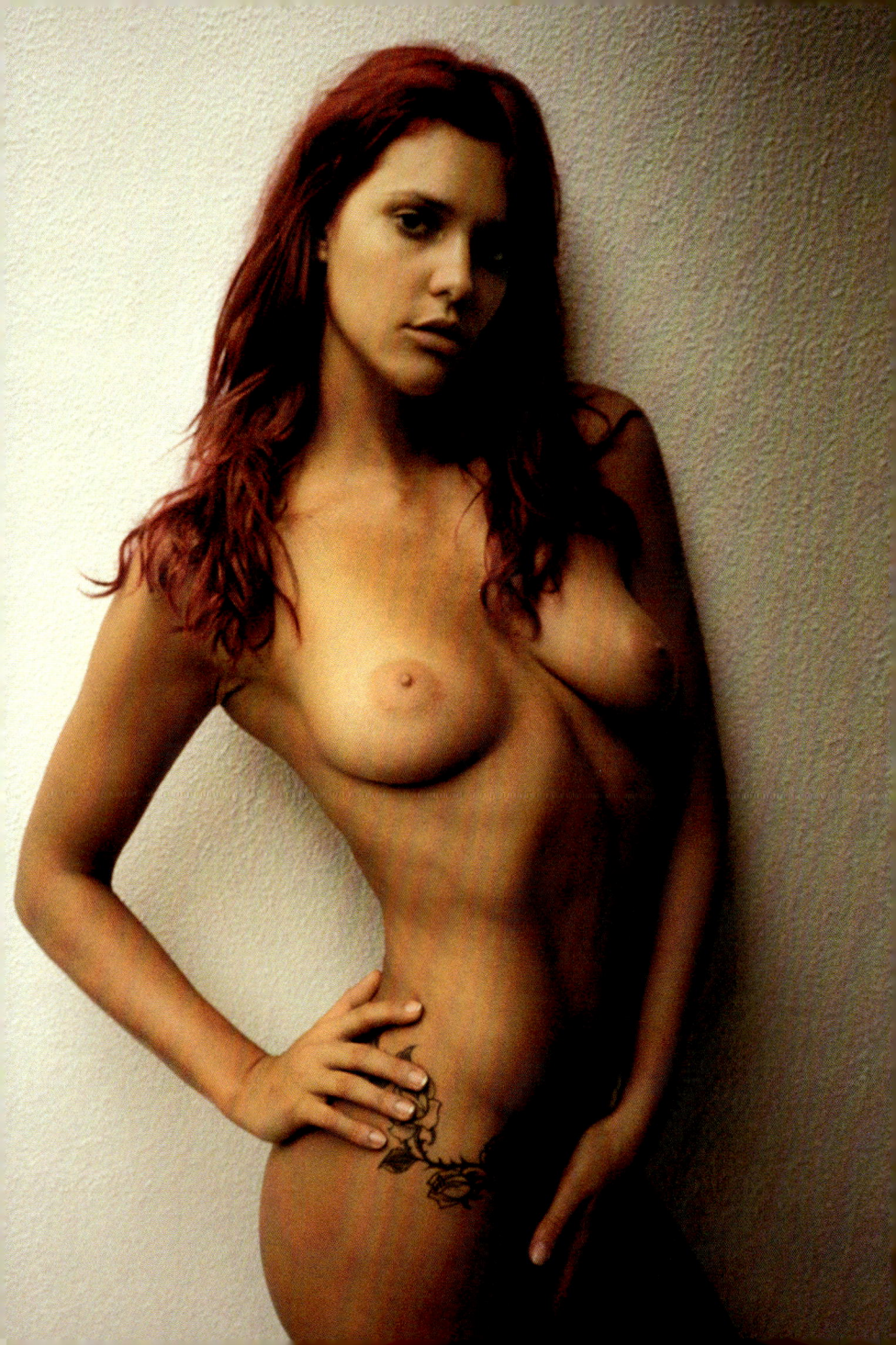

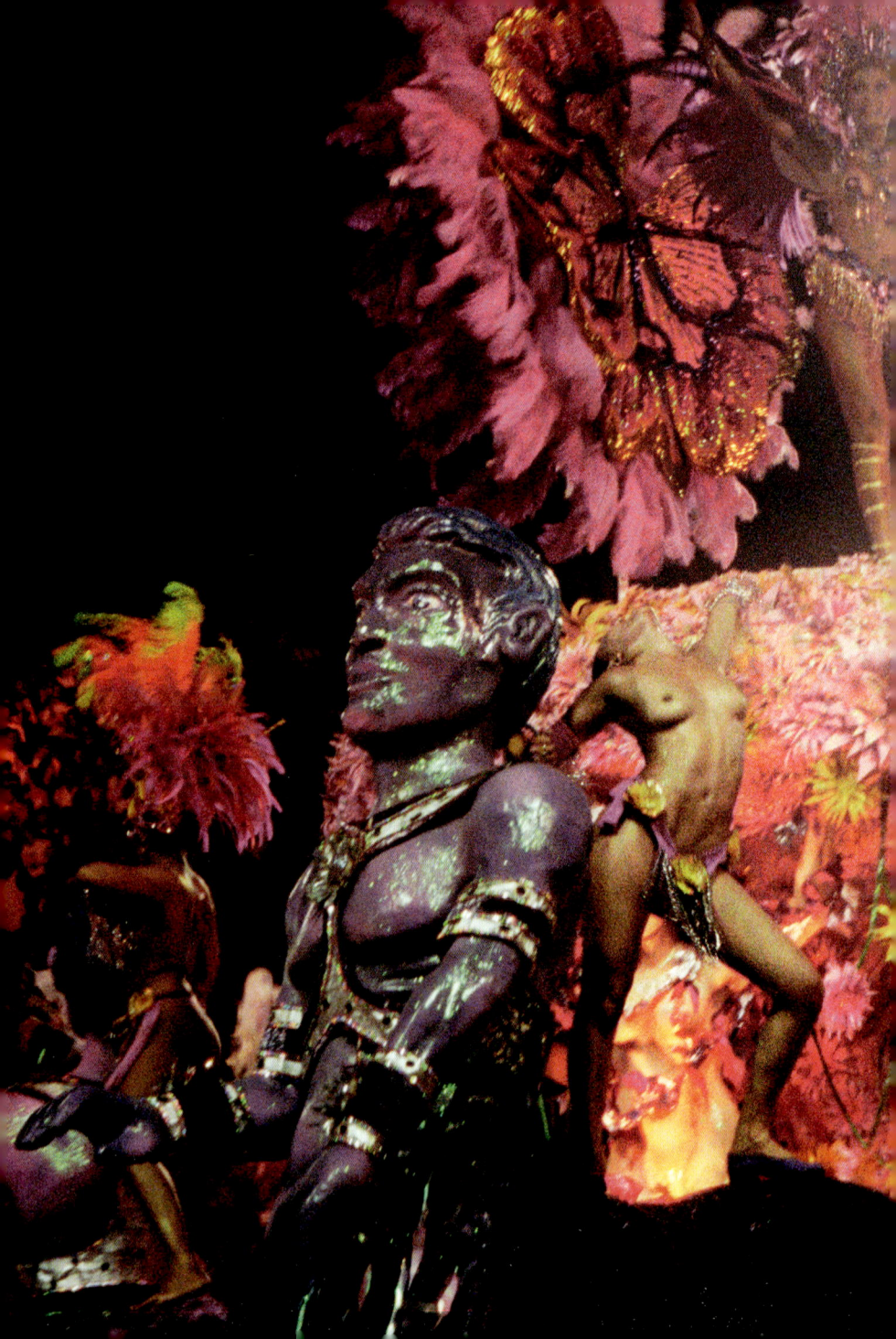

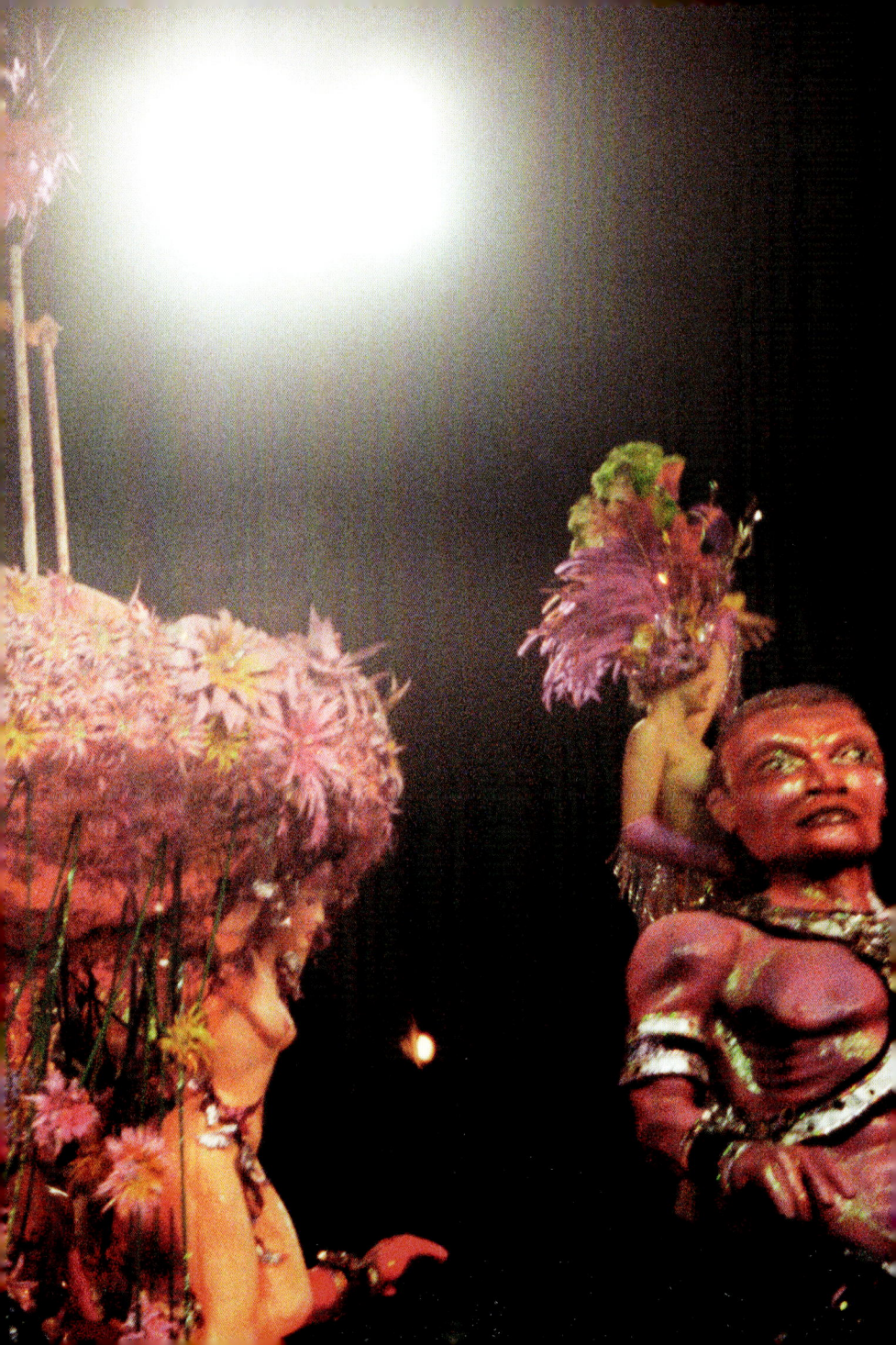

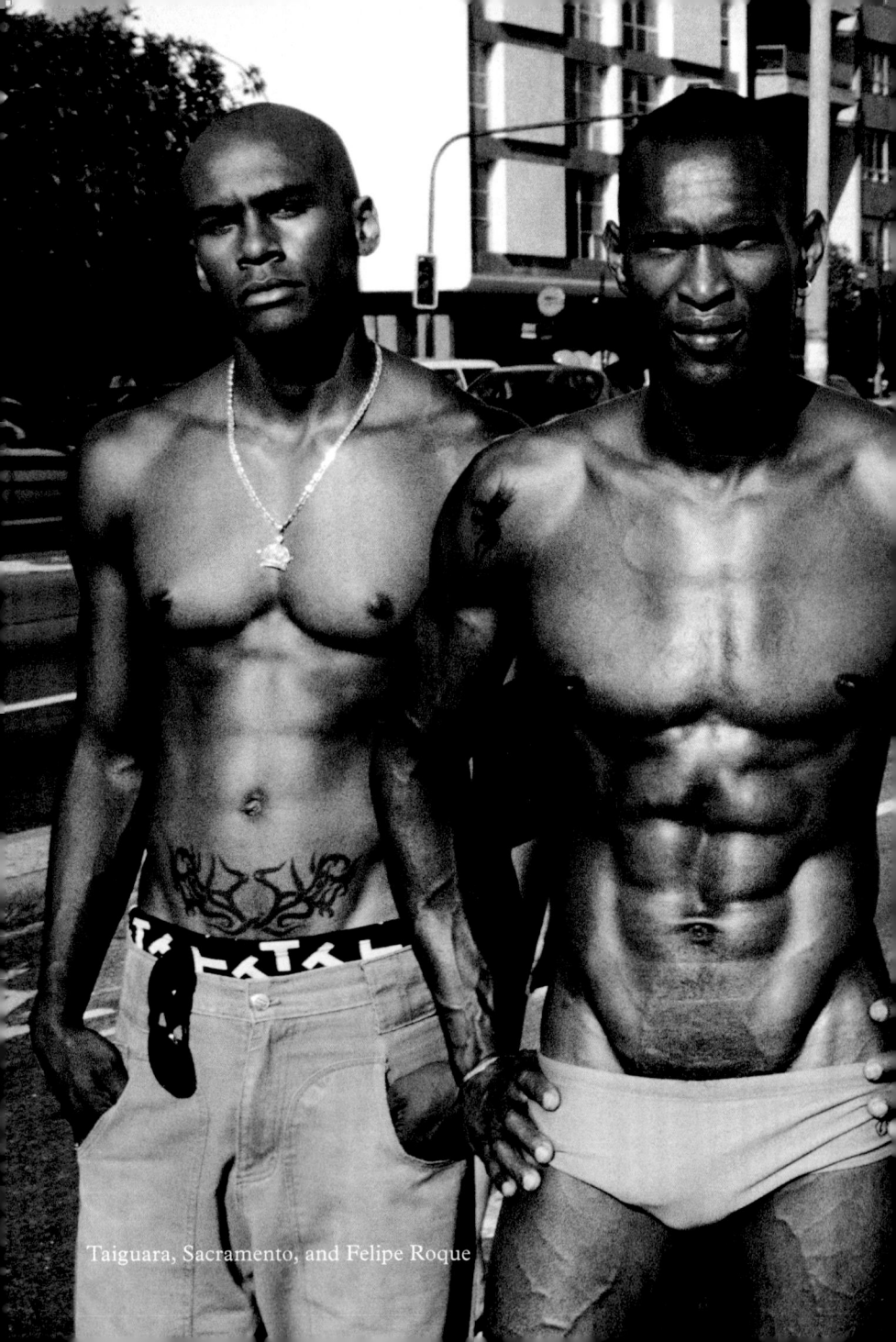

Taiguara, Sacramento, and Felipe Roque

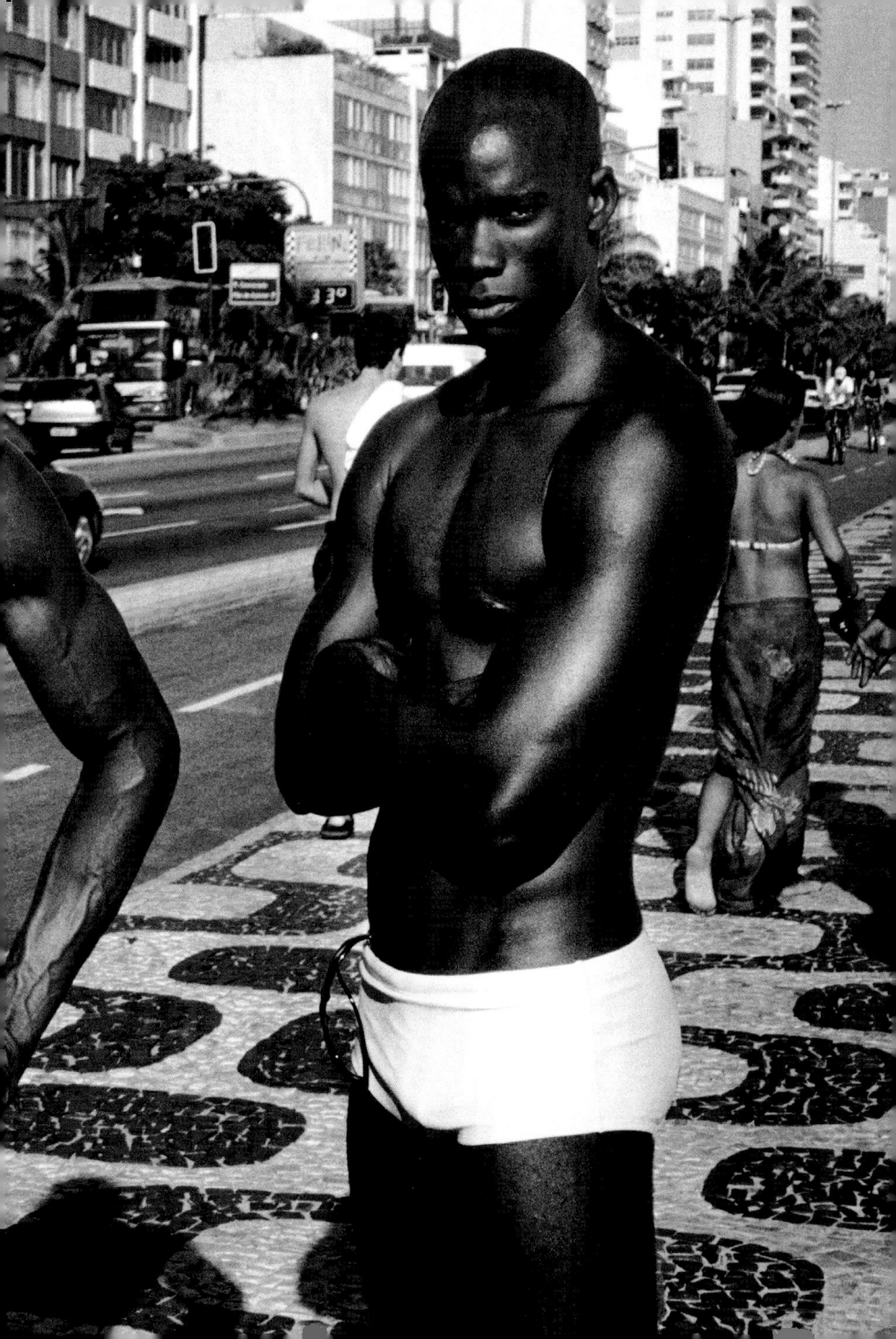

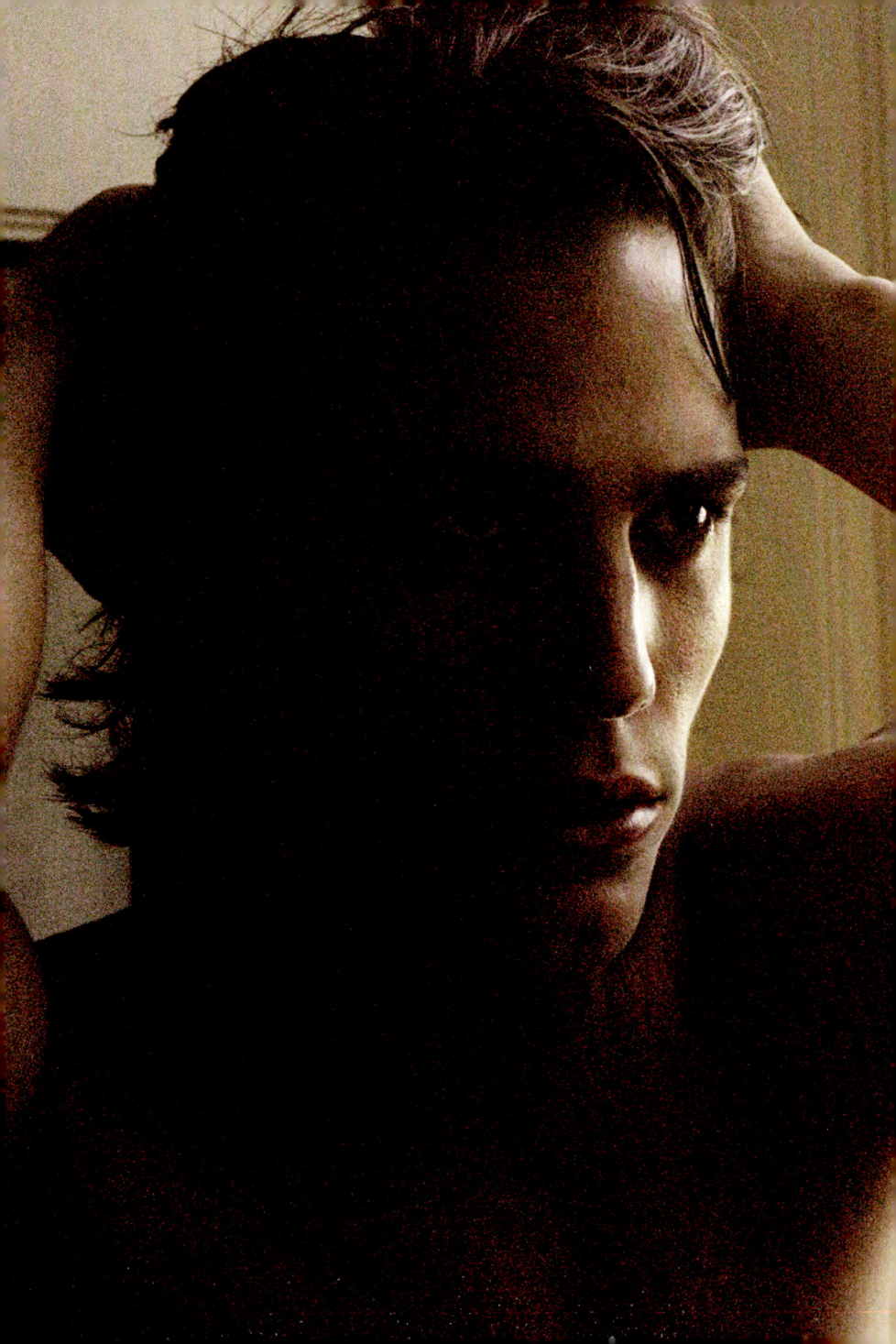

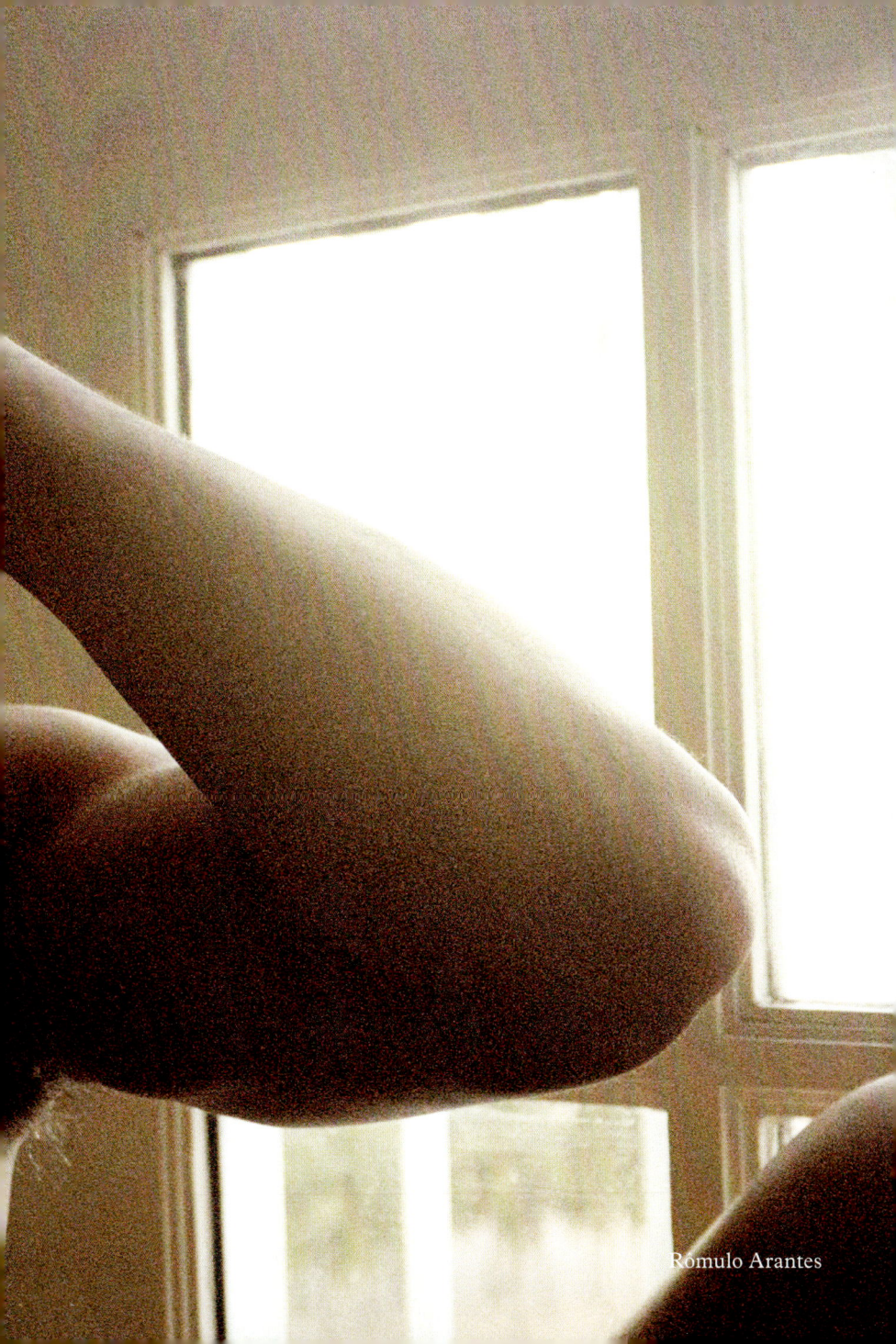

Rômulo Arantes

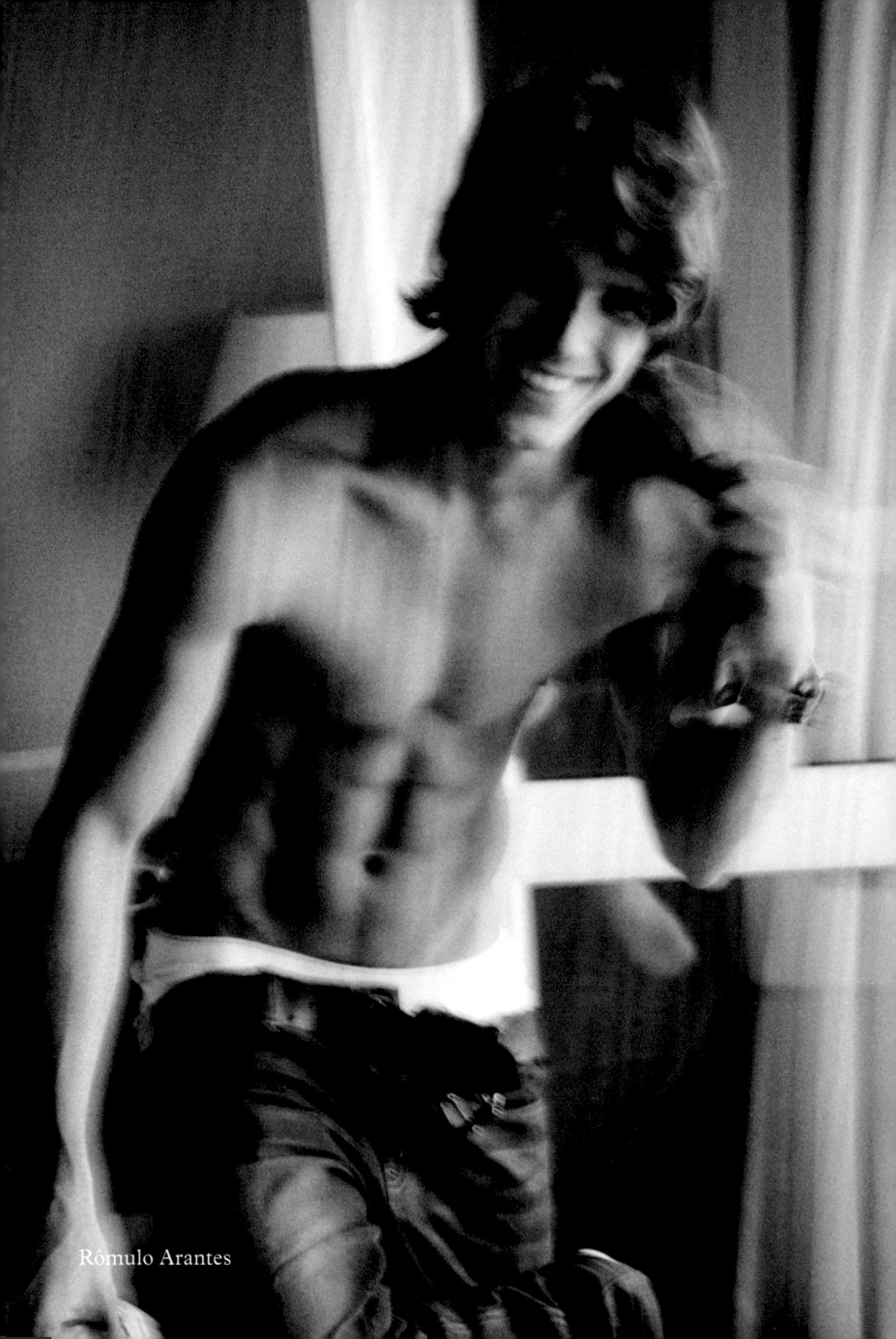
Rômulo Arantes

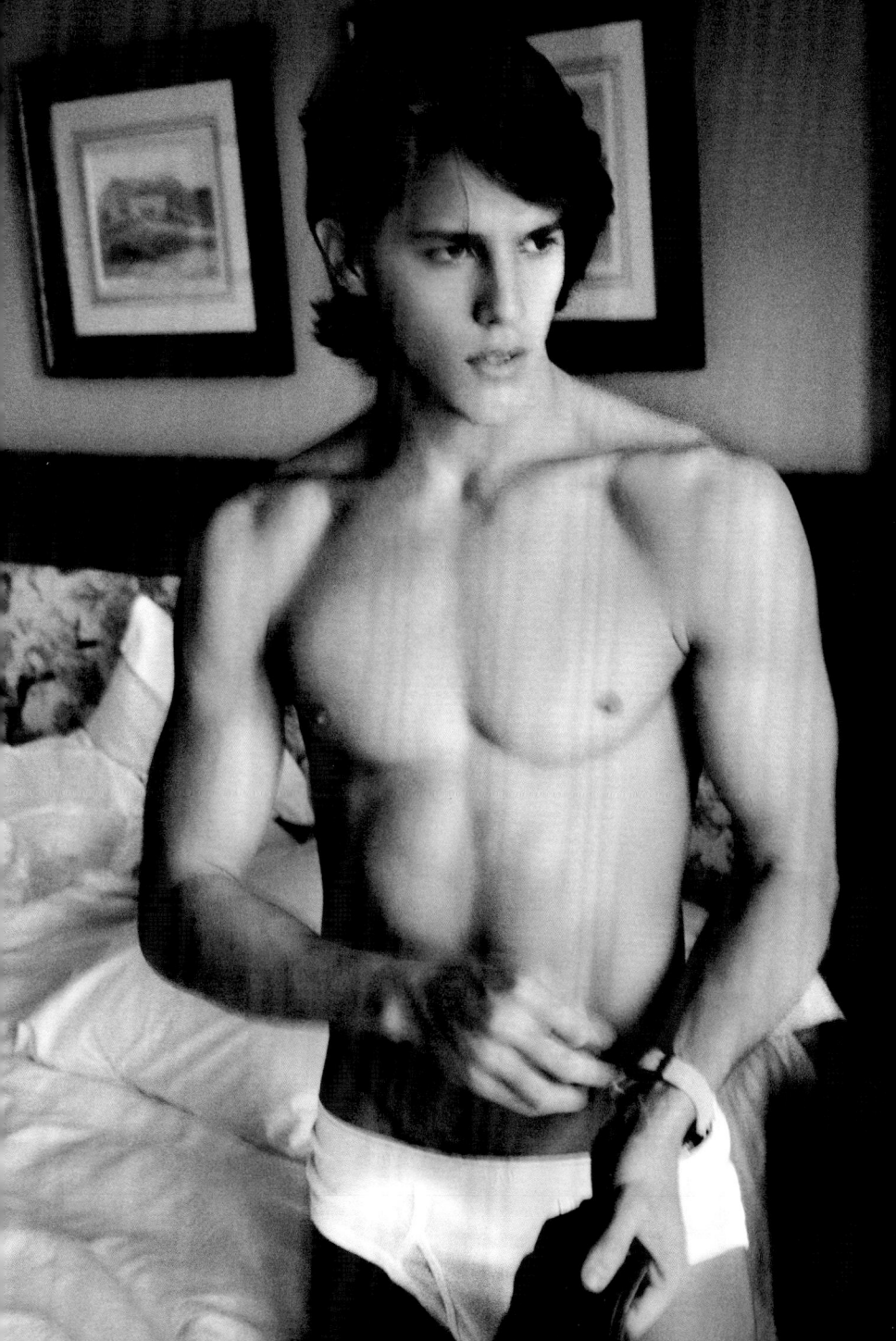

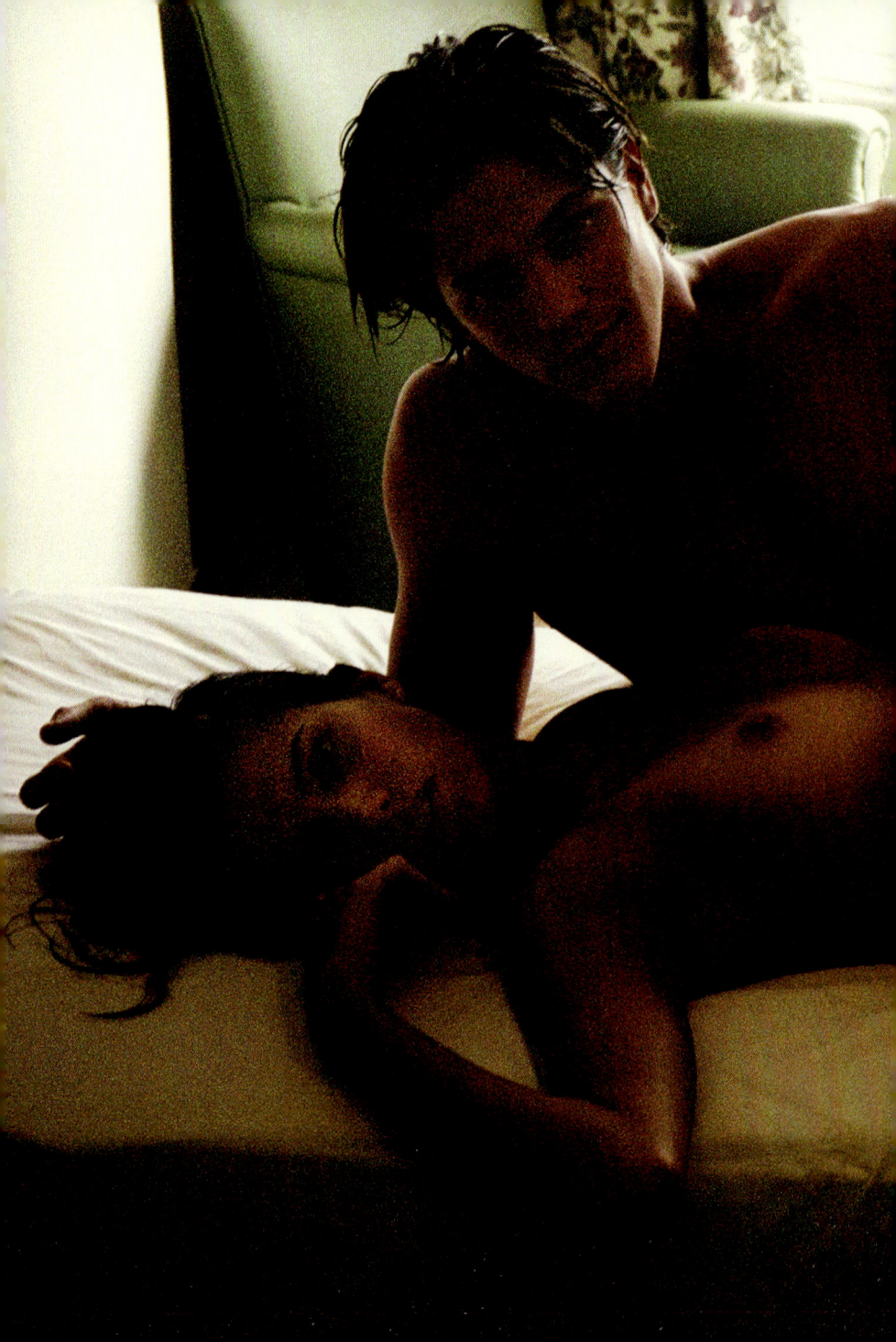

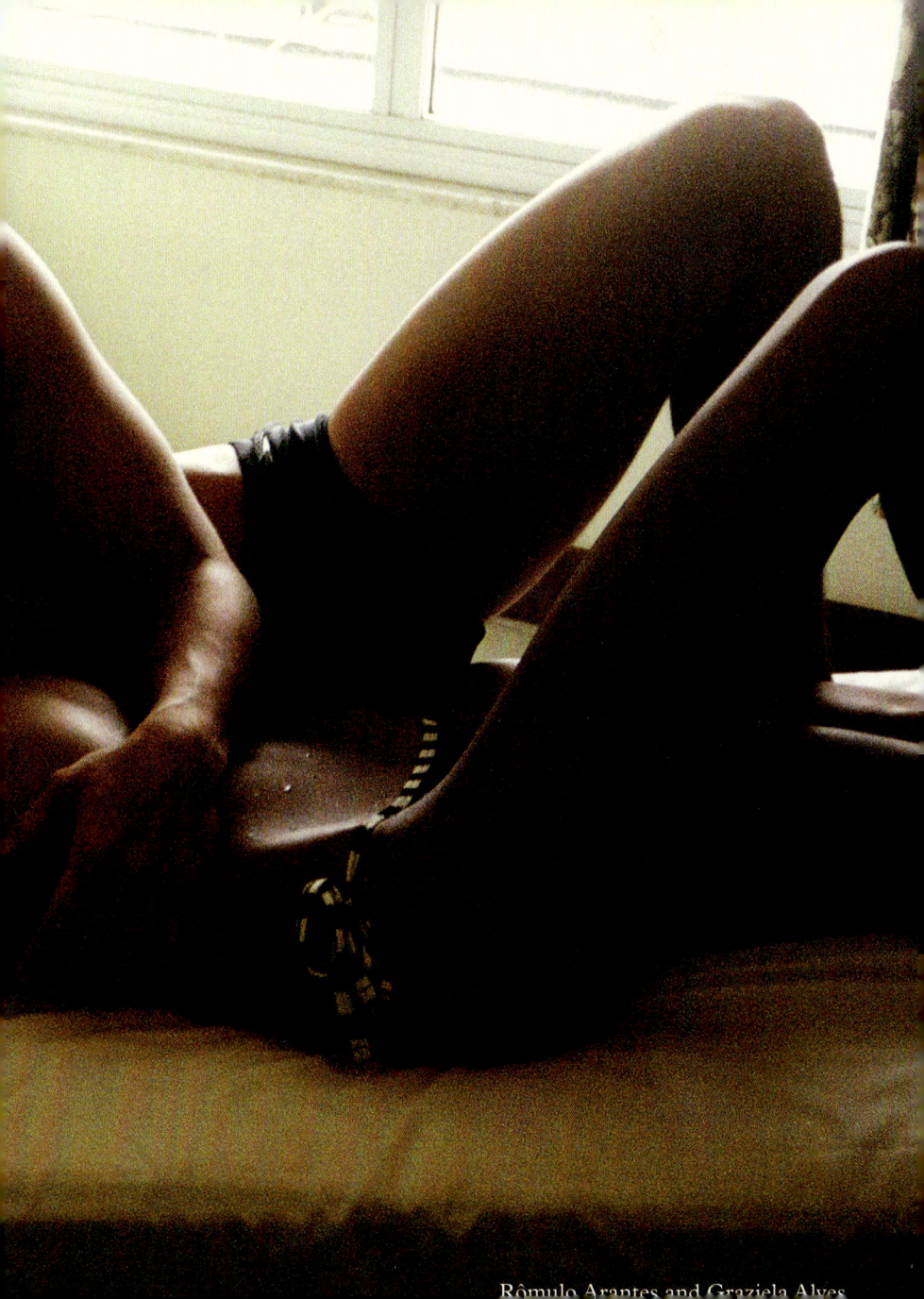

Rômulo Arantes and Graziela Alves

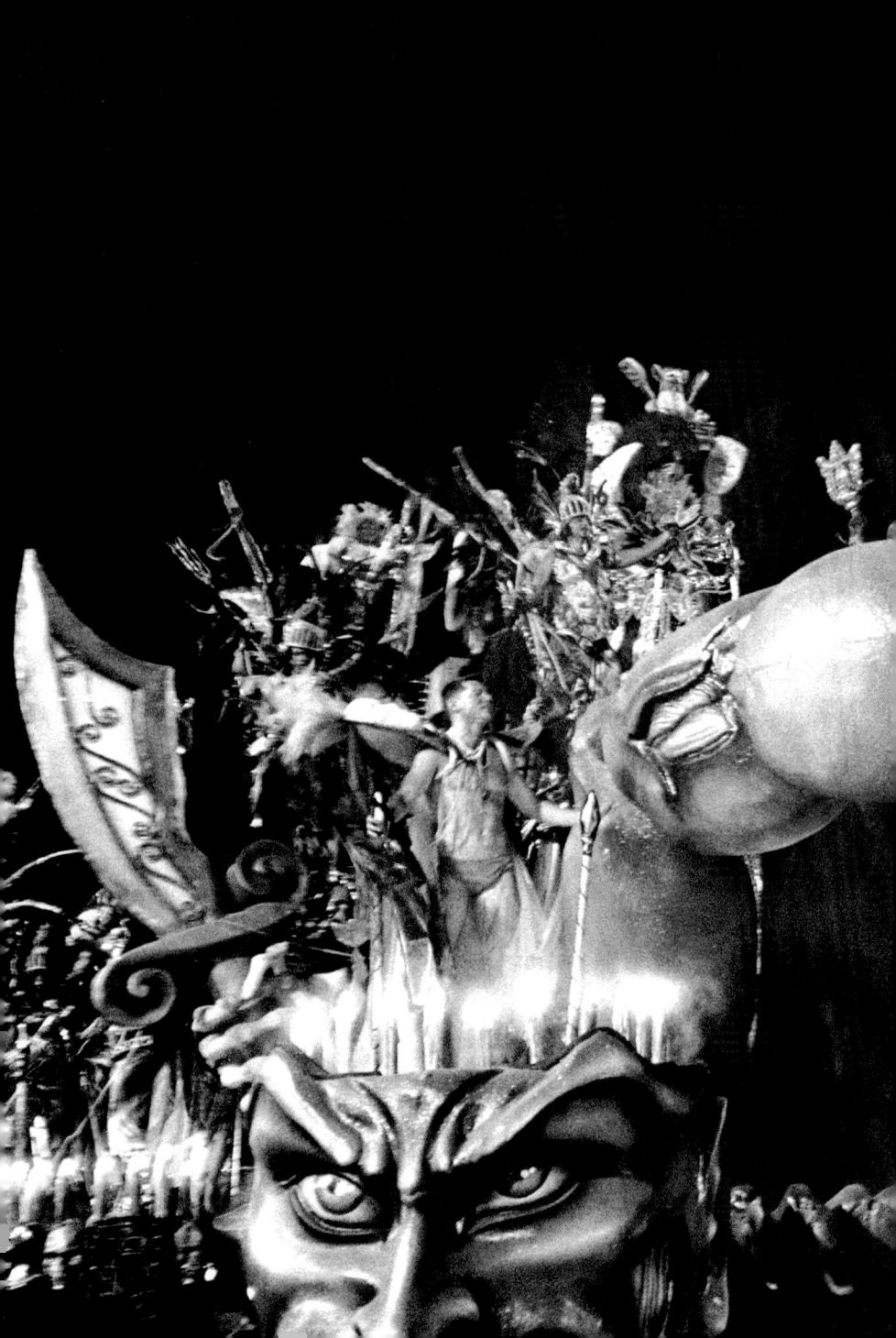

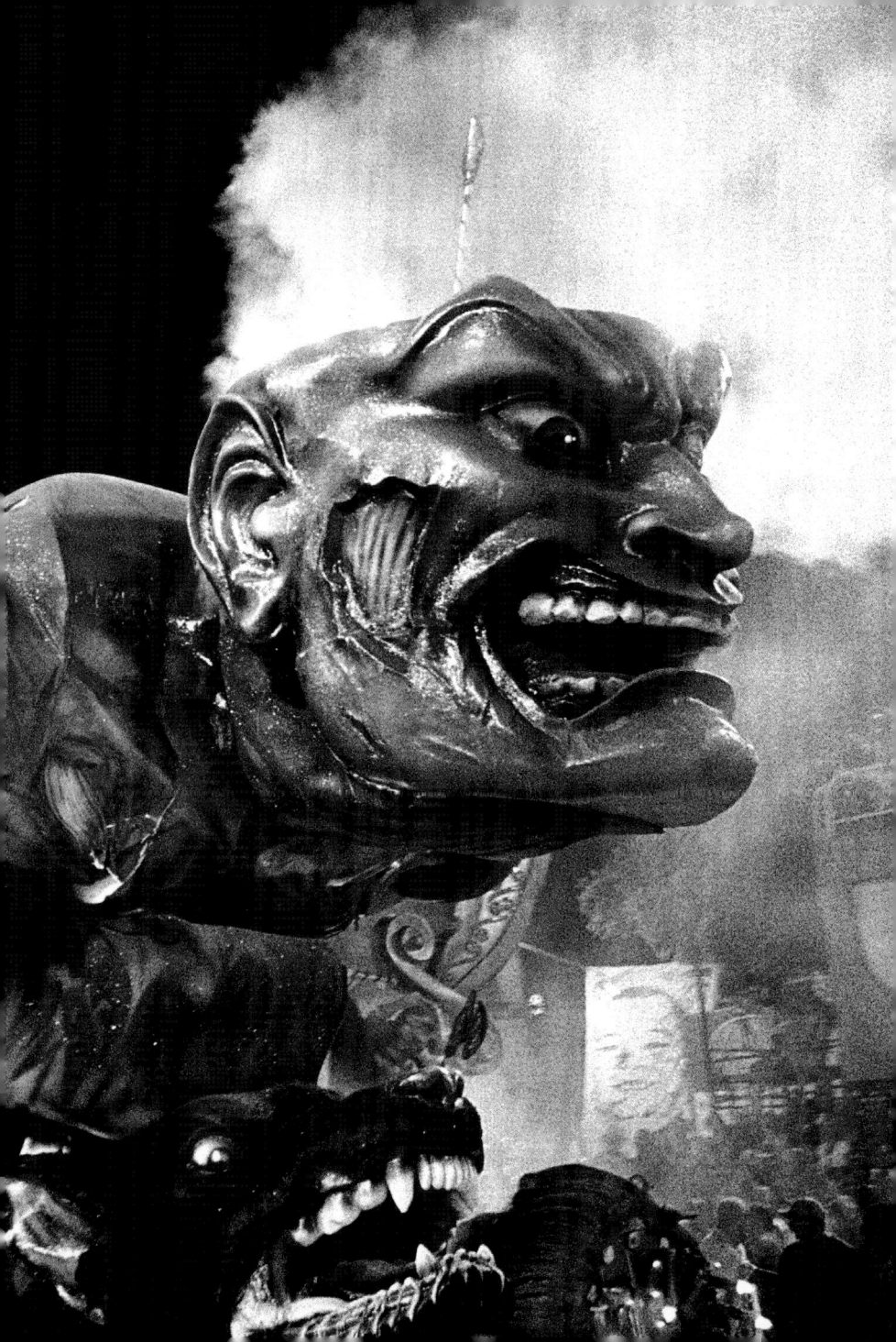

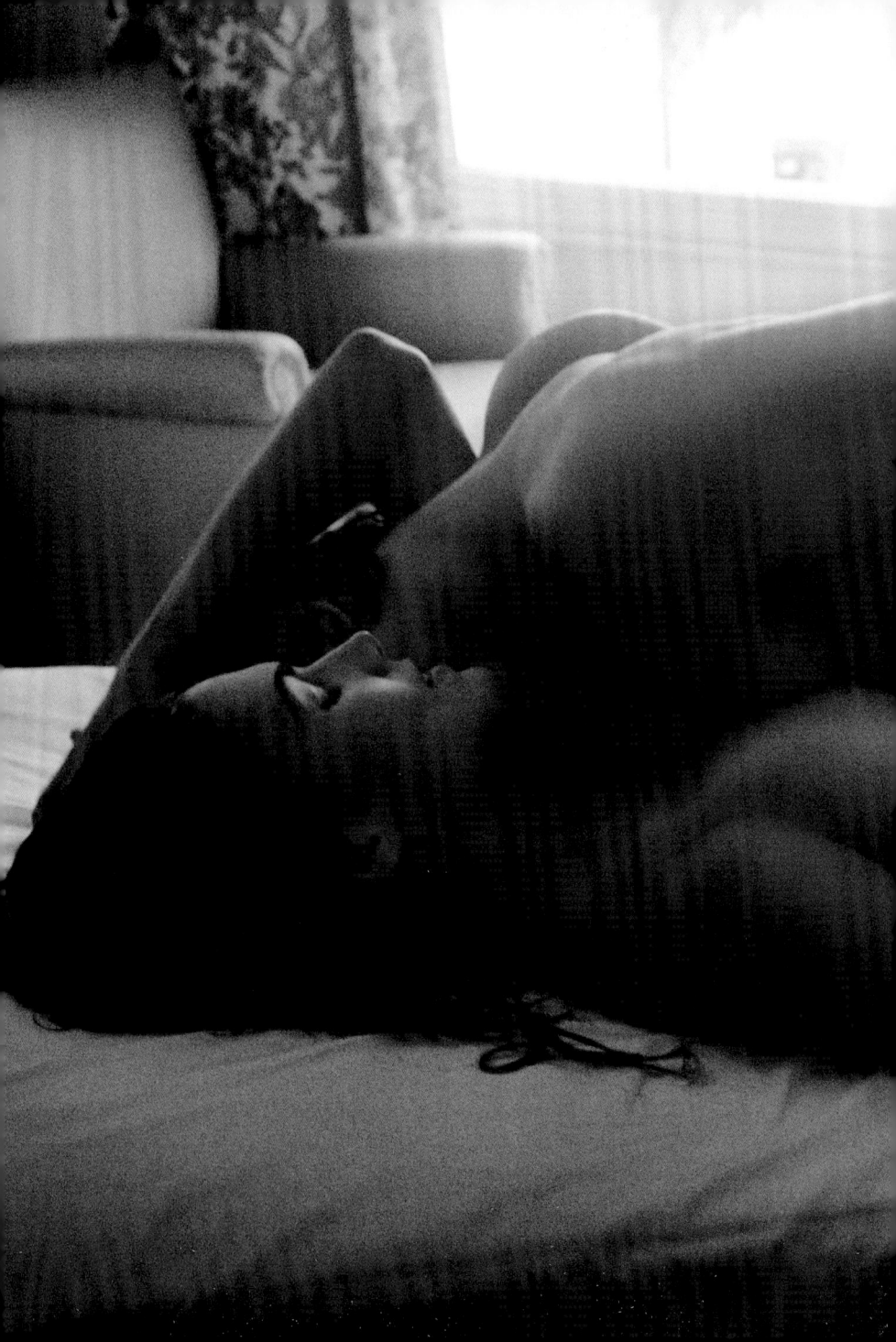

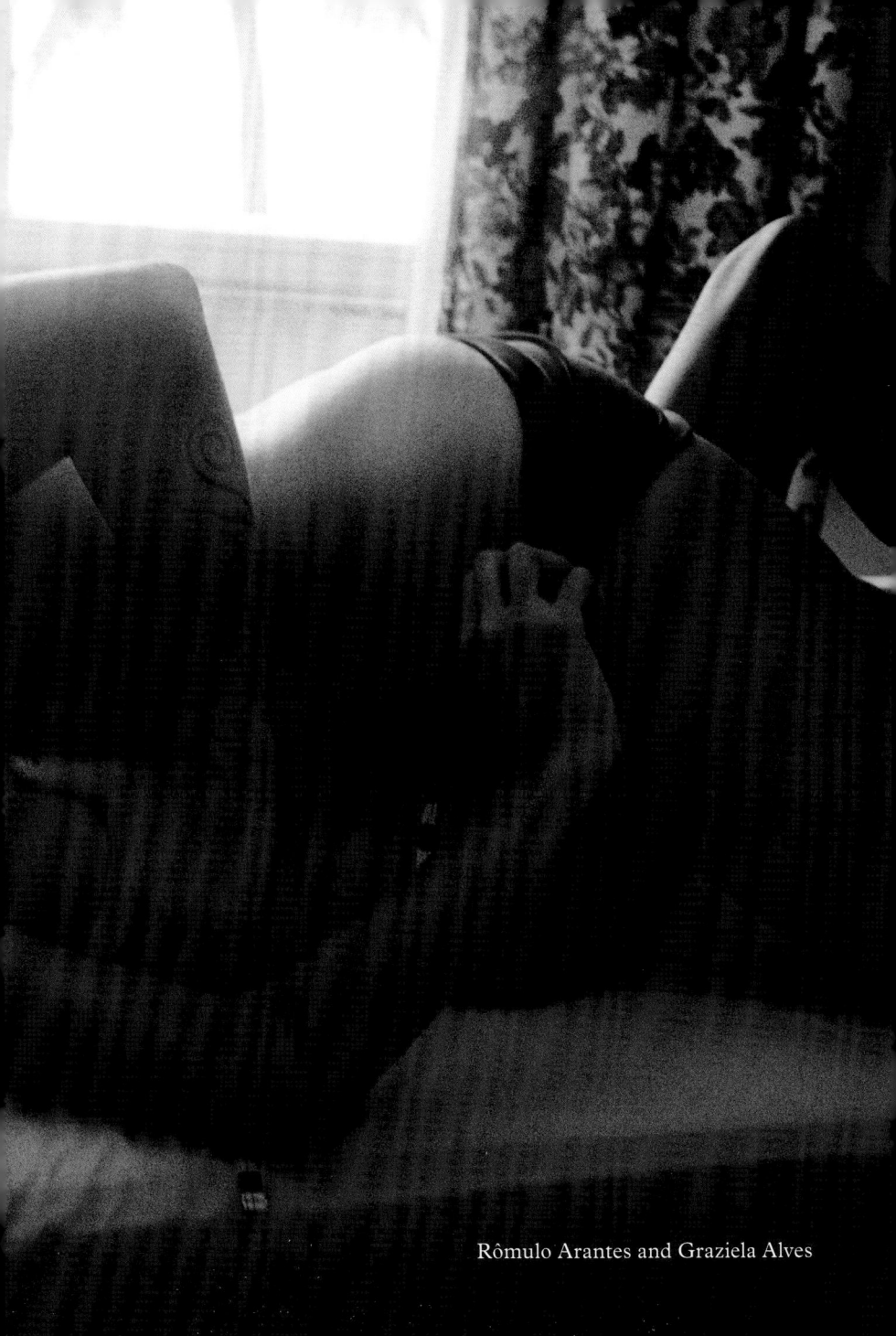

Rômulo Arantes and Graziela Alves

Grazielli Massafera

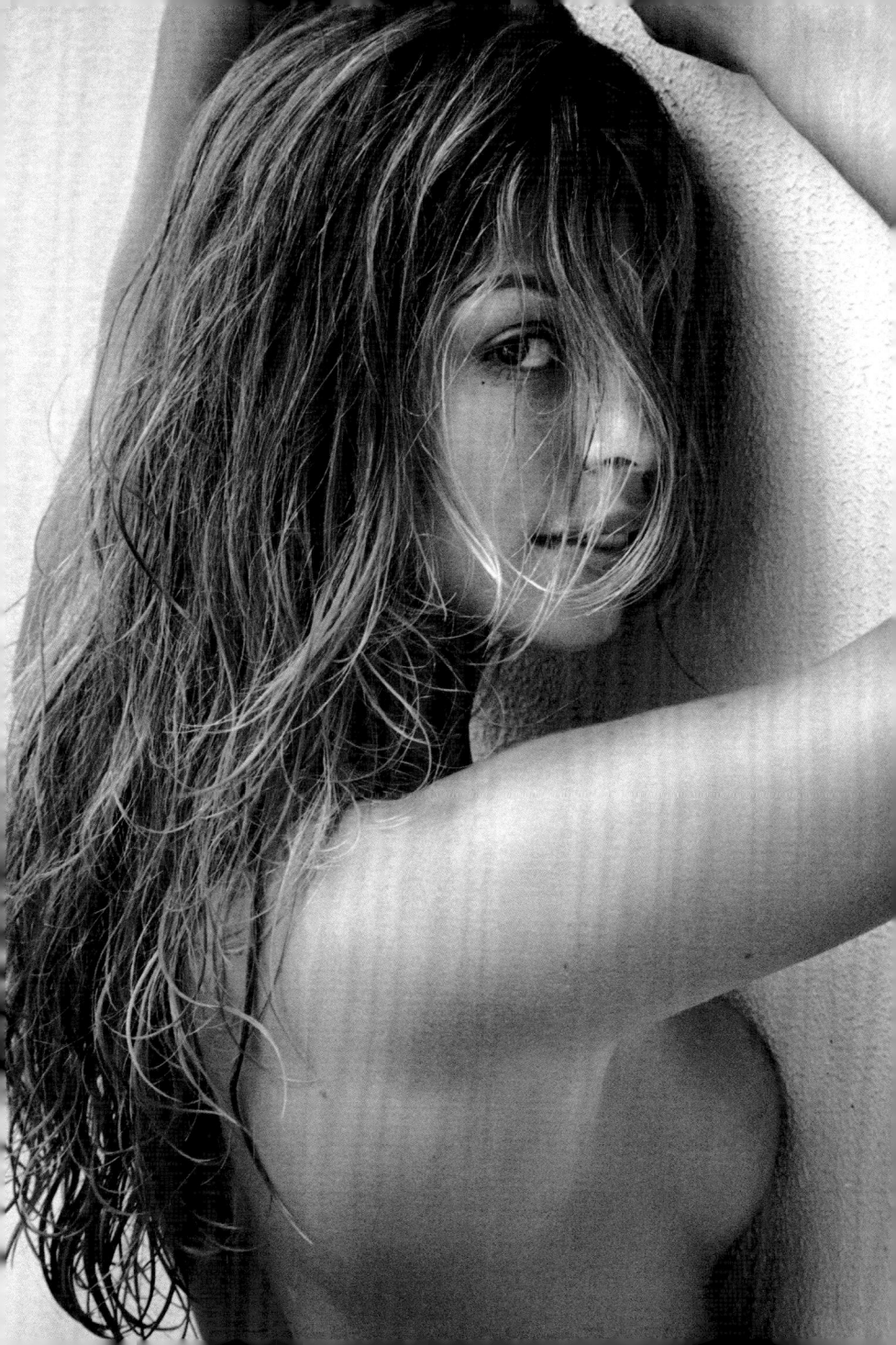

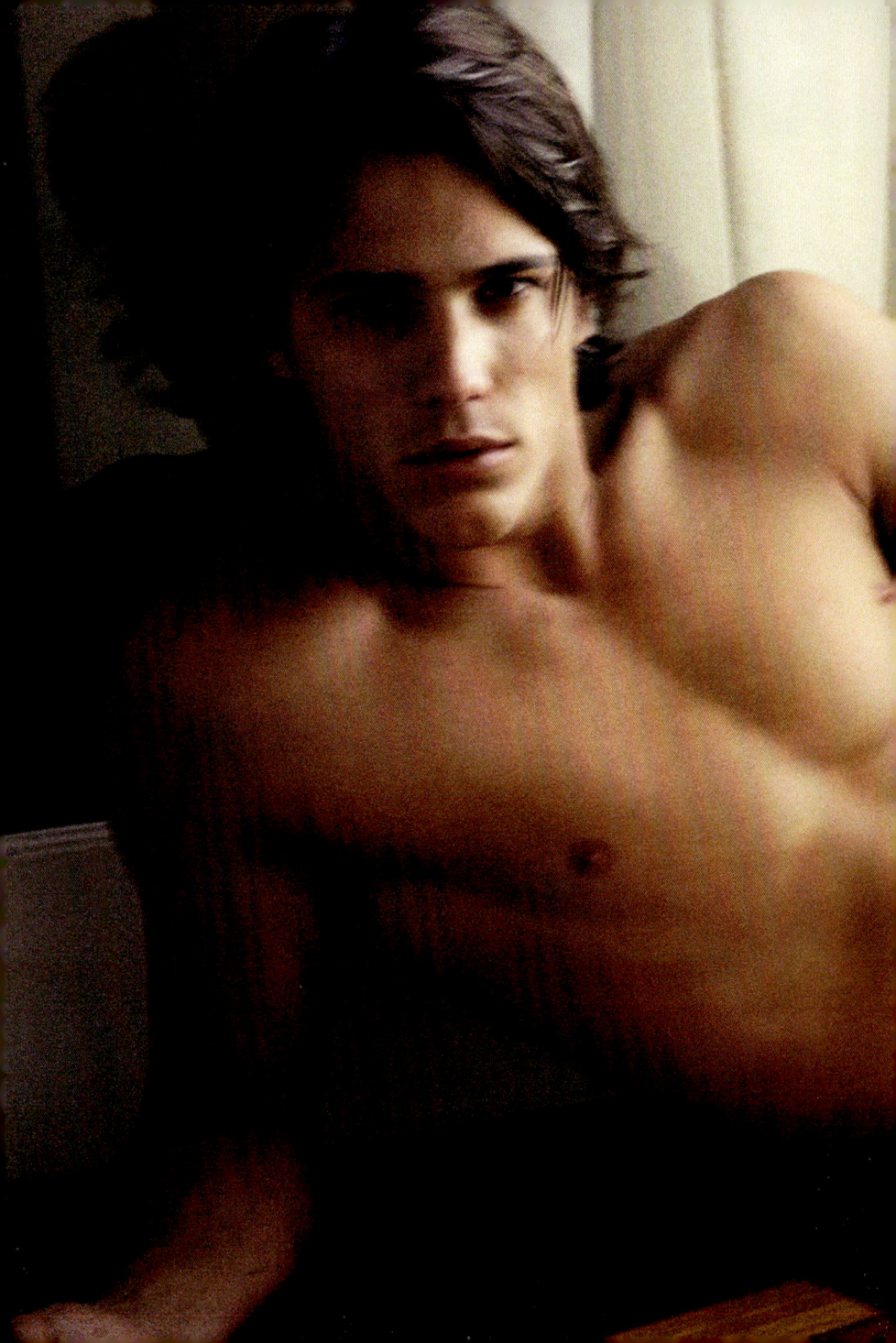

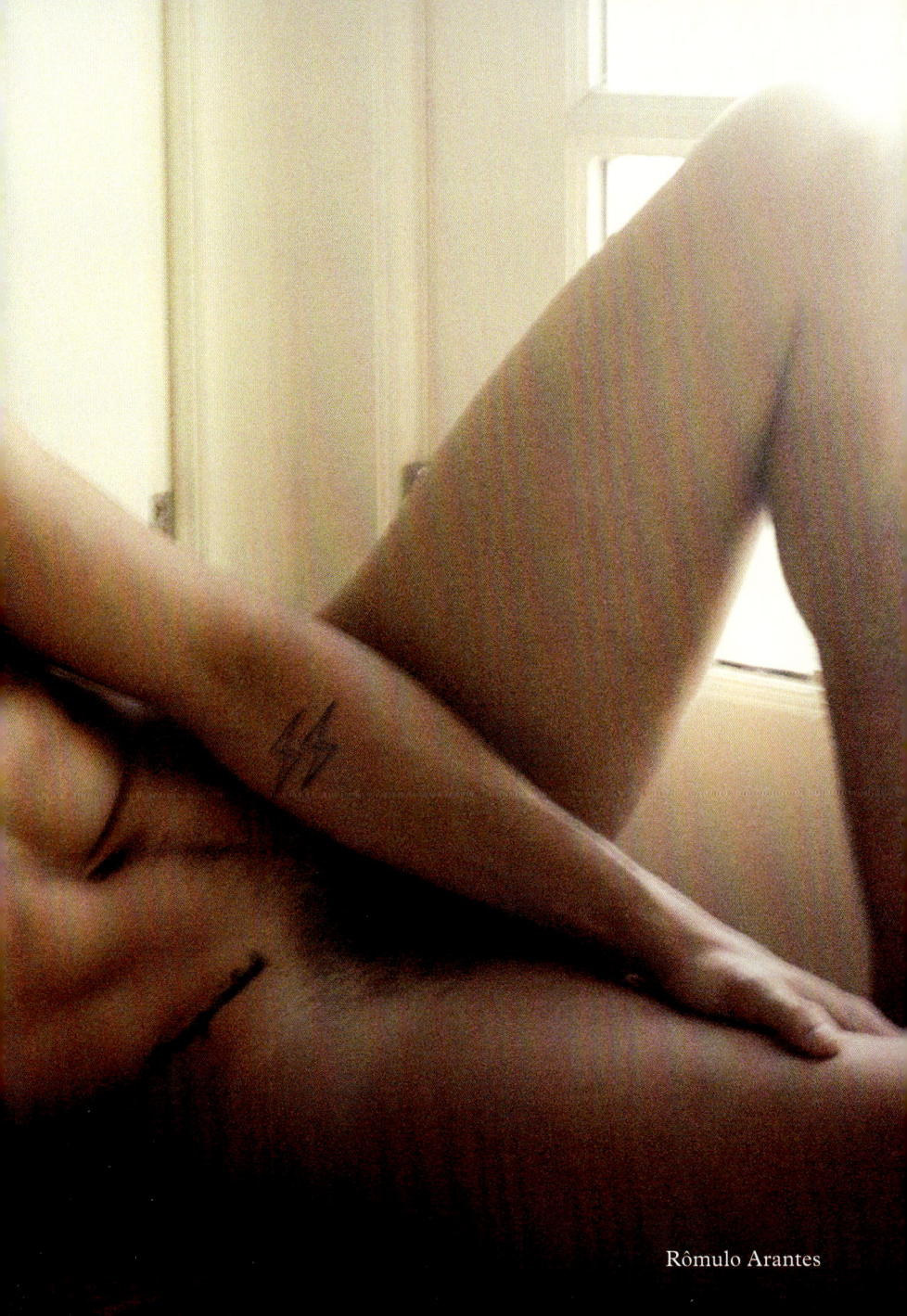

Rômulo Arantes

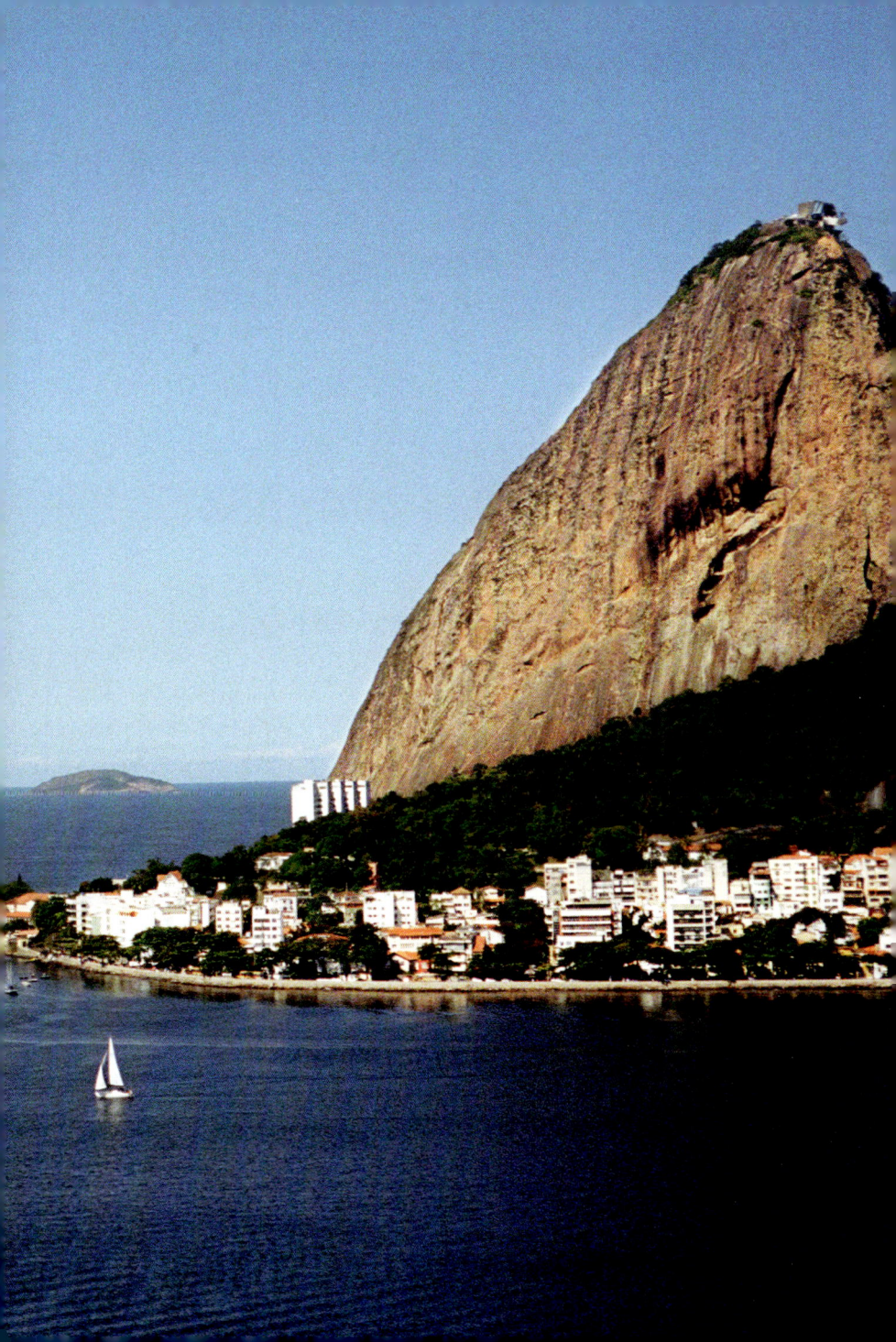

Rodrigo Hilbert

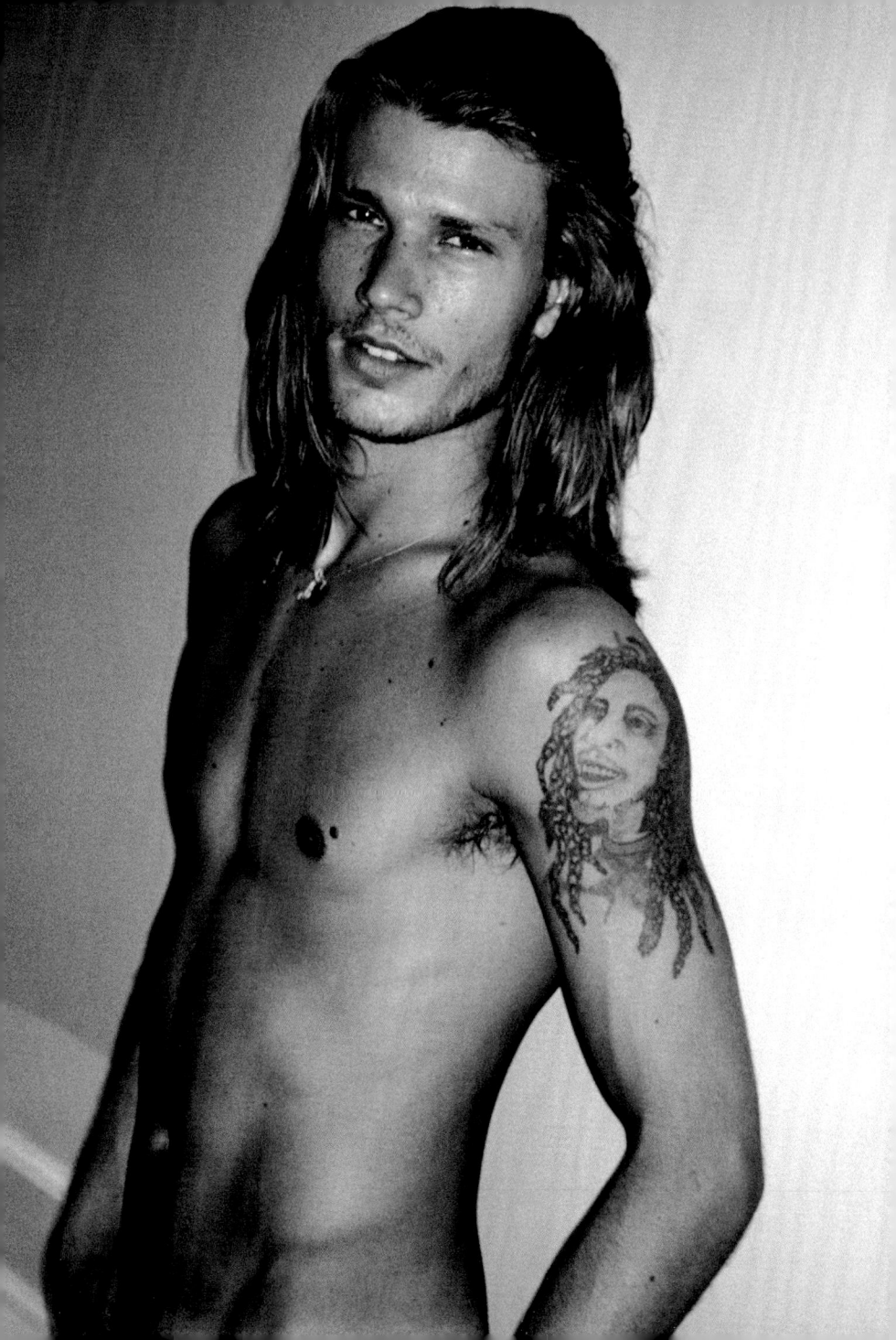

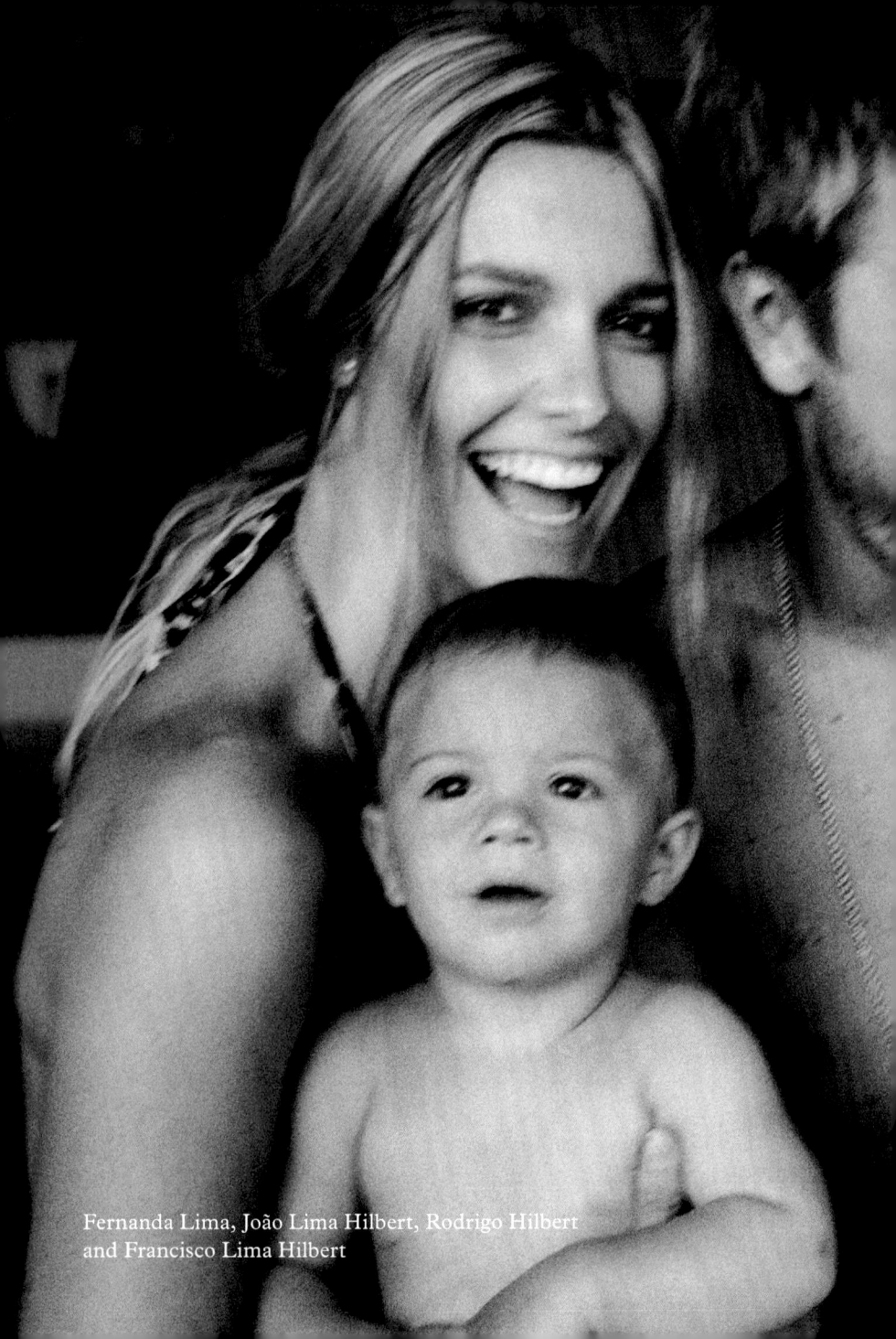

Fernanda Lima, João Lima Hilbert, Rodrigo Hilbert
and Francisco Lima Hilbert

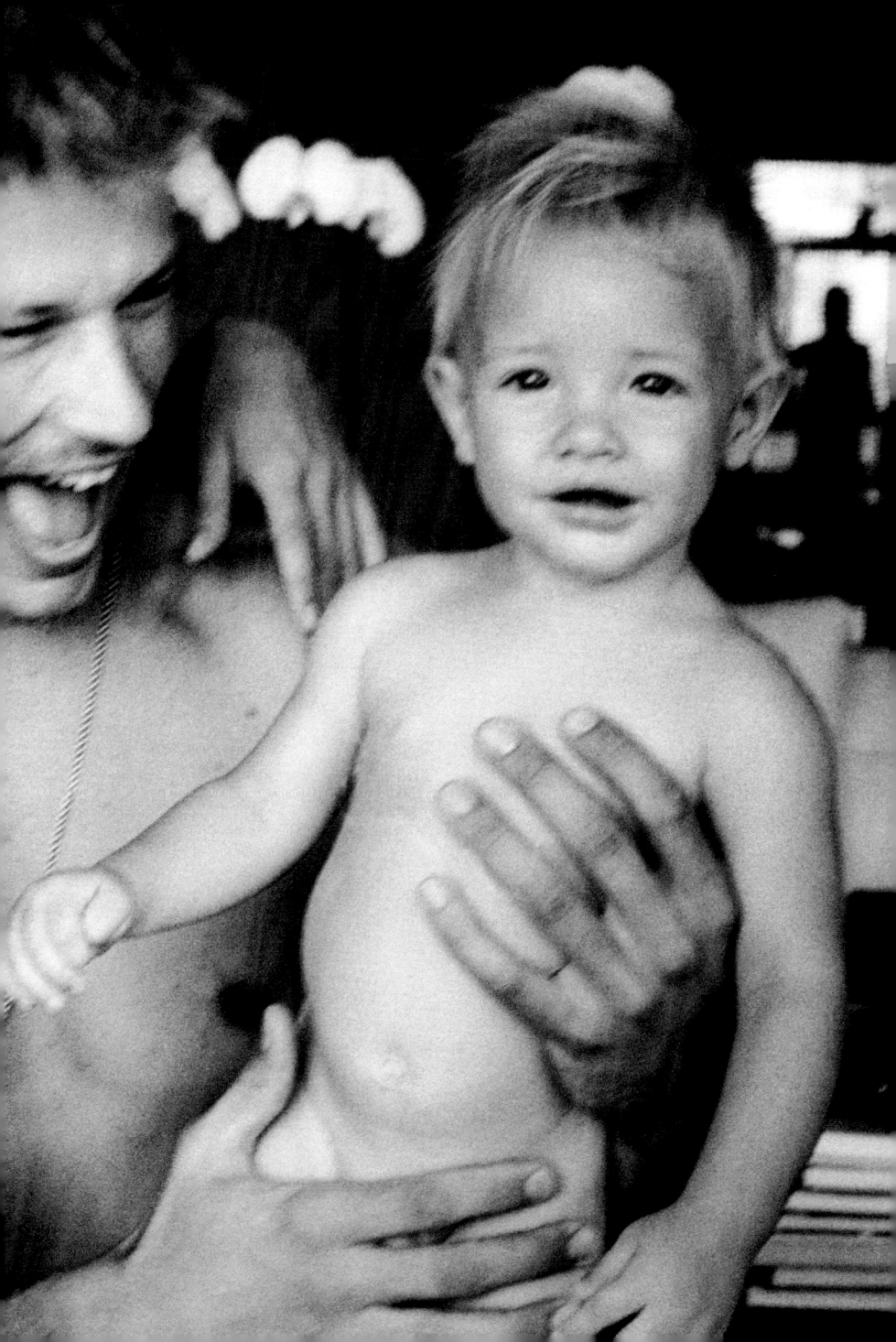

Tiago and Daniel Lo

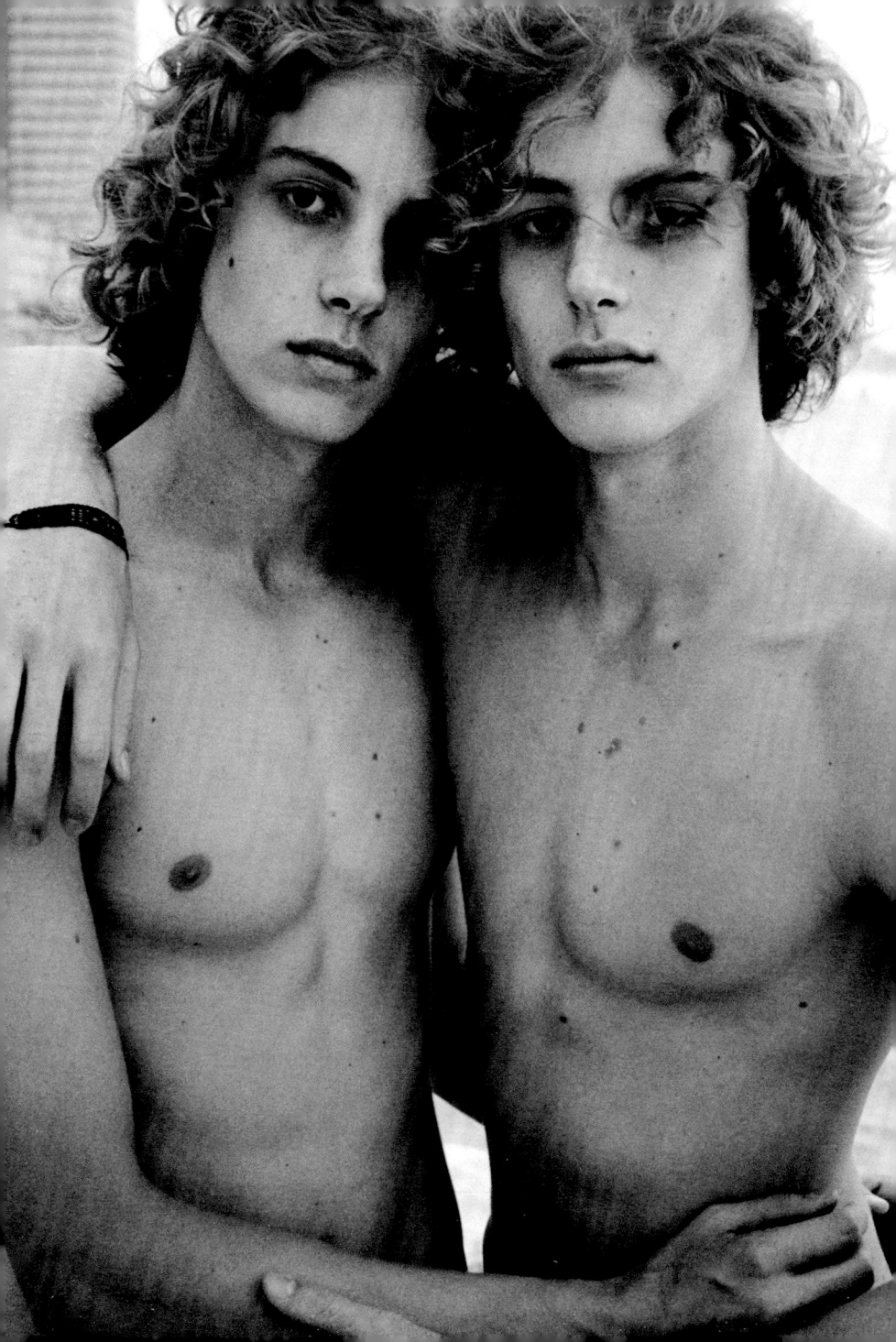

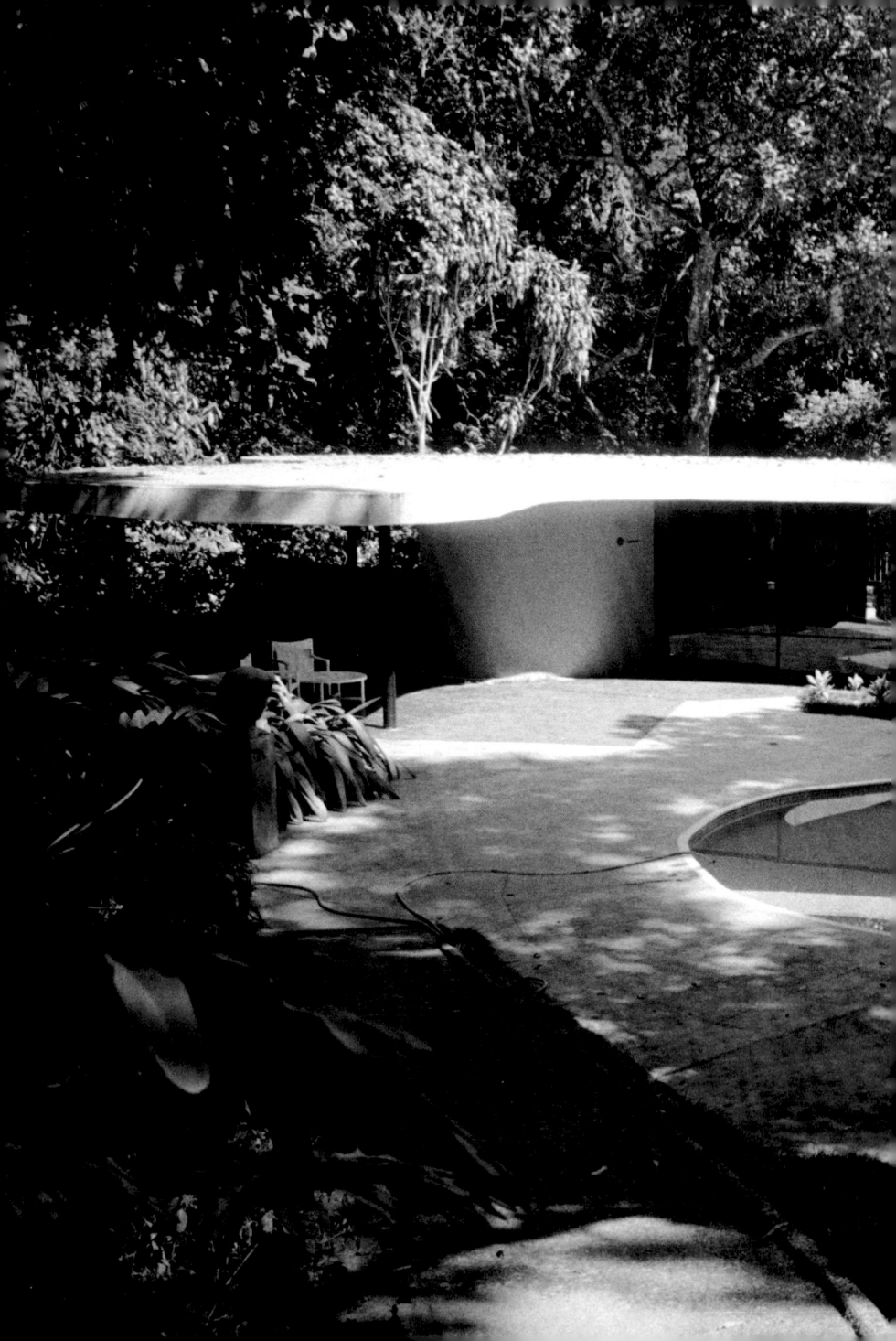

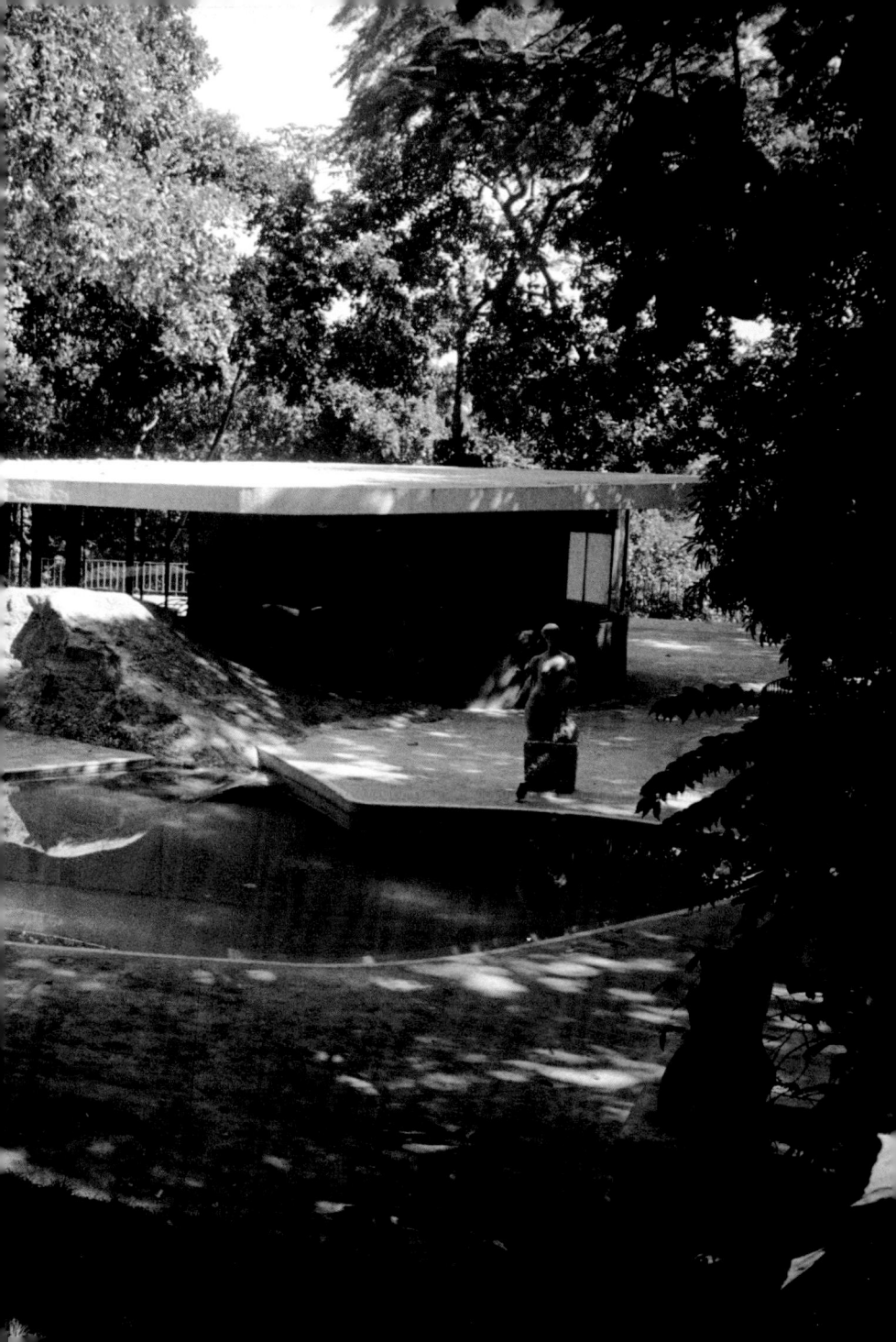

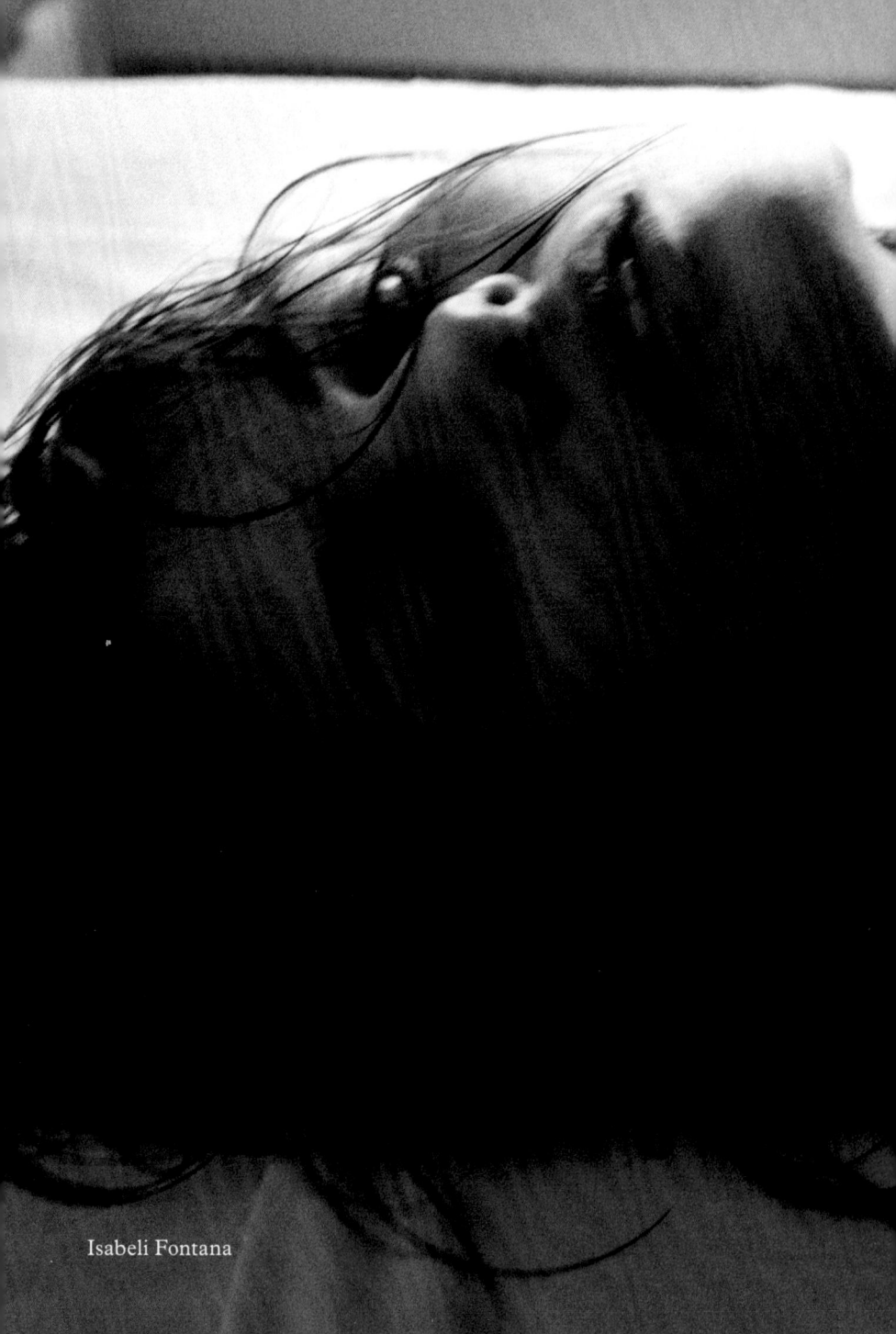

Isabeli Fontana

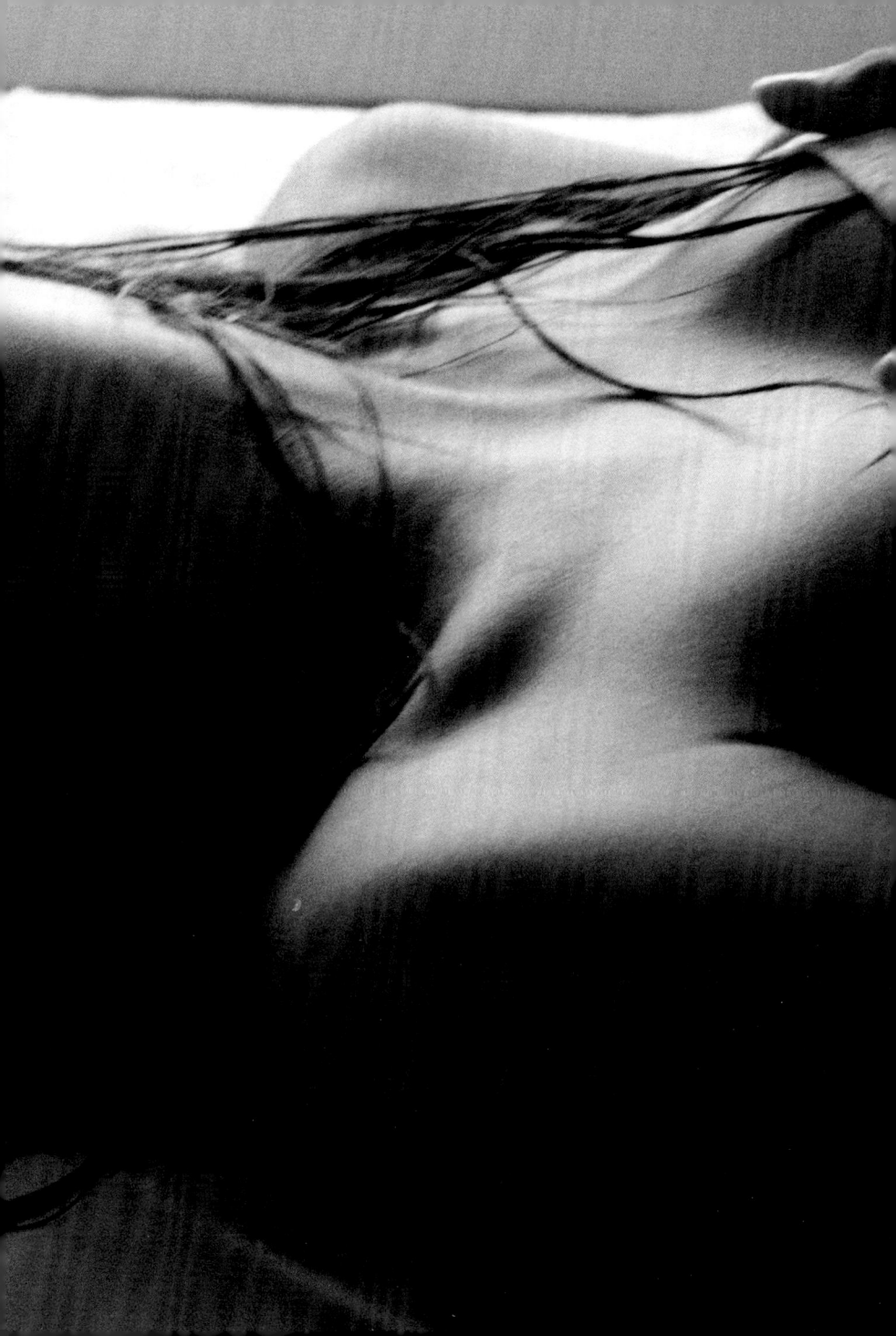

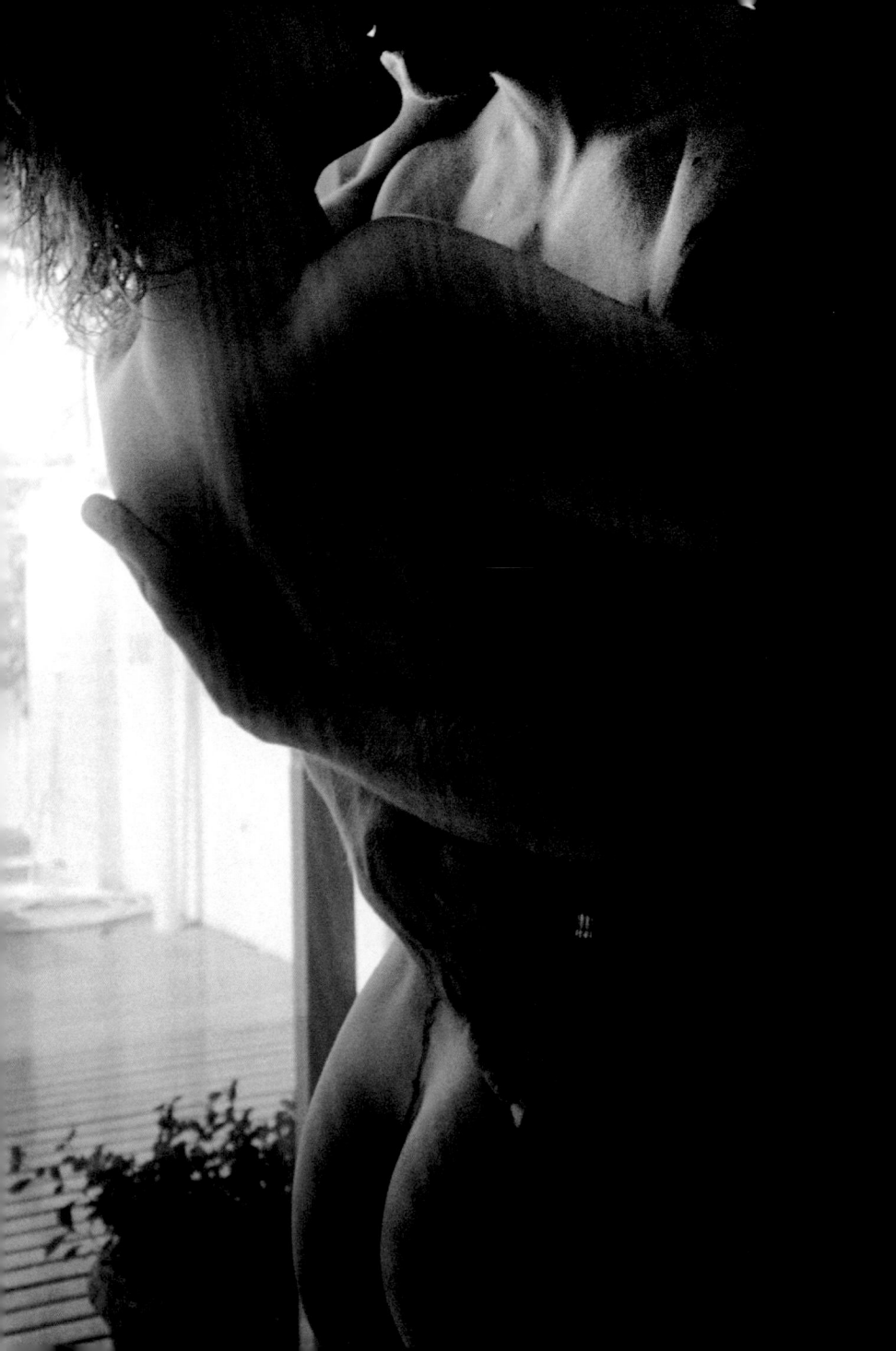

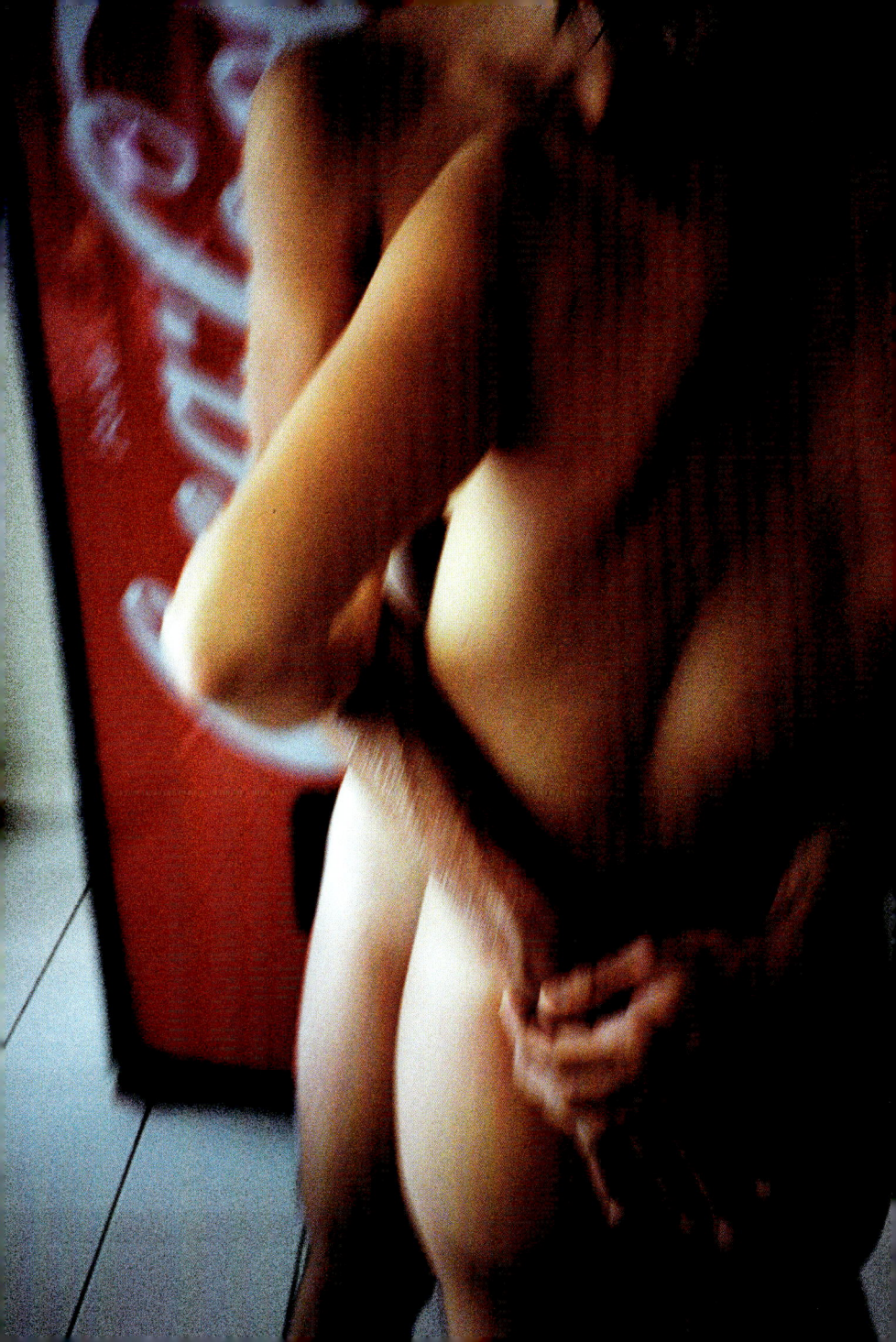

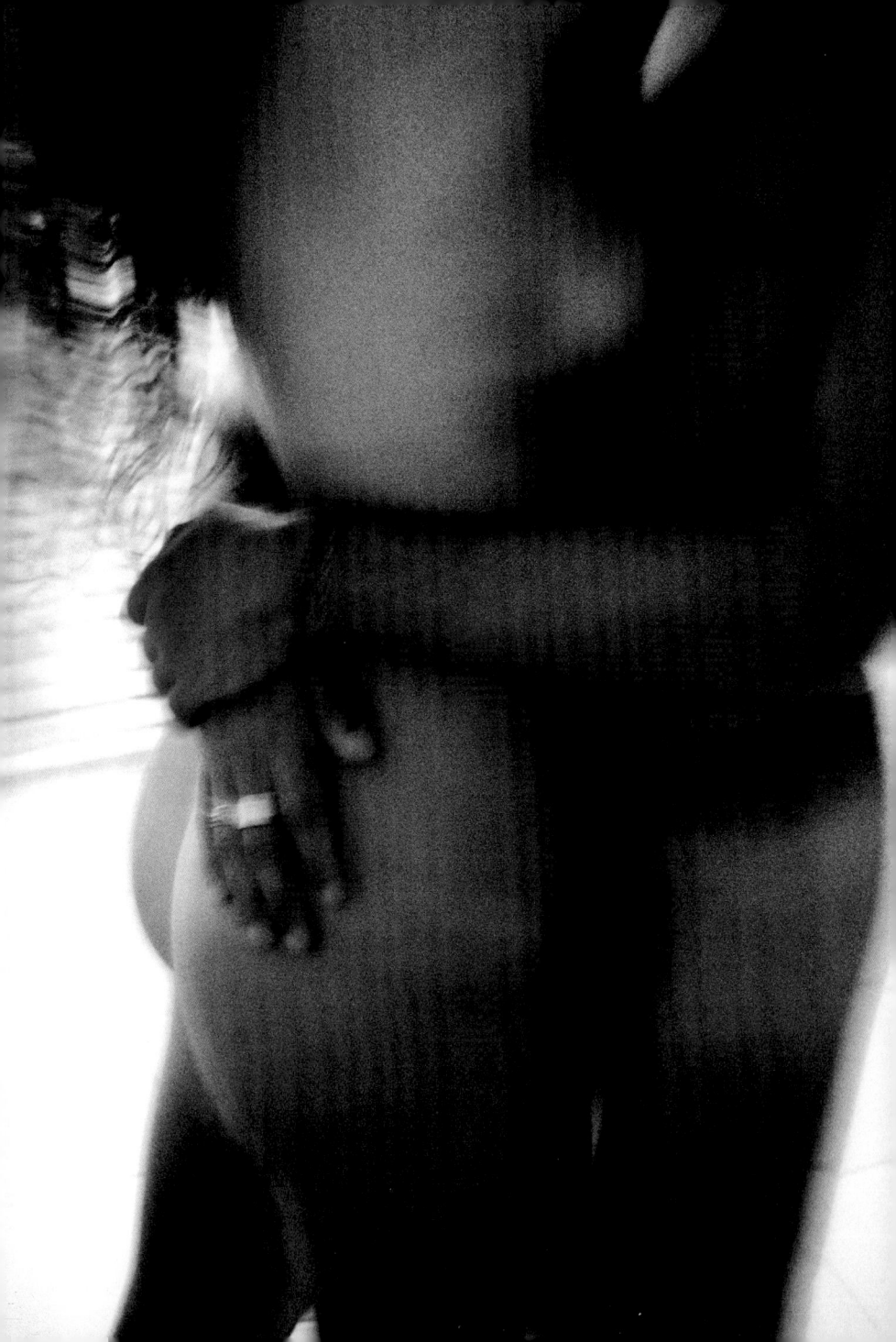

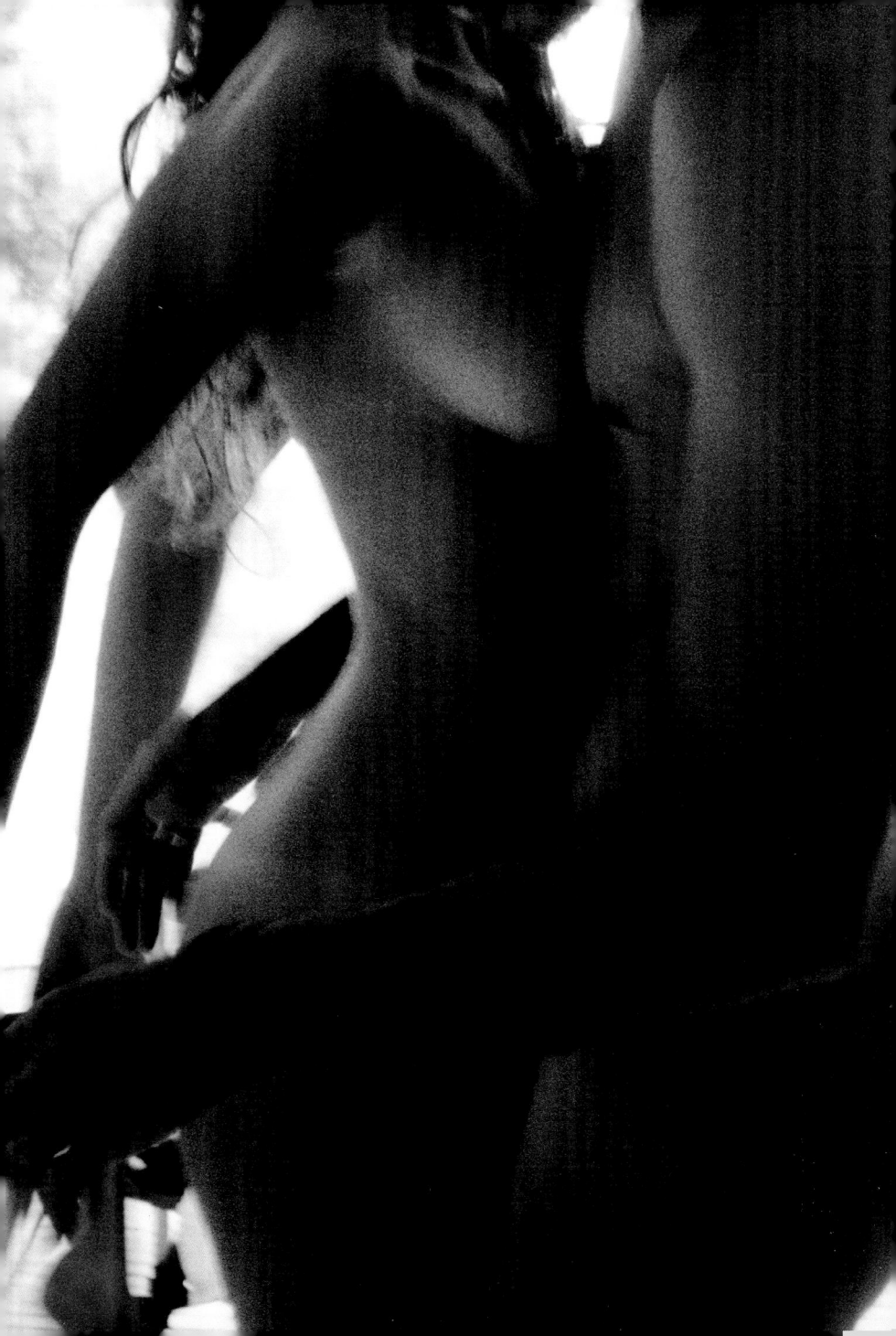

Felipe Hulse, Ana Beatriz Barros, João Vellutini,
and Rômulo Arantes

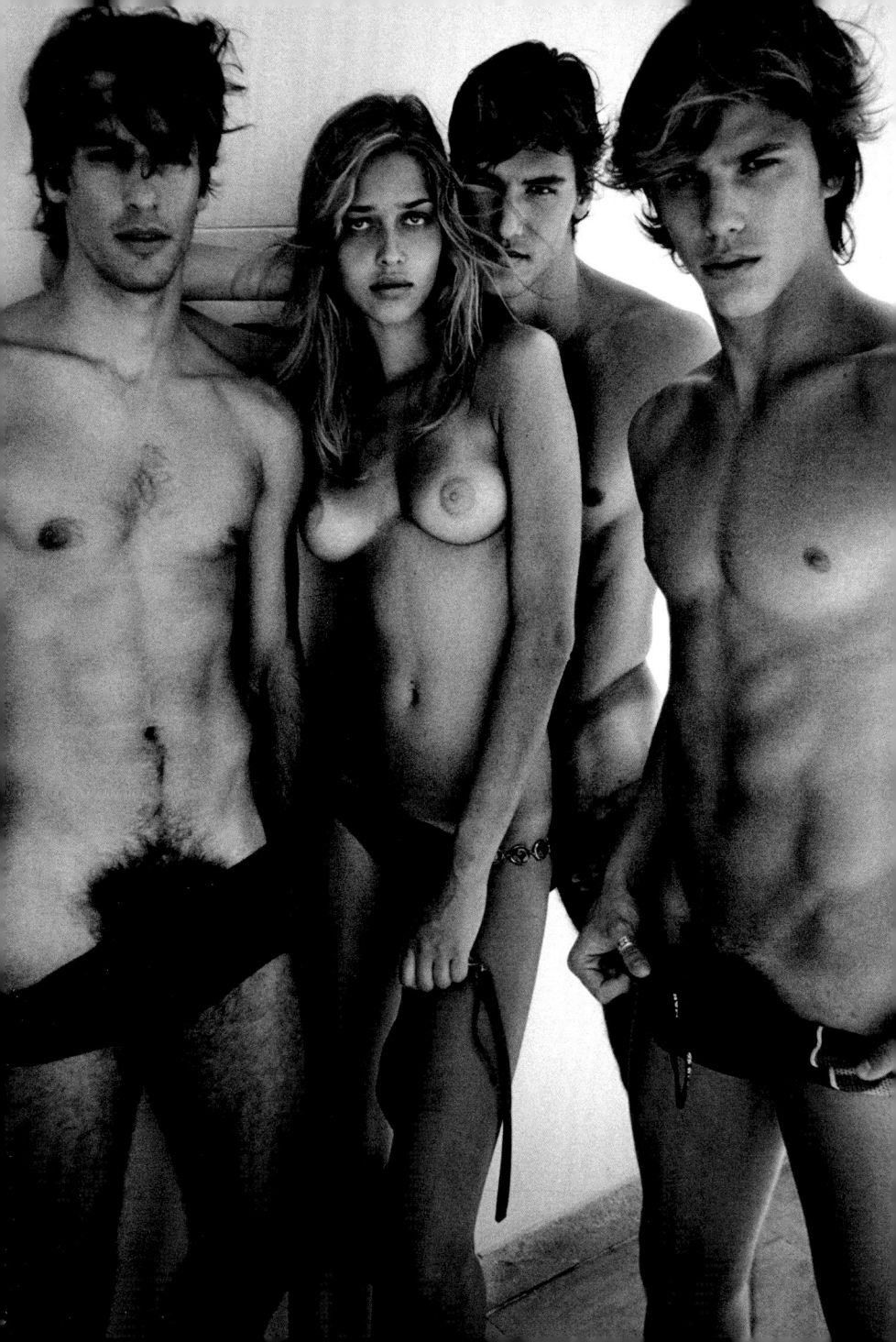

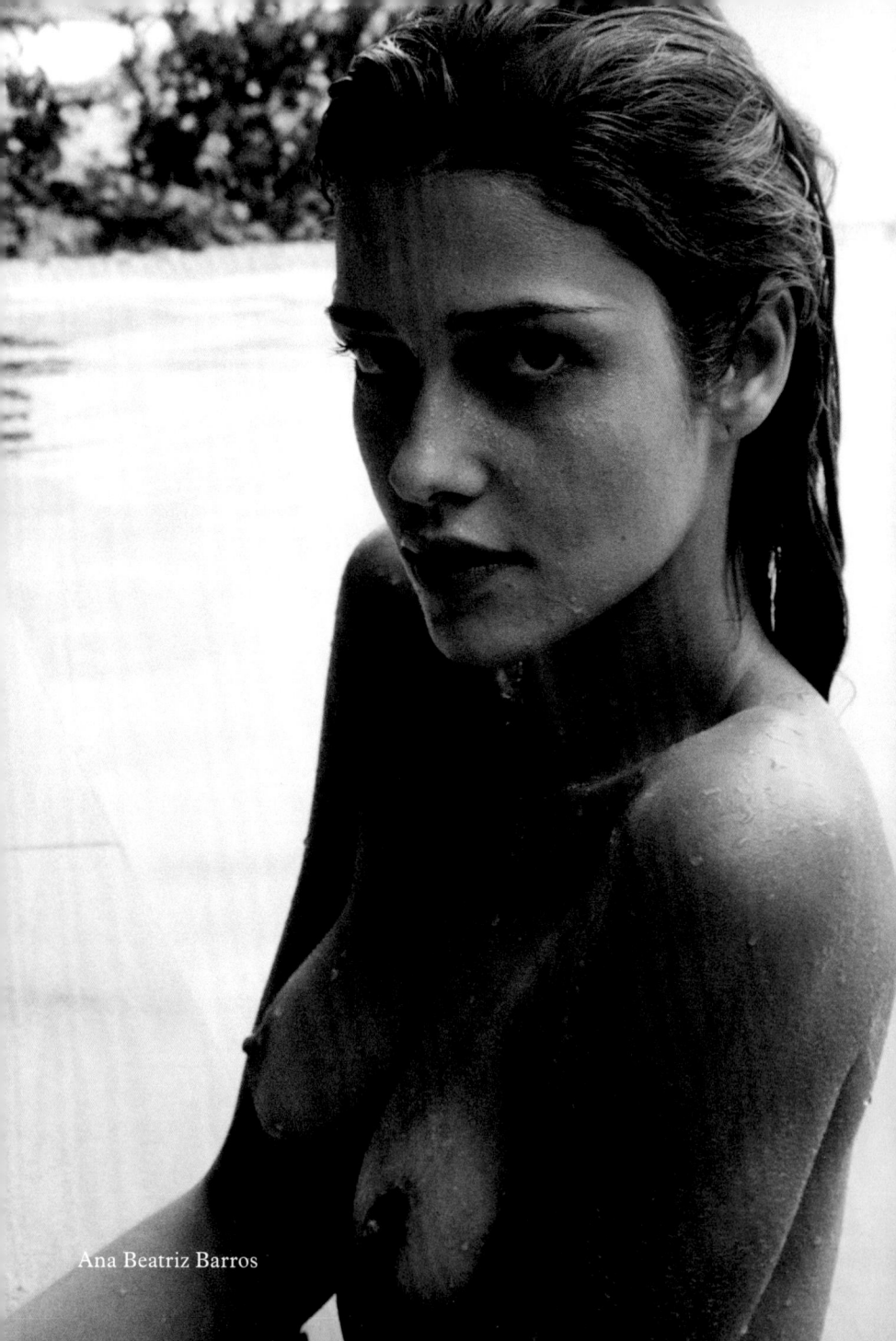

Ana Beatriz Barros

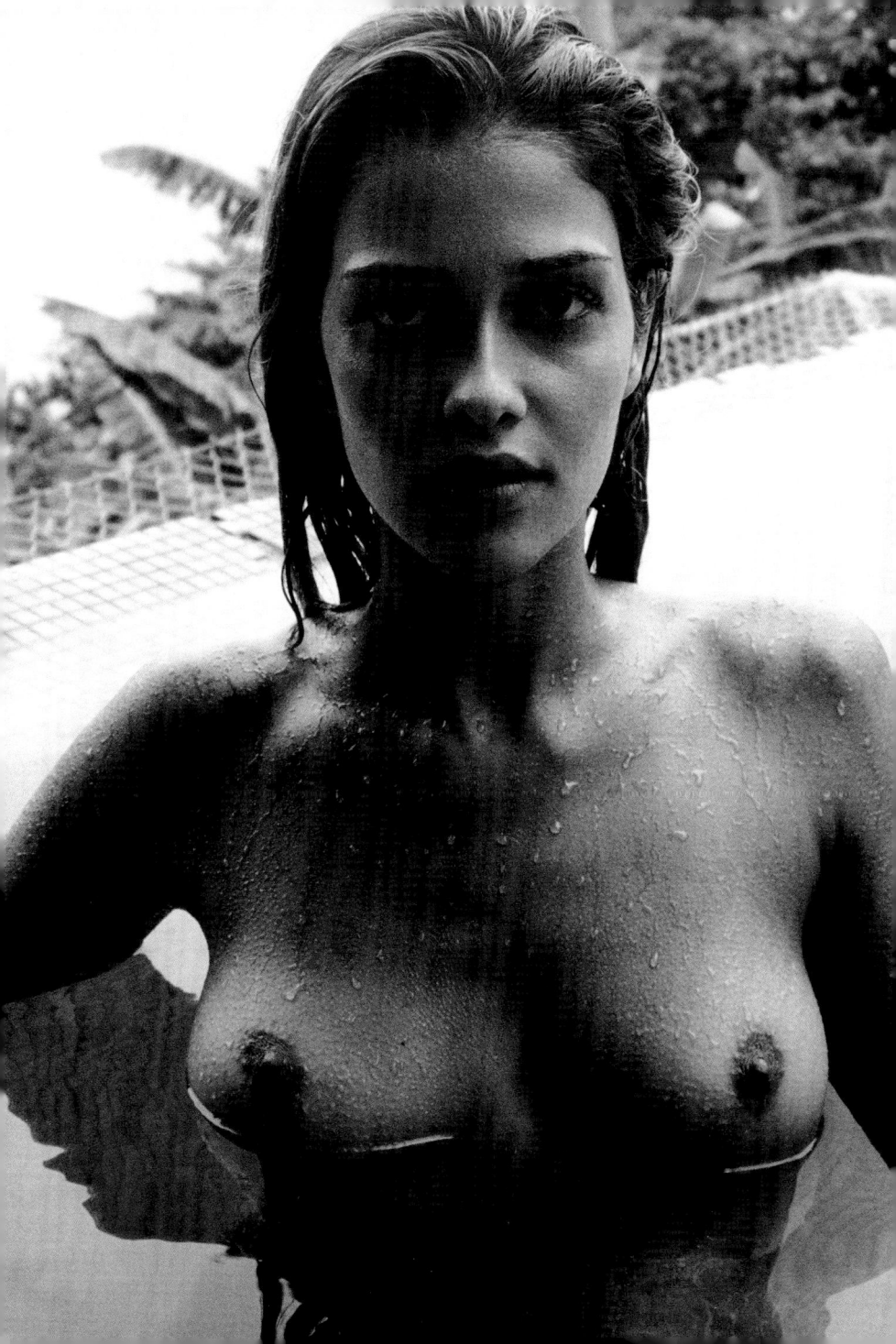

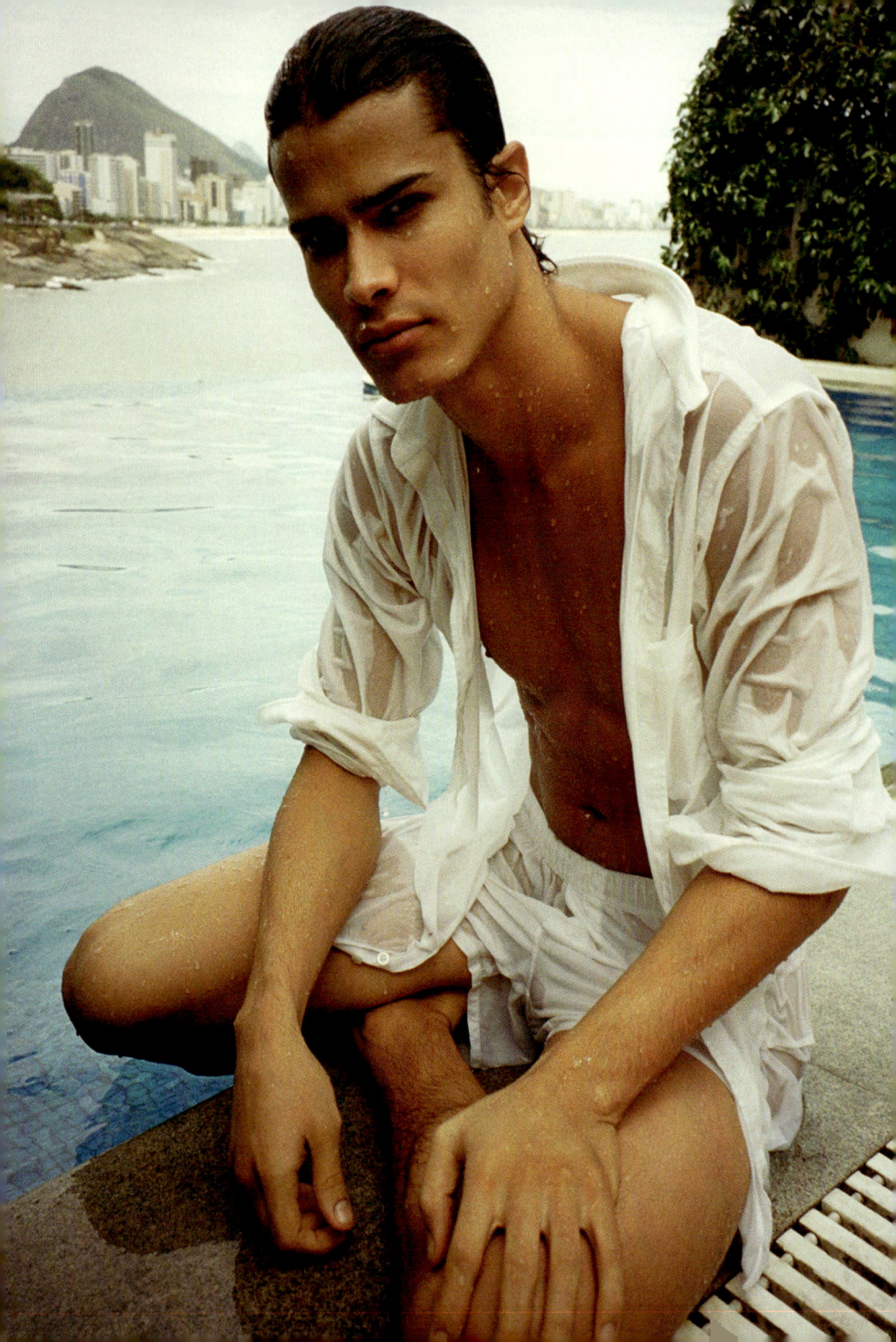

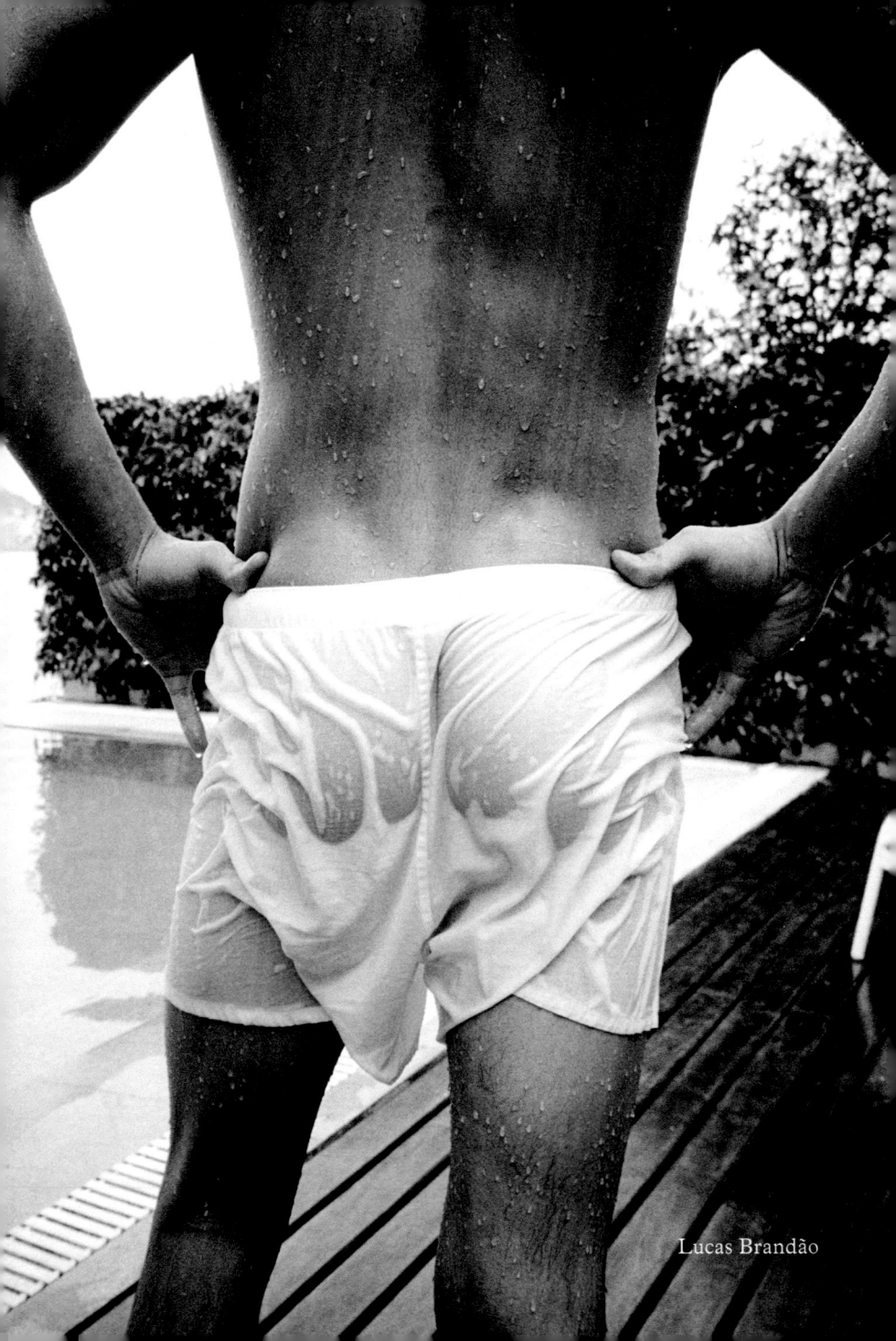
Lucas Brandão

Lucas Brandão

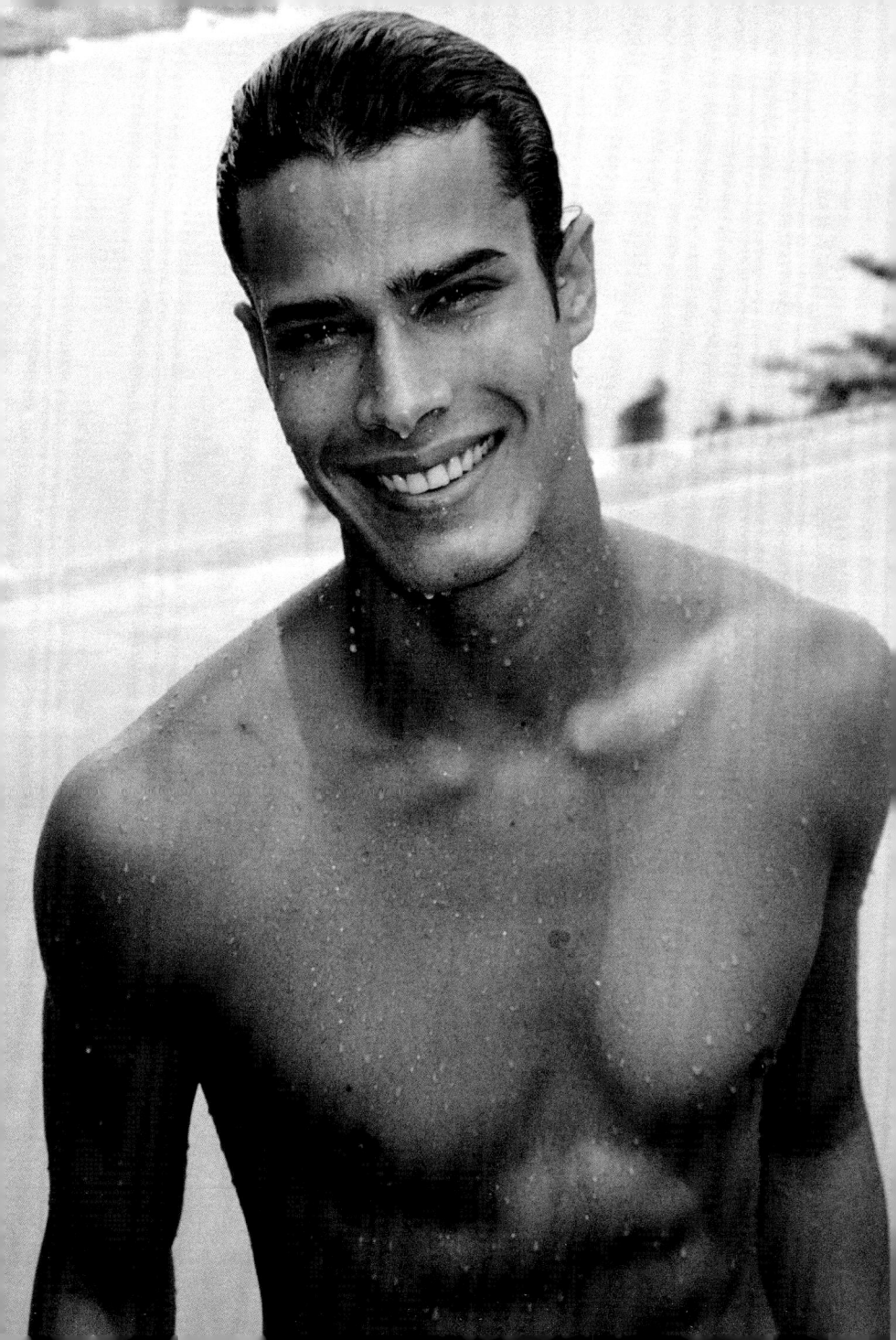

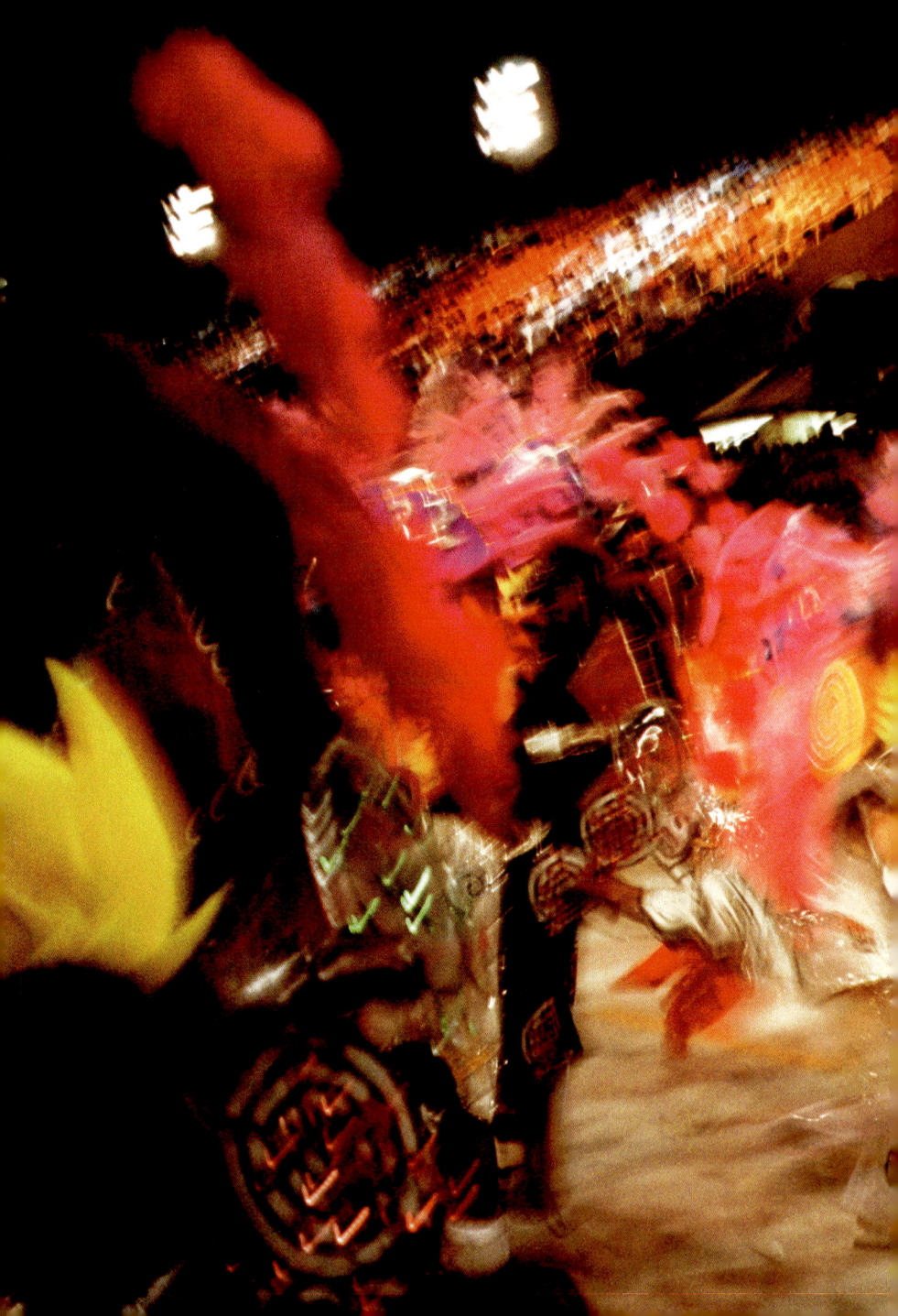

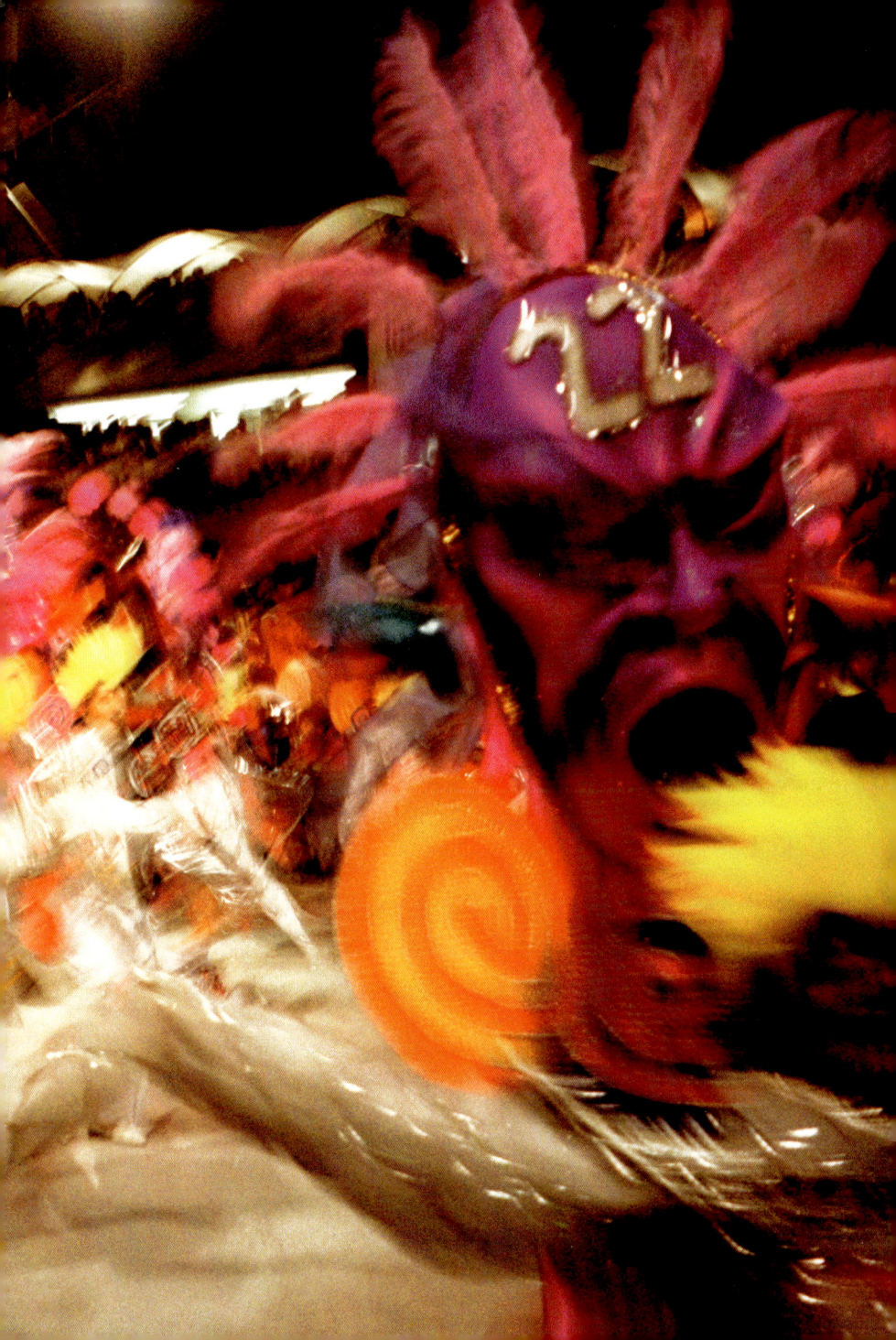

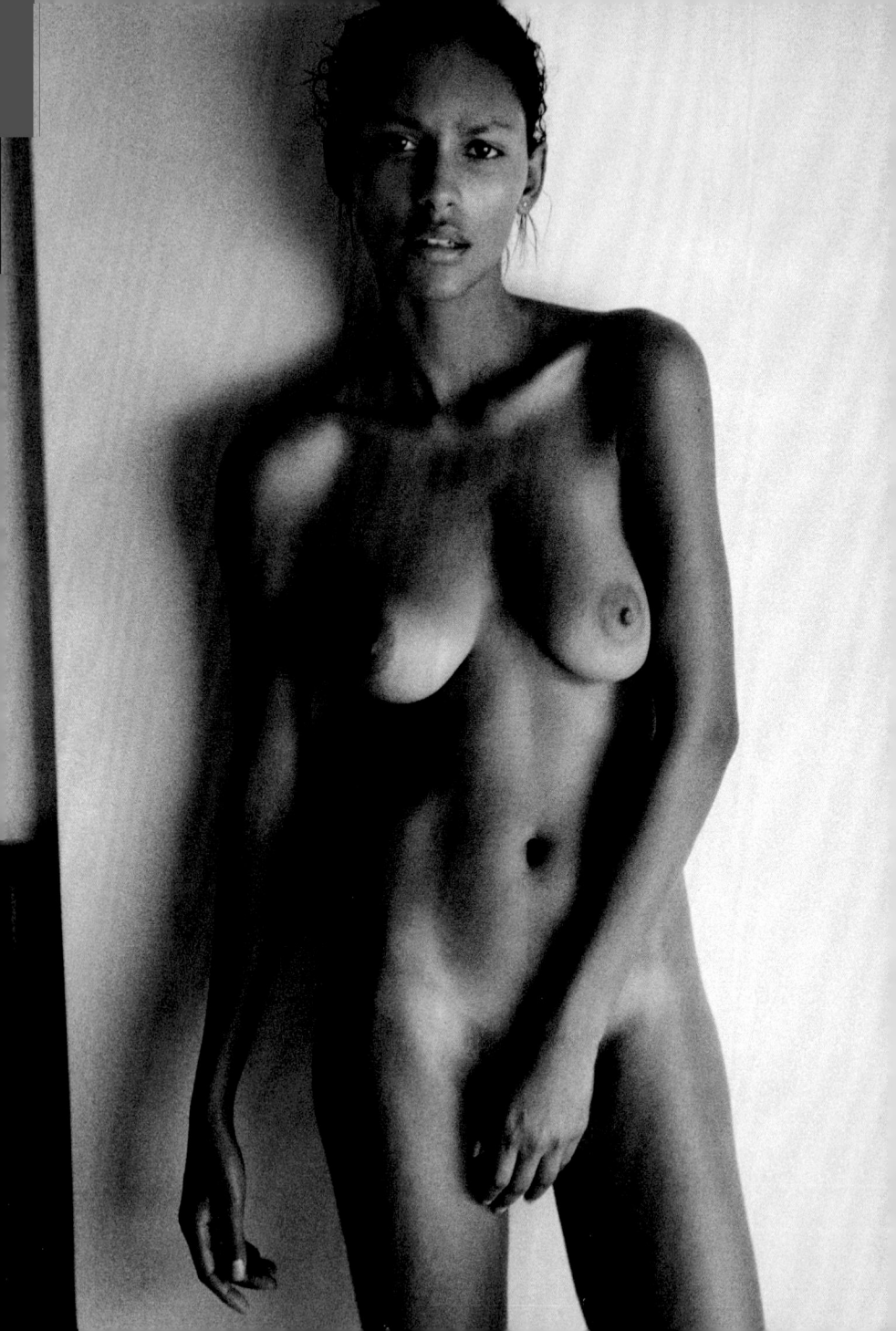

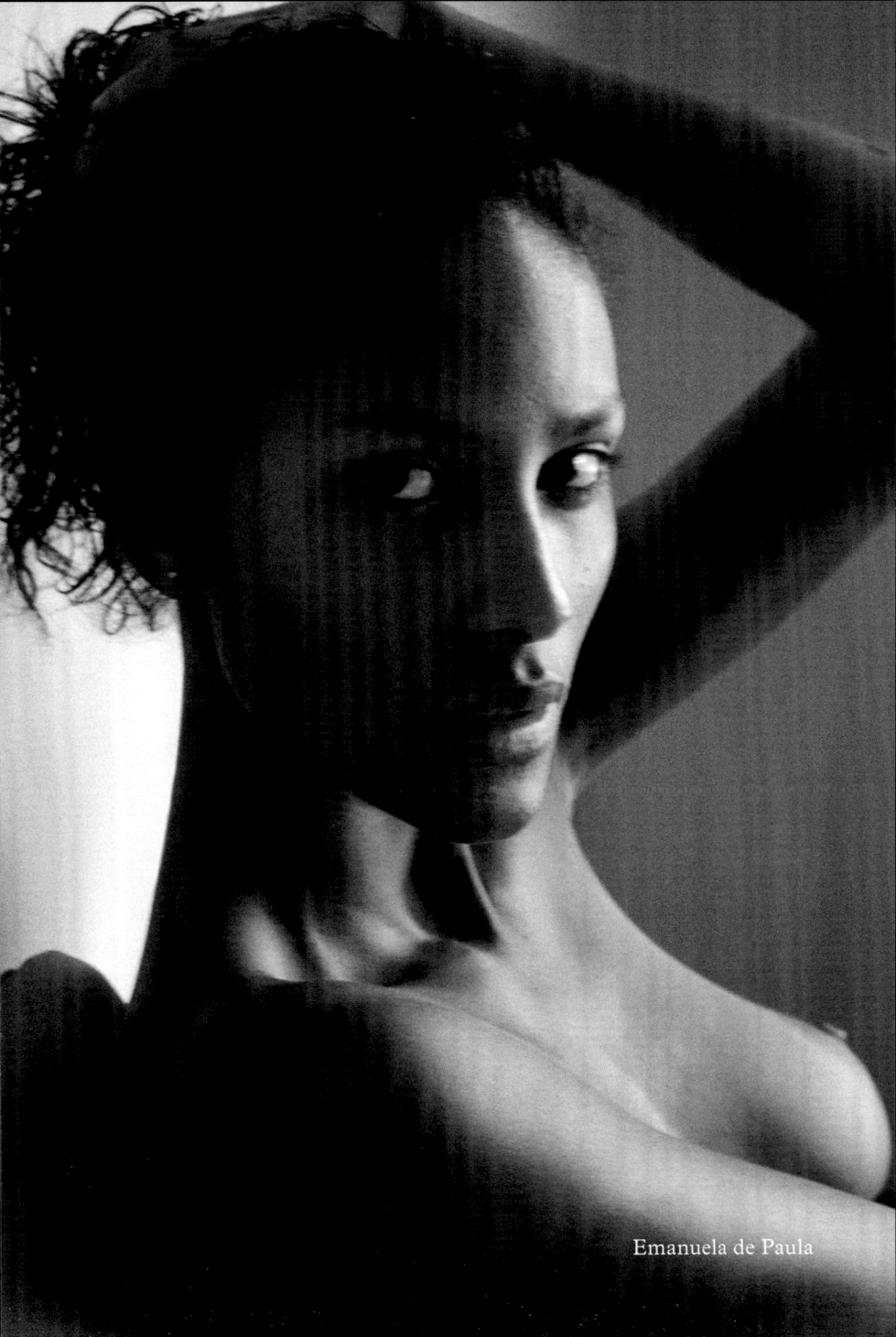

Emanuela de Paula

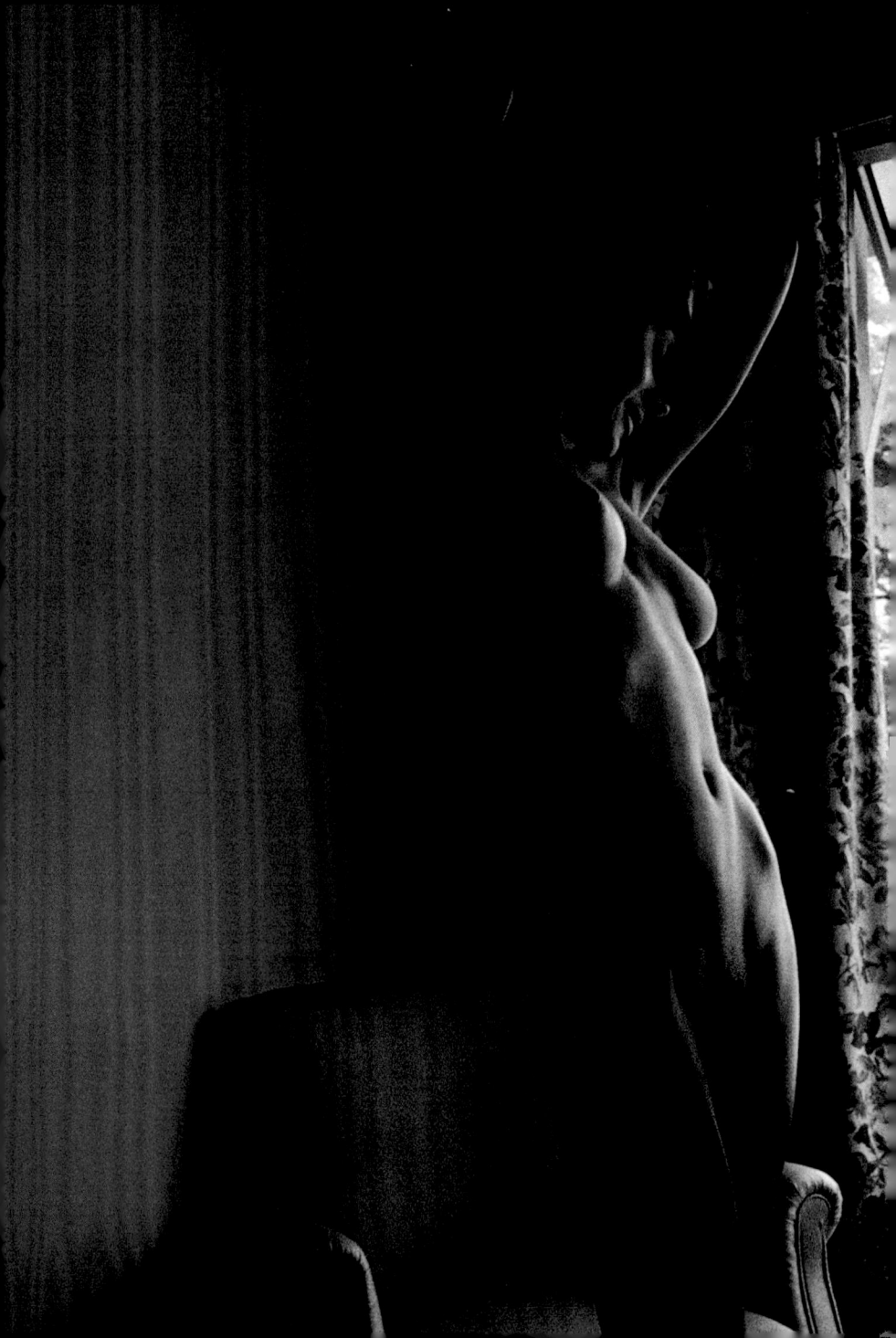

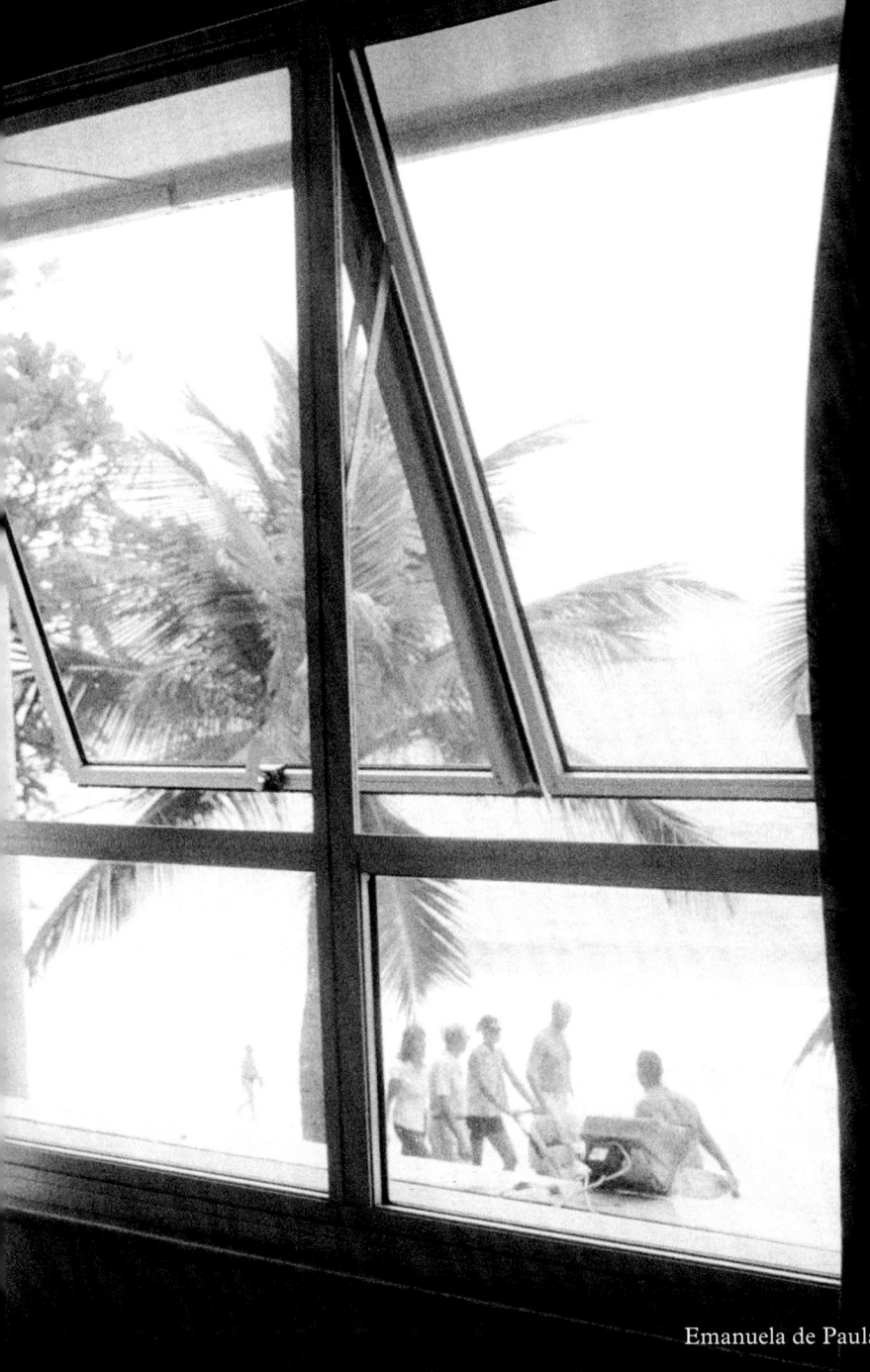

Emanuela de Paula

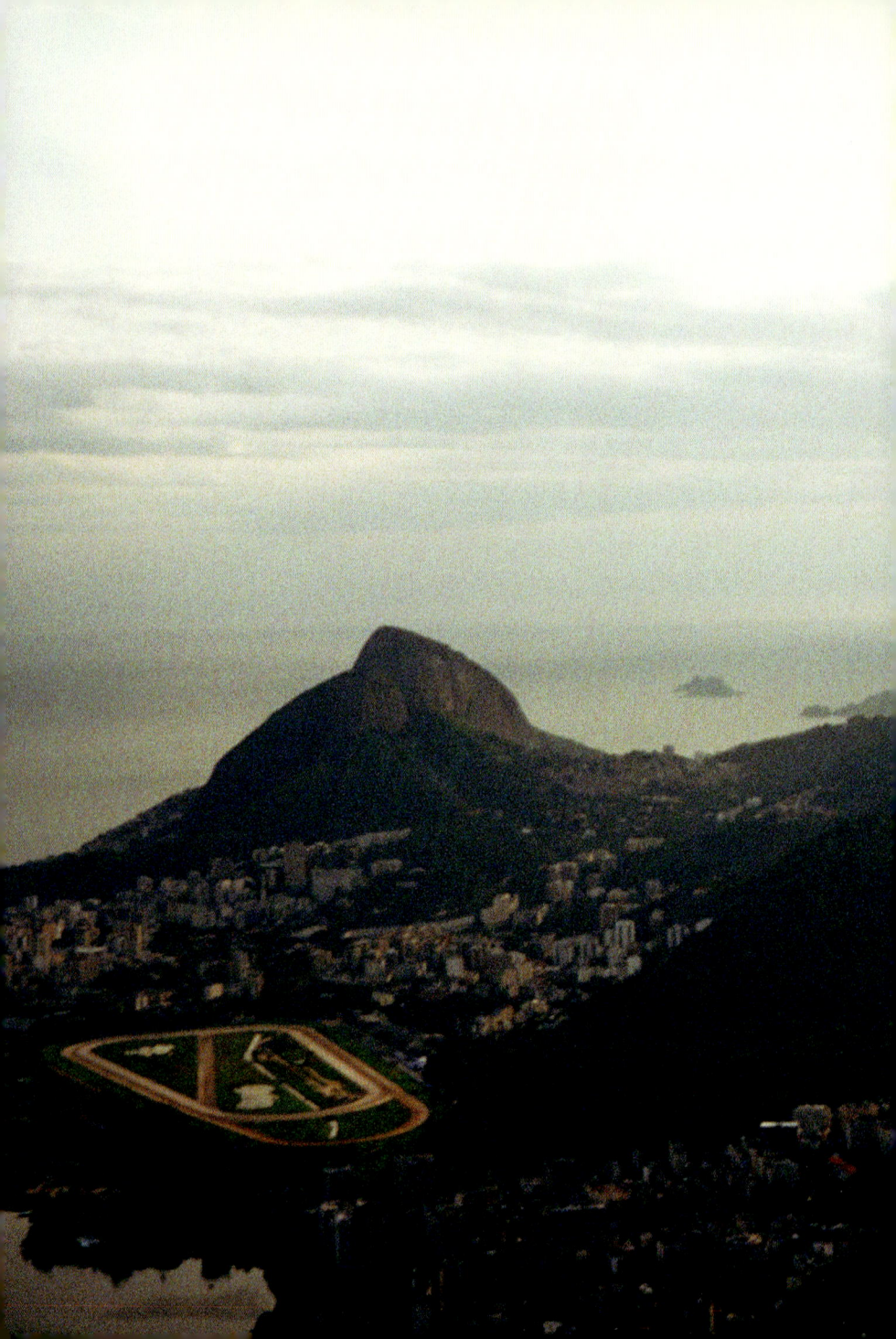

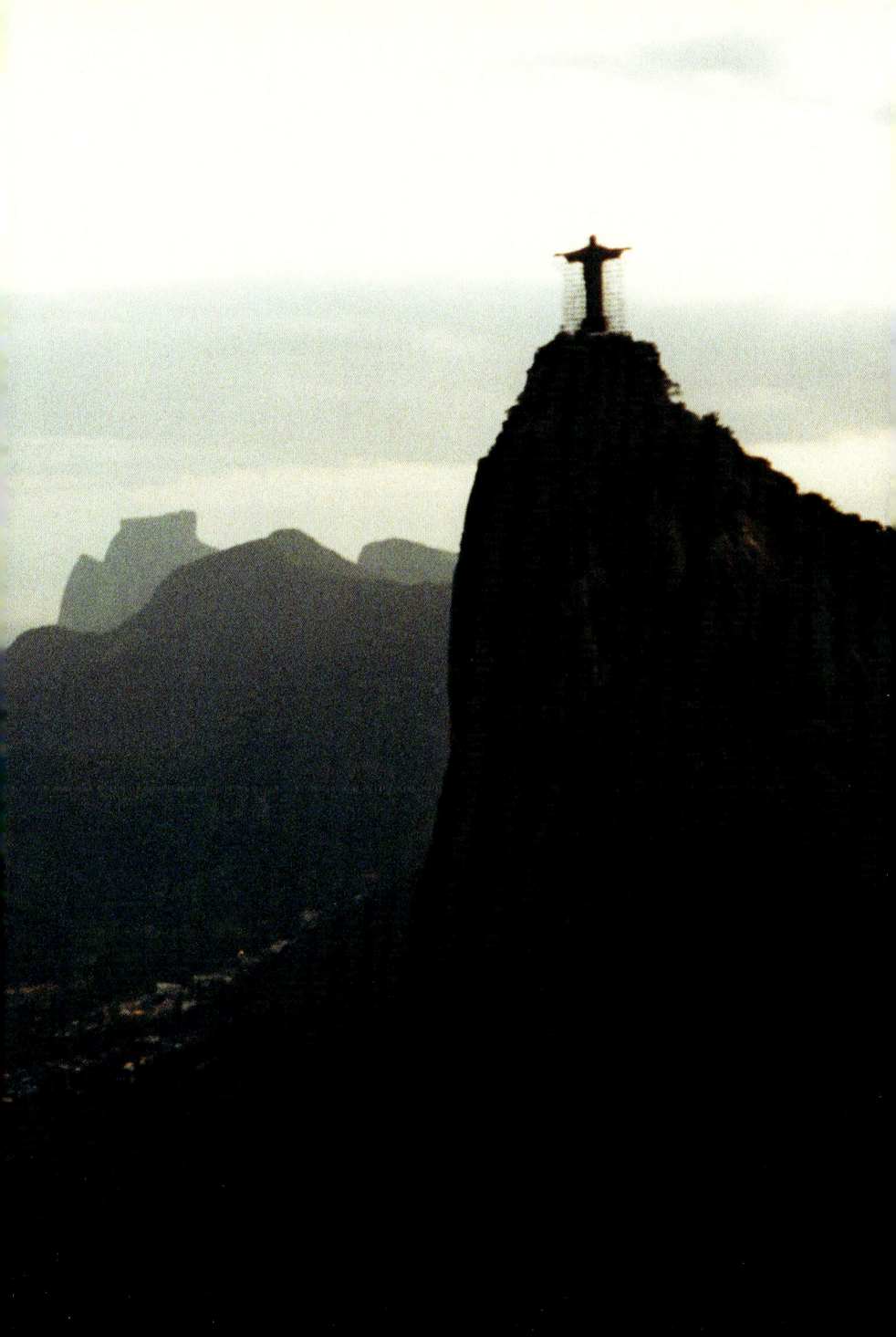

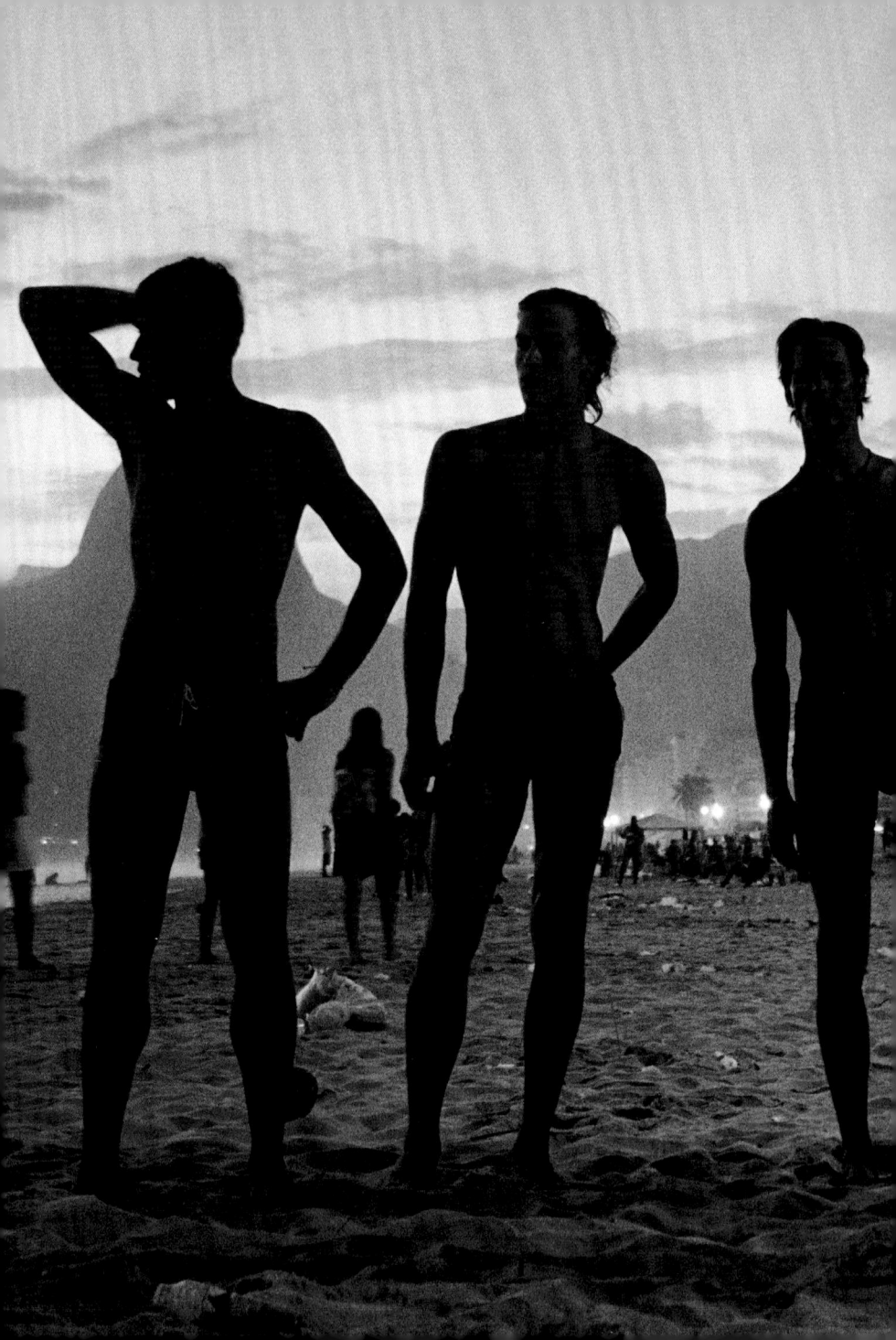

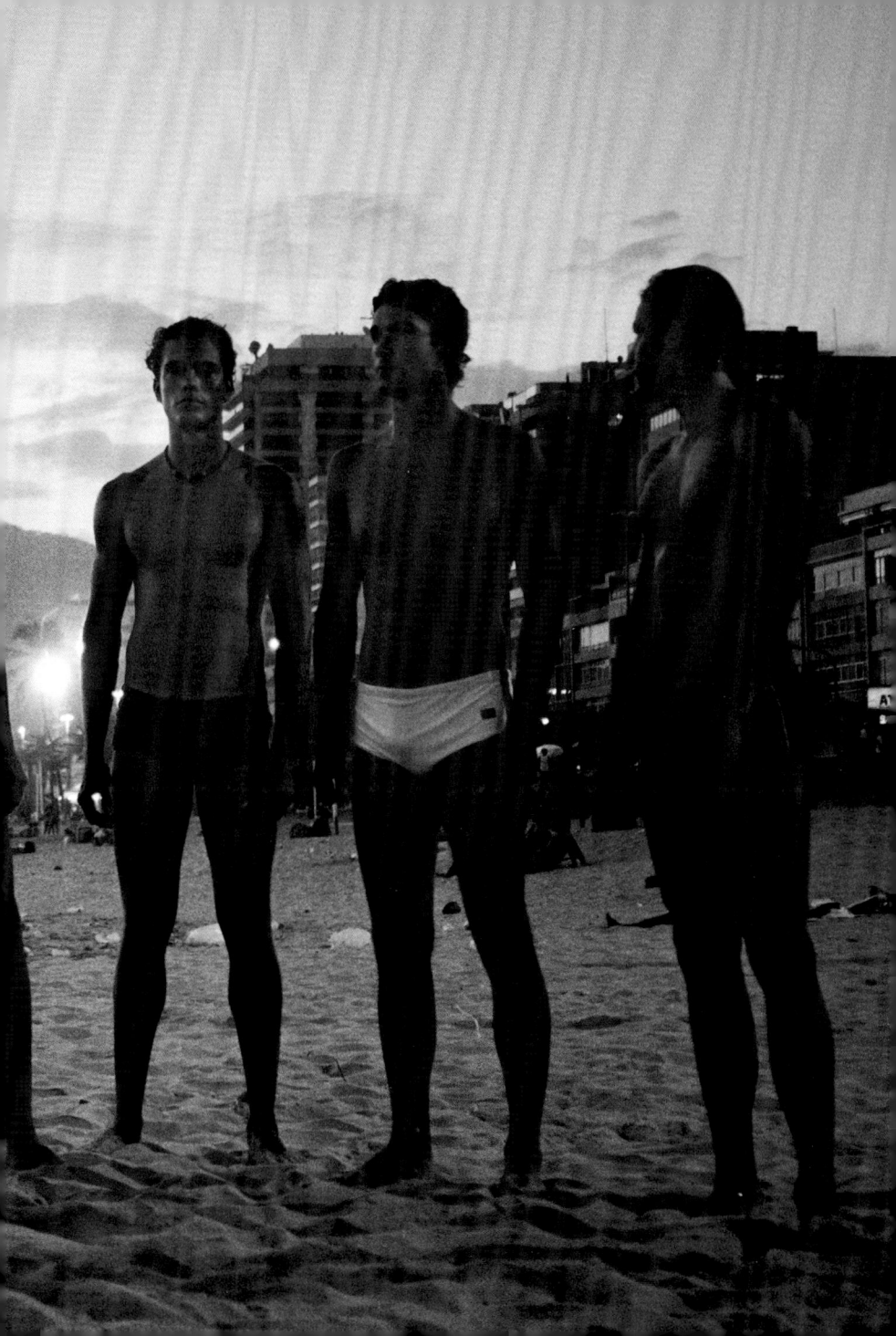

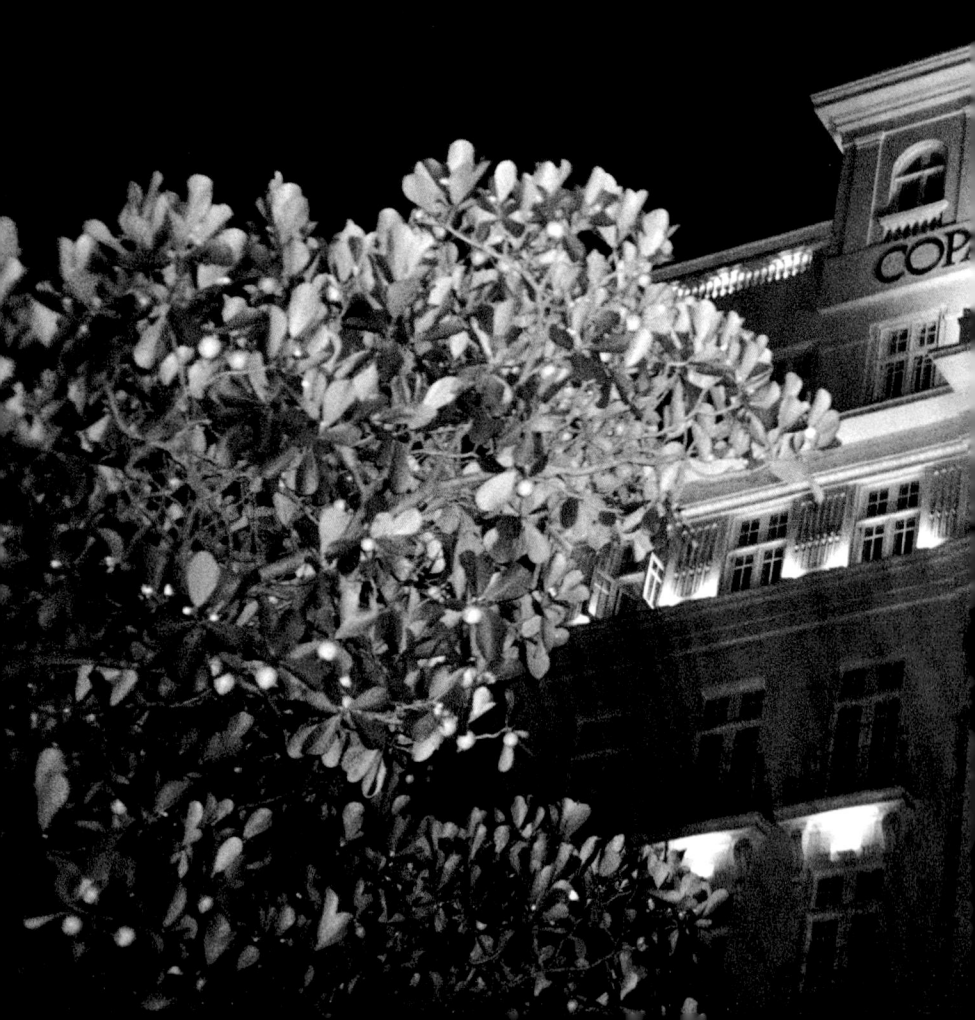

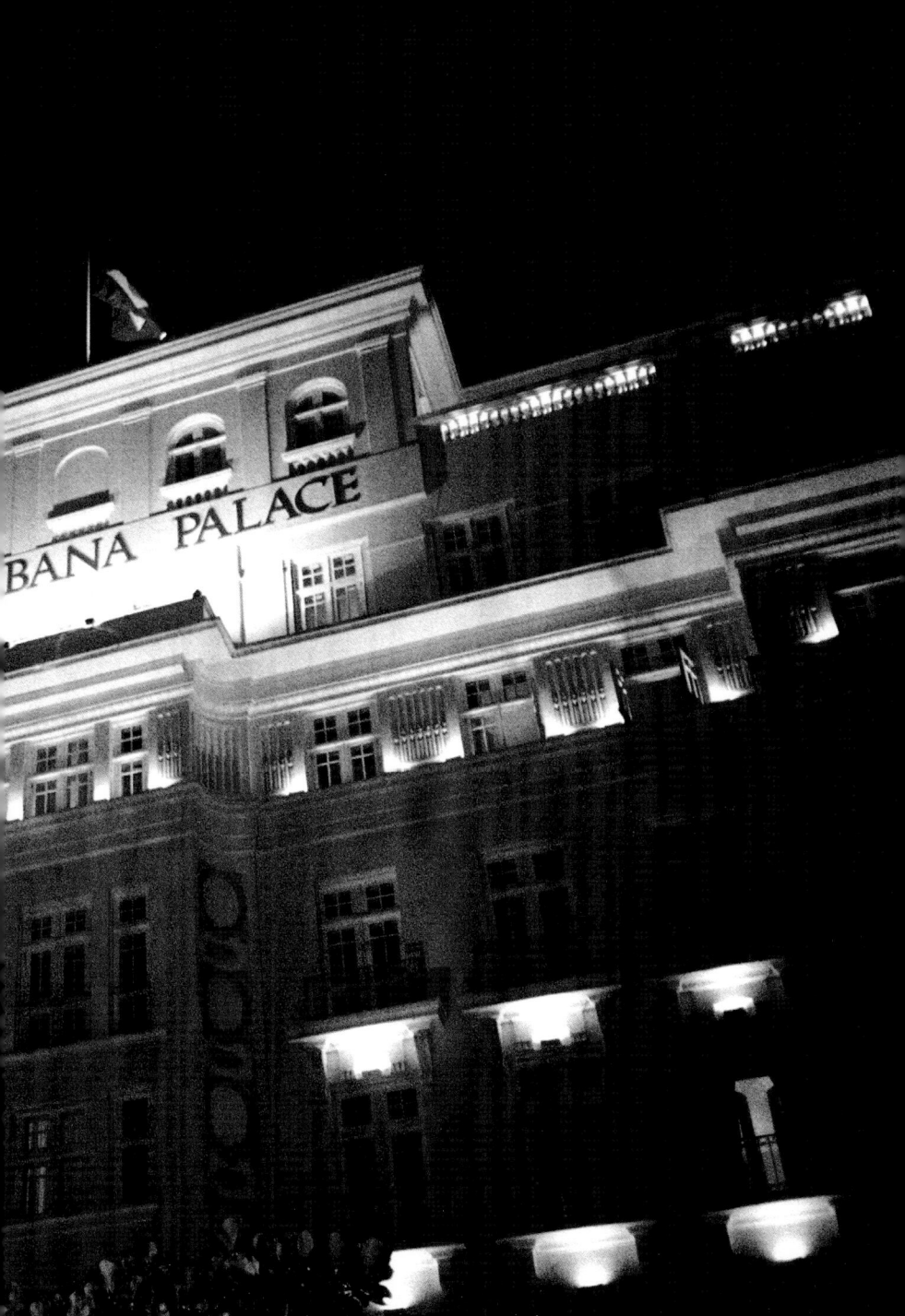

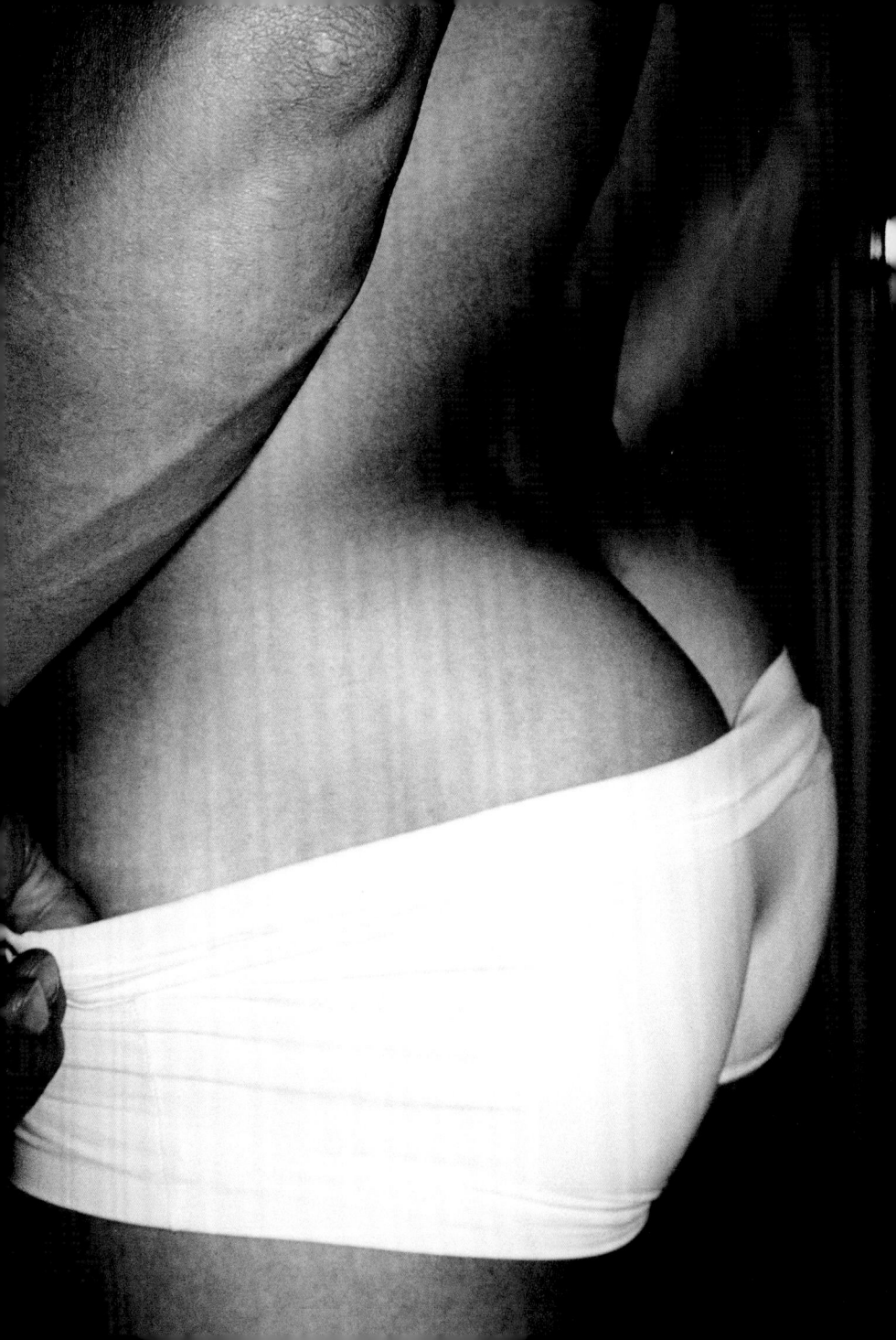

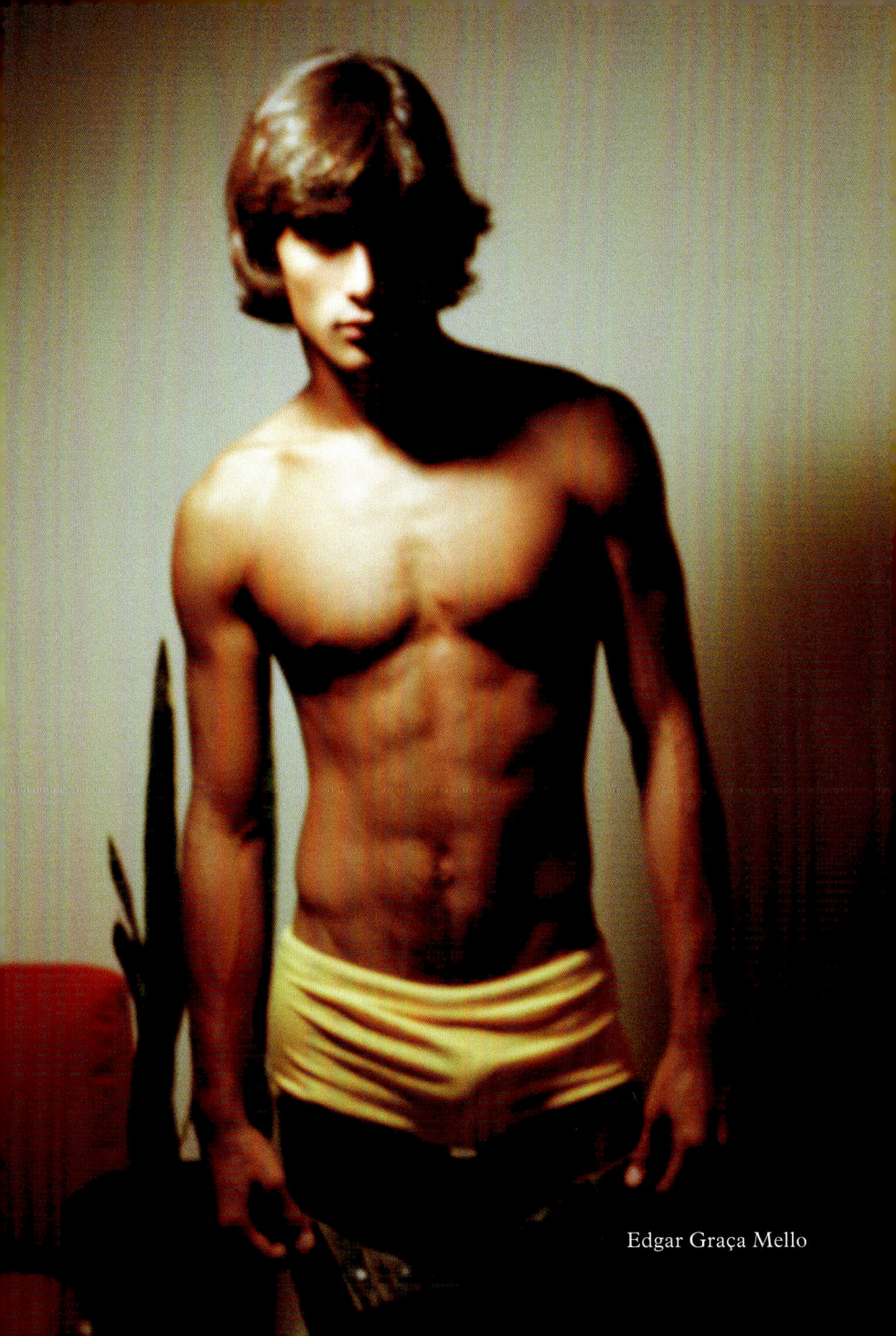

Edgar Graça Mello

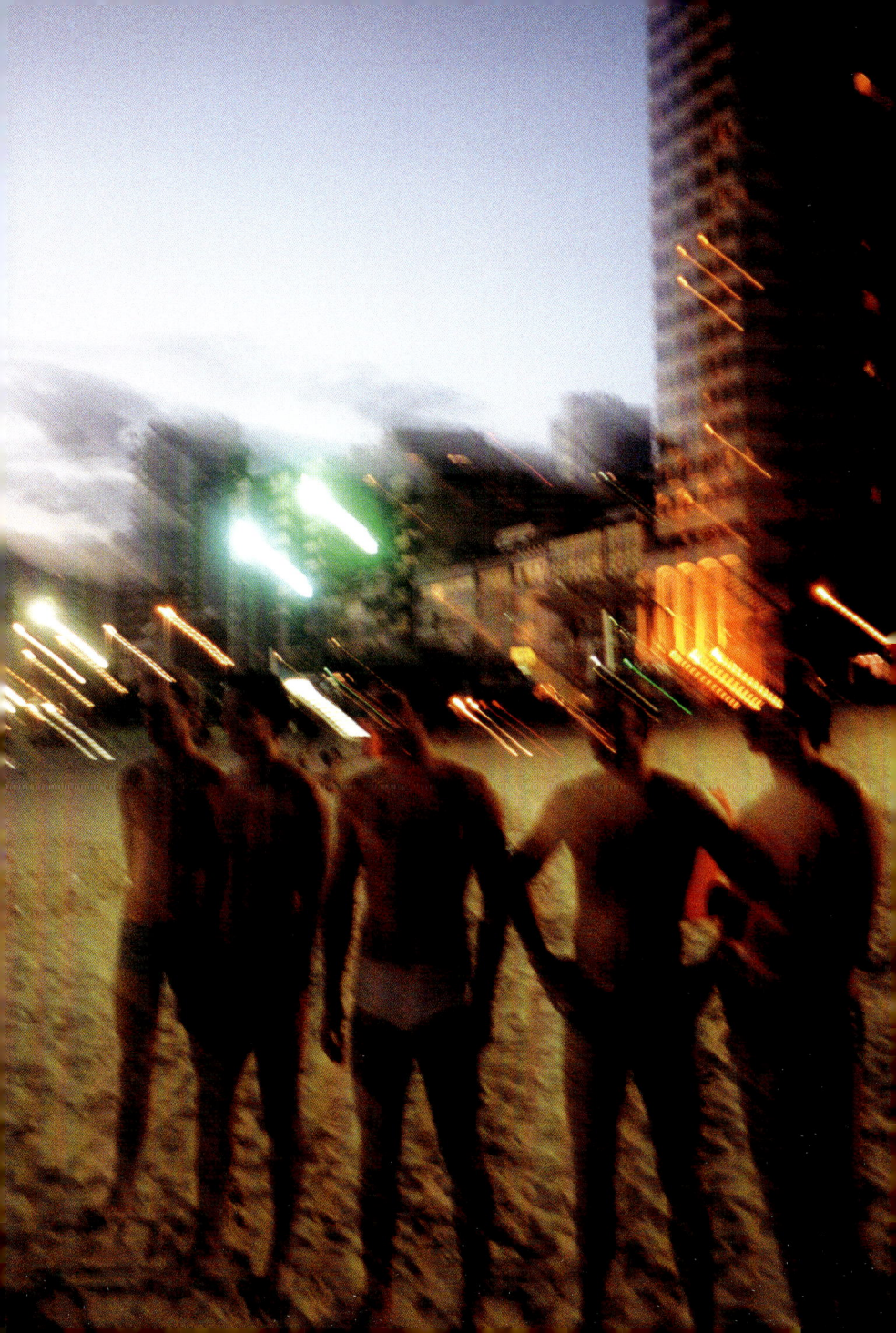

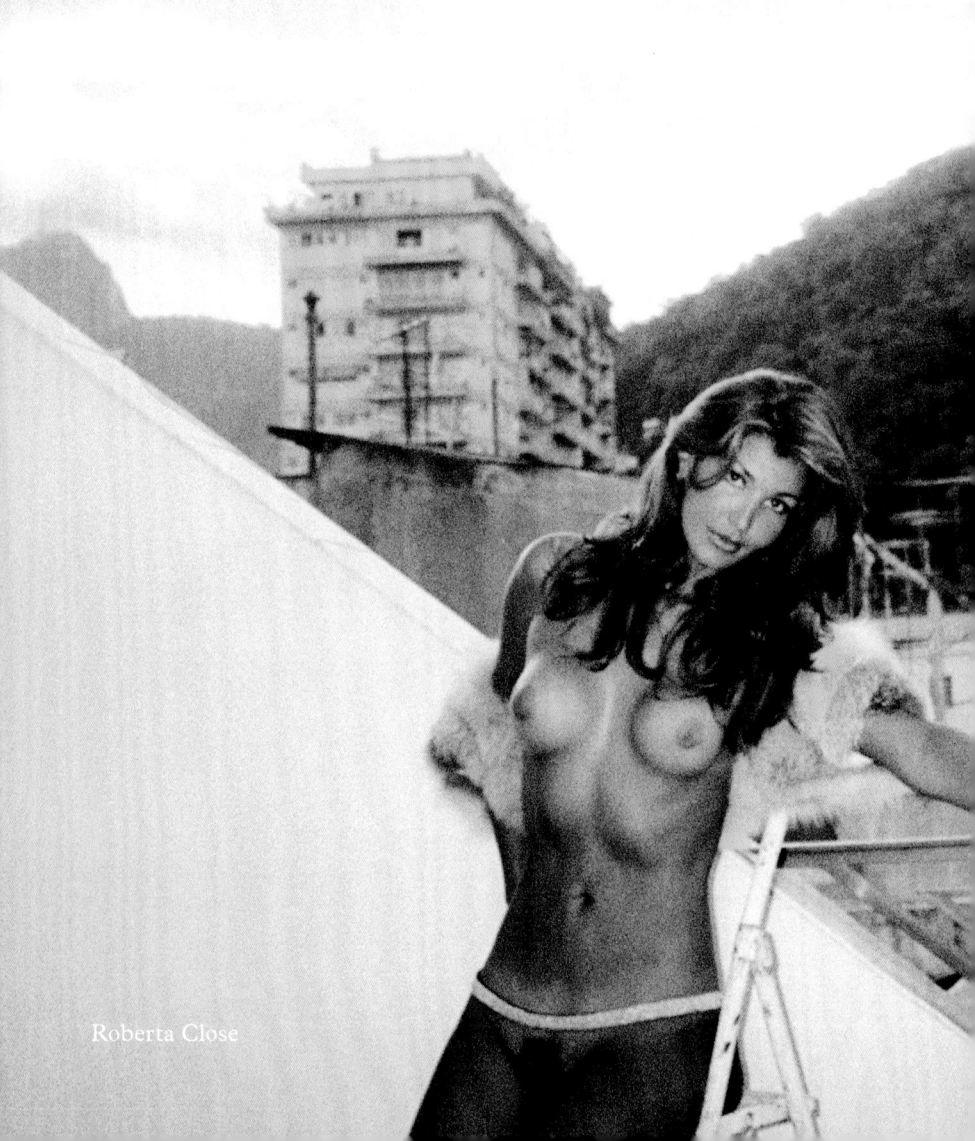

Roberta Close

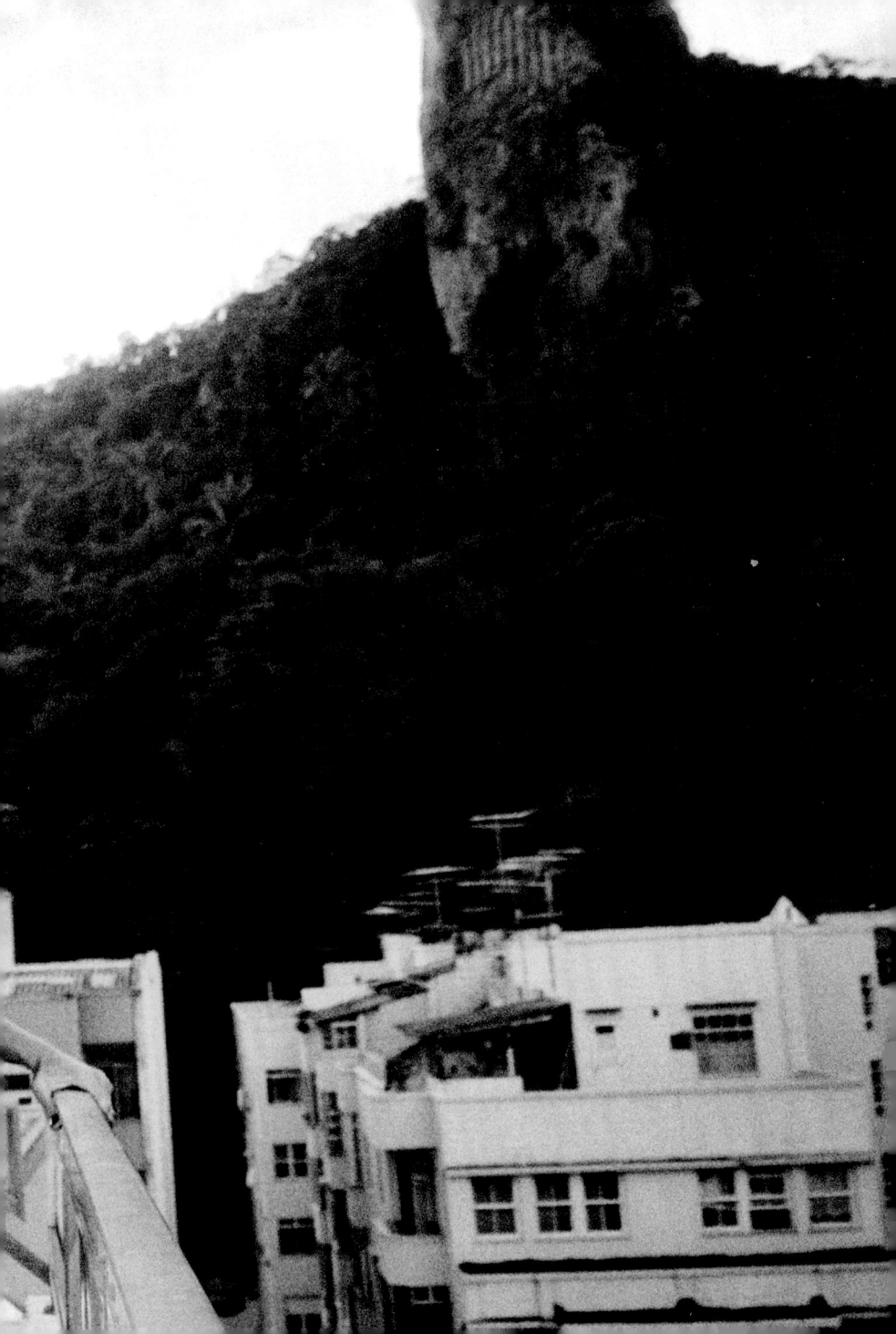

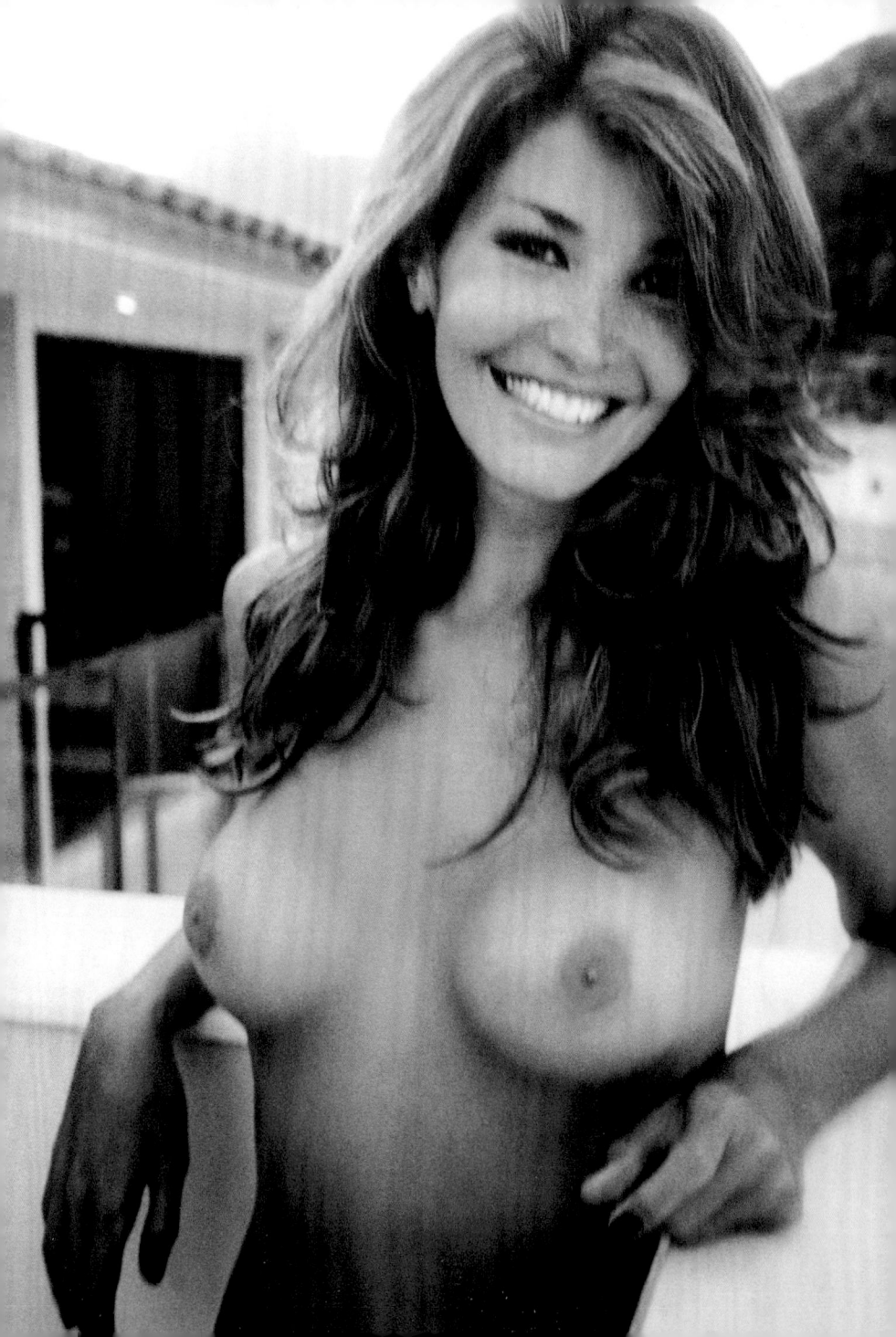

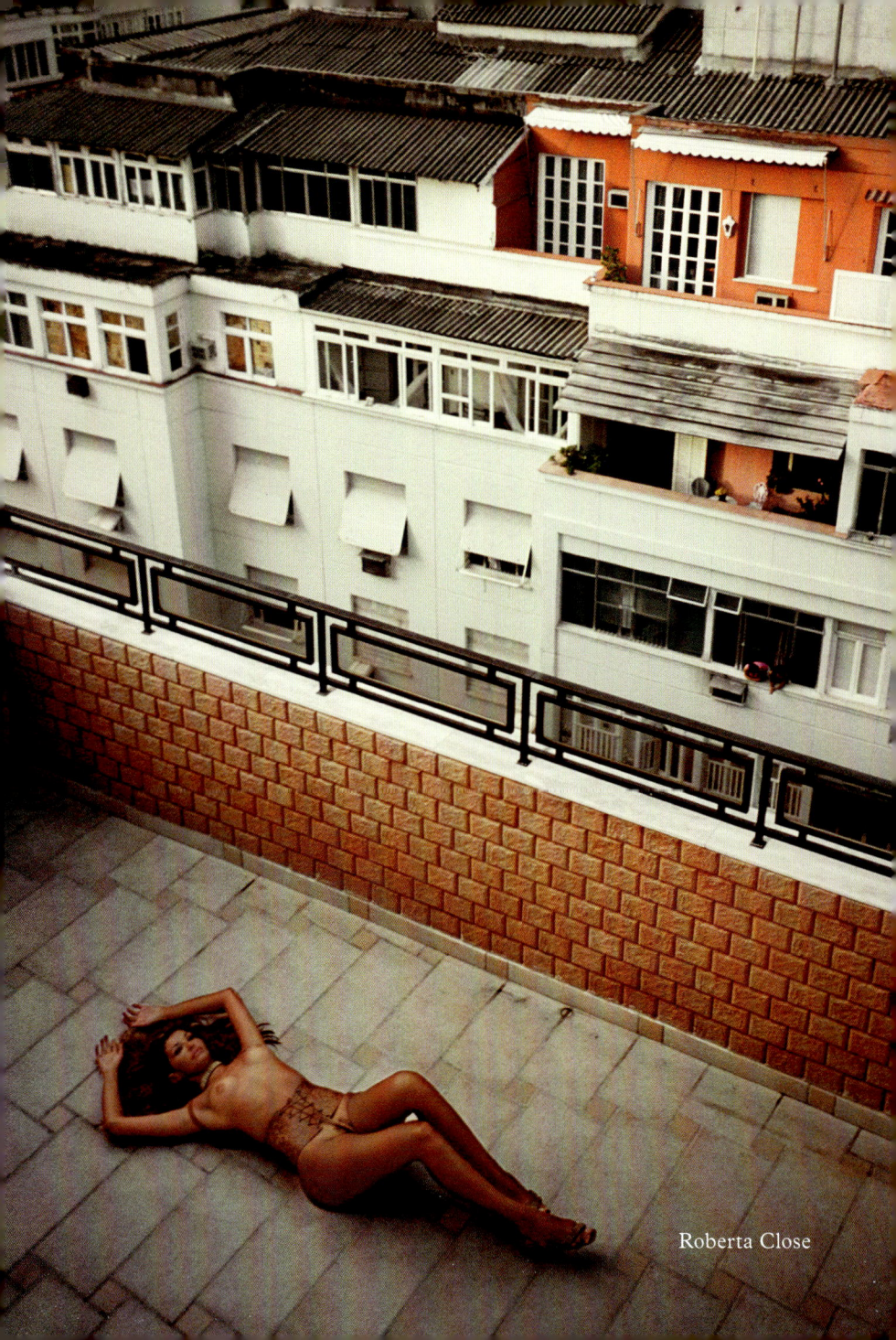

Roberta Close

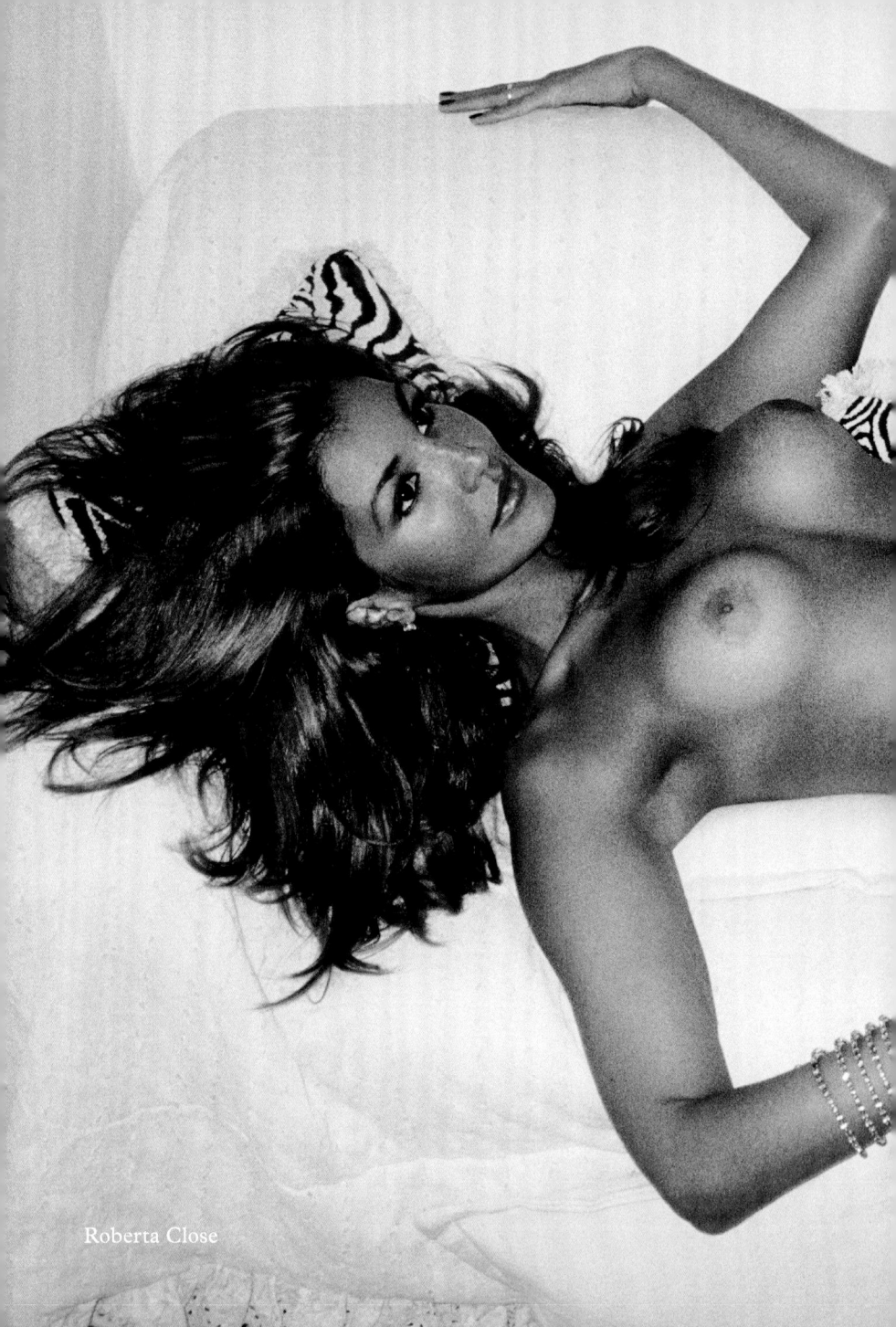

Roberta Close

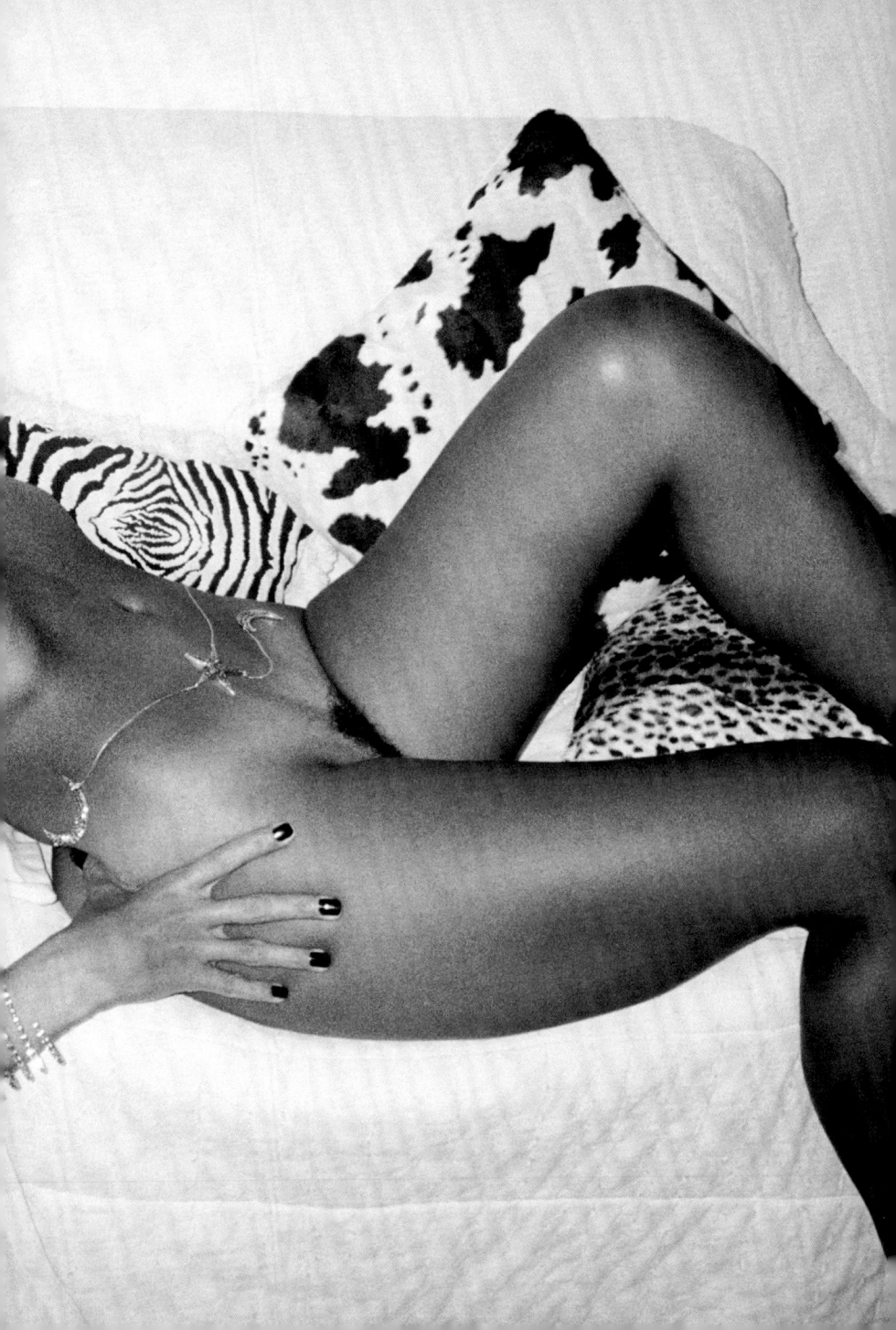

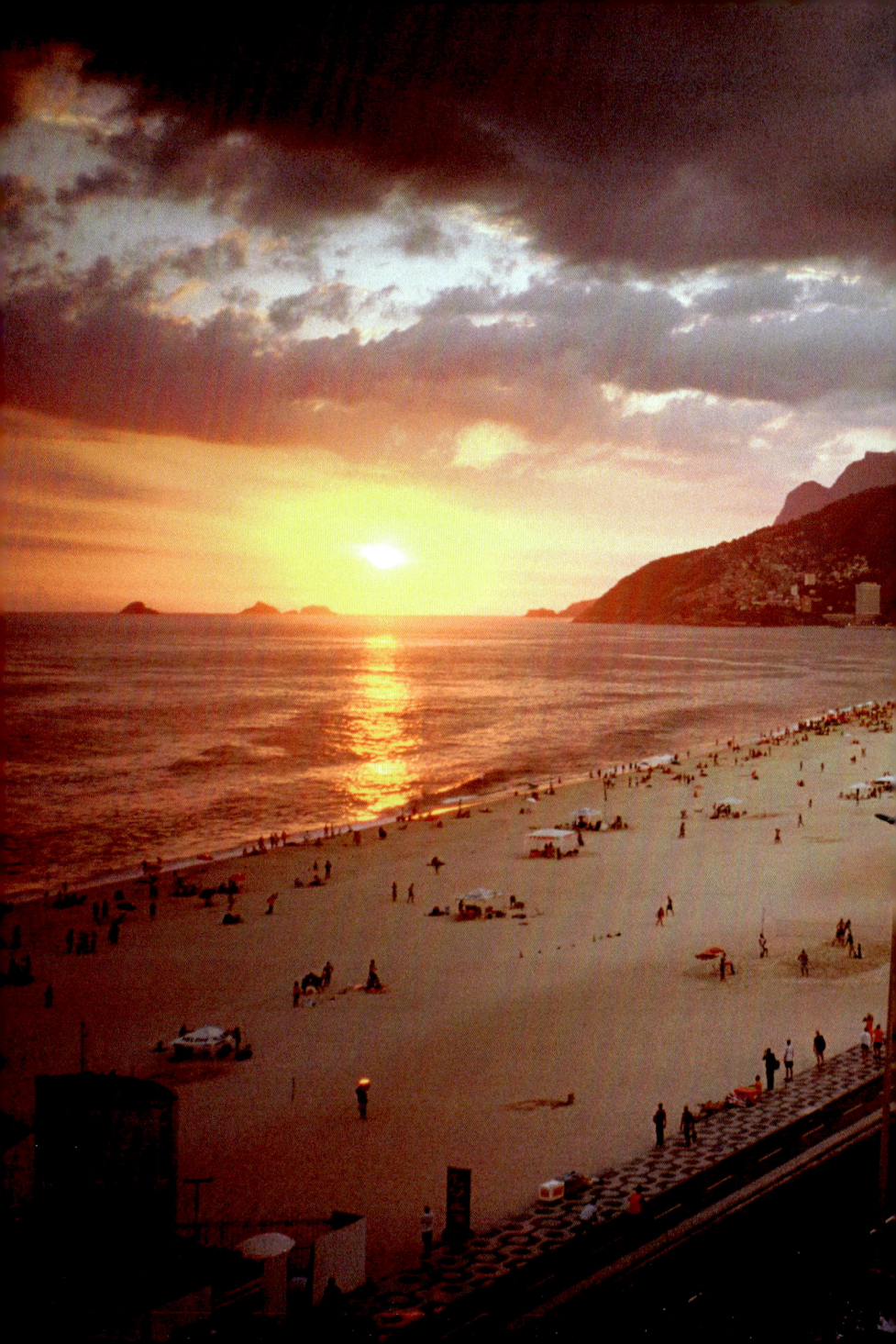

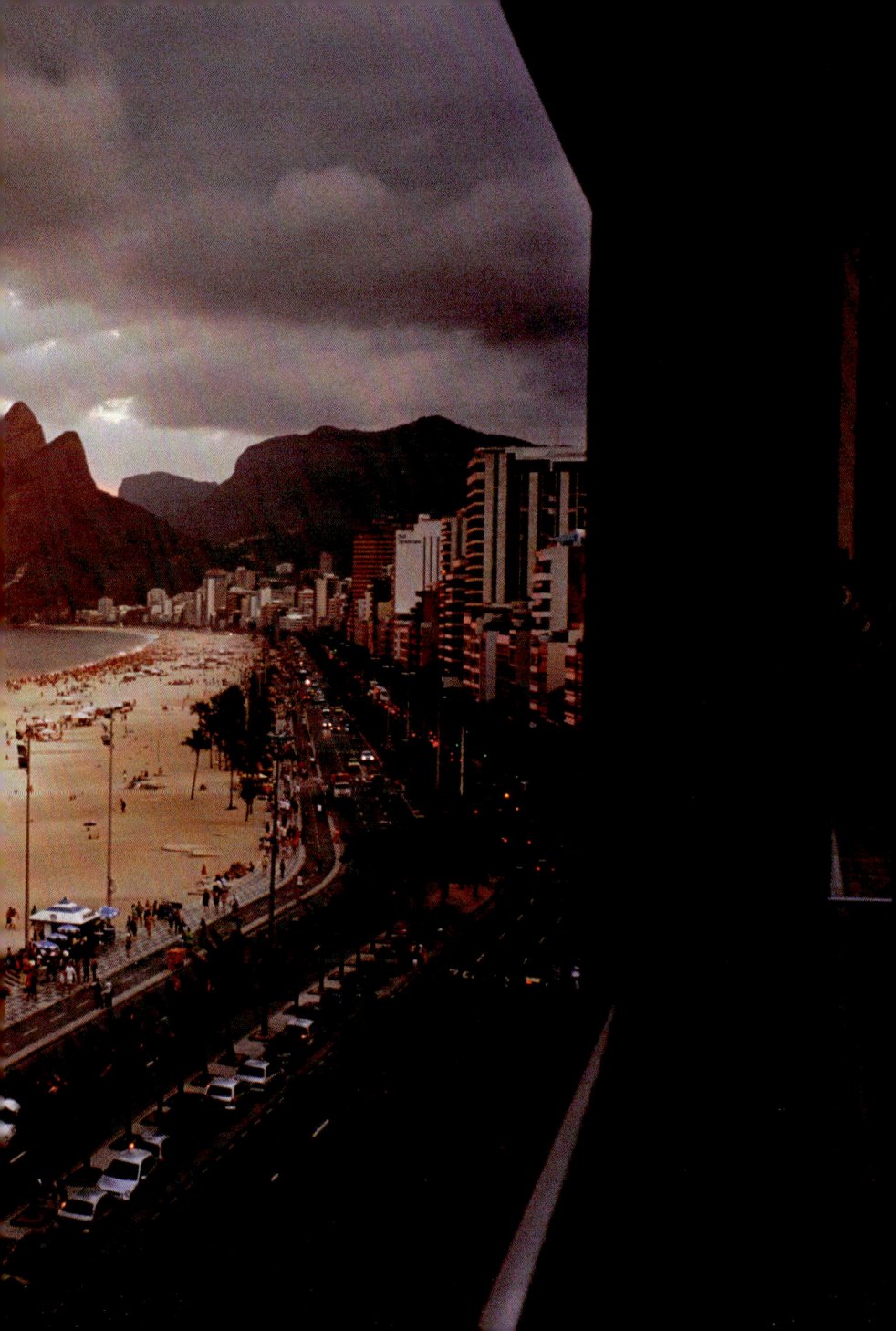

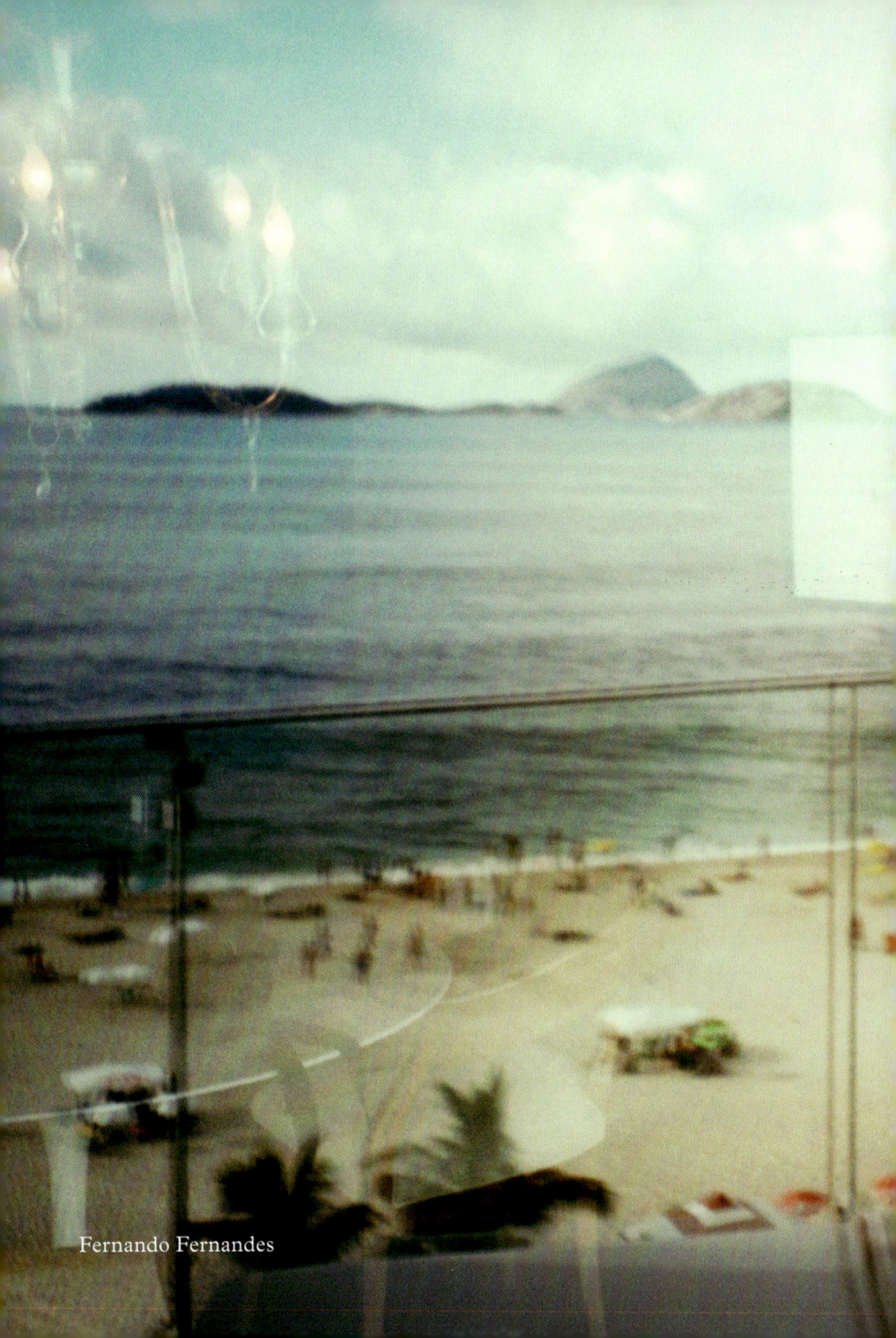

Fernando Fernandes

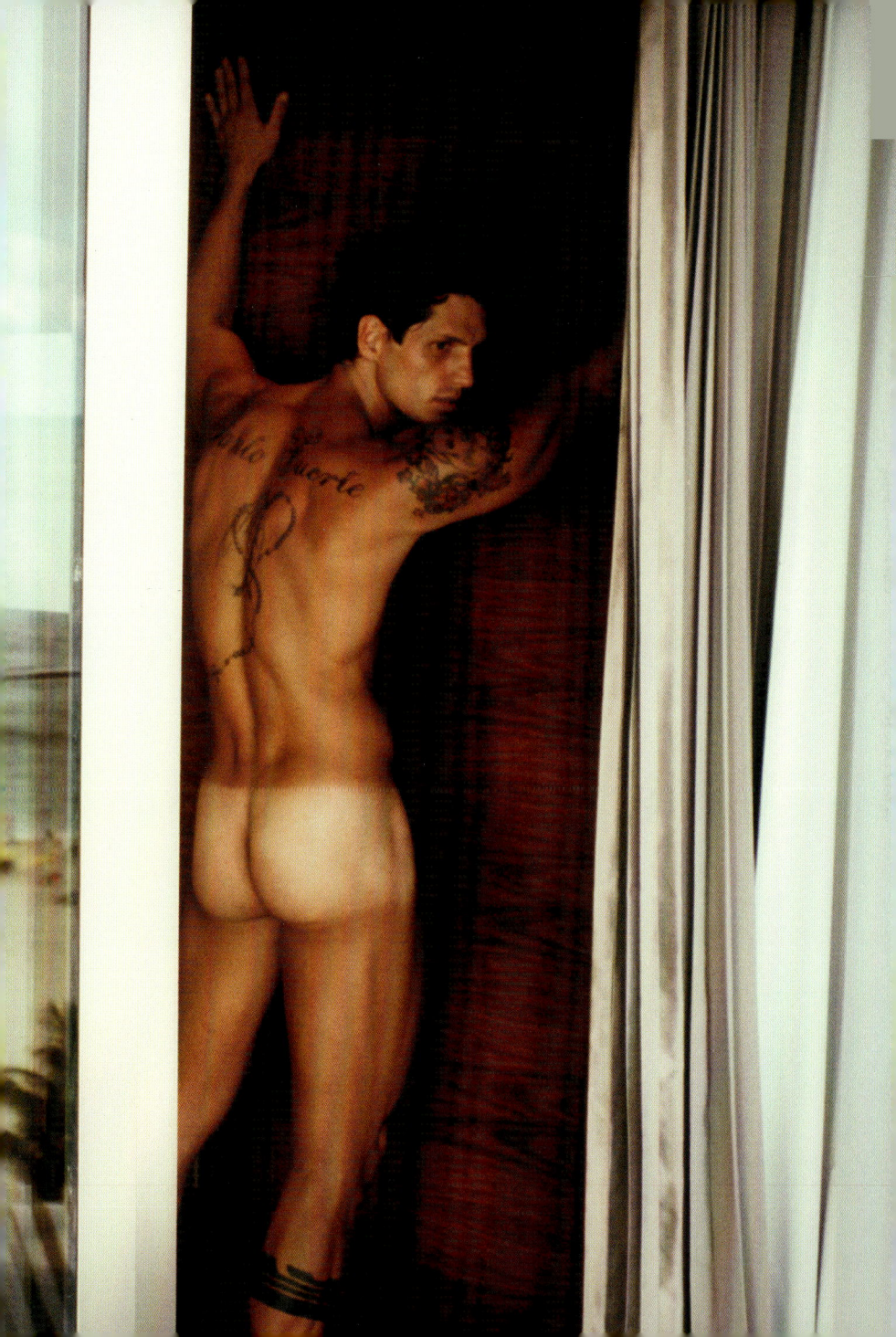

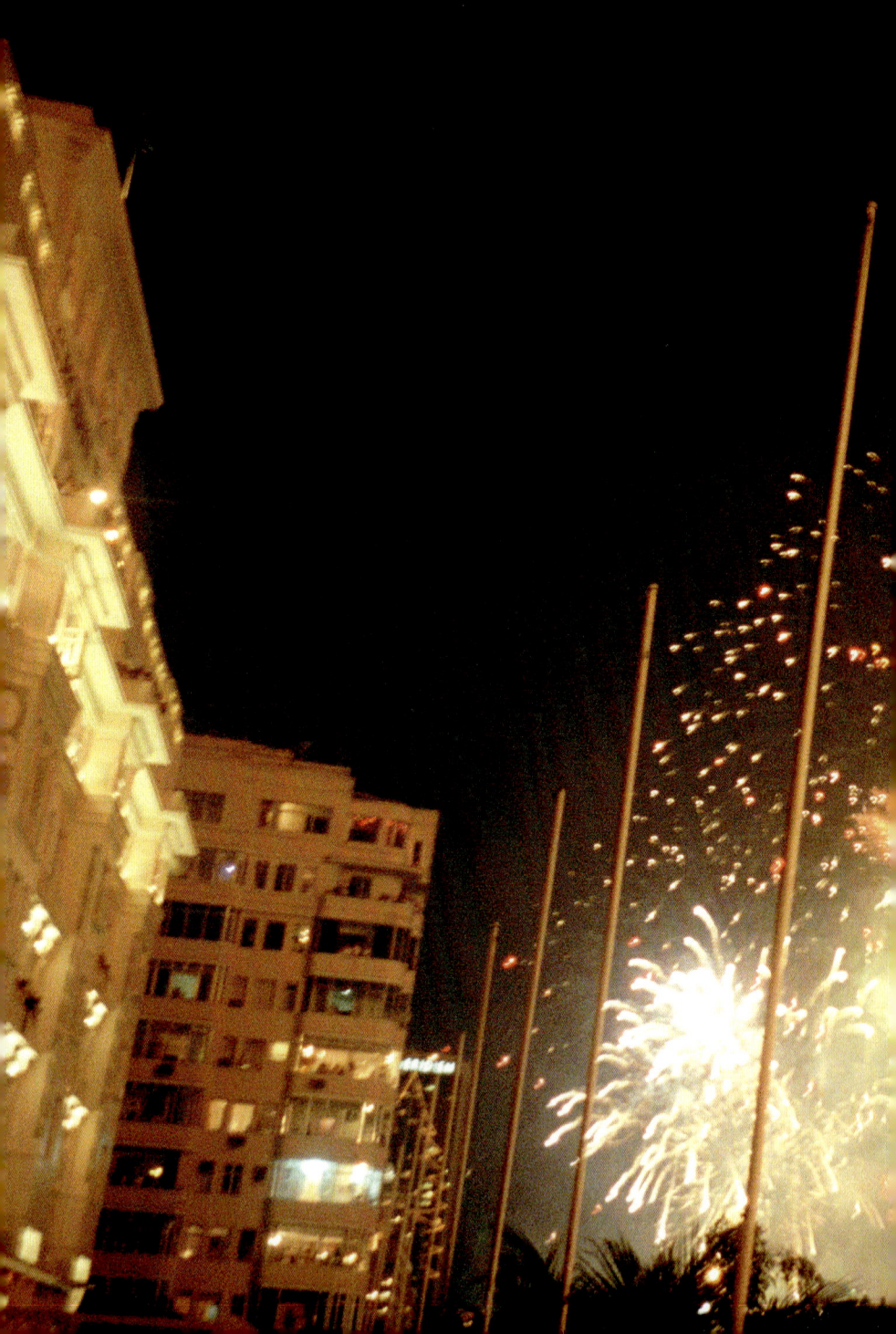

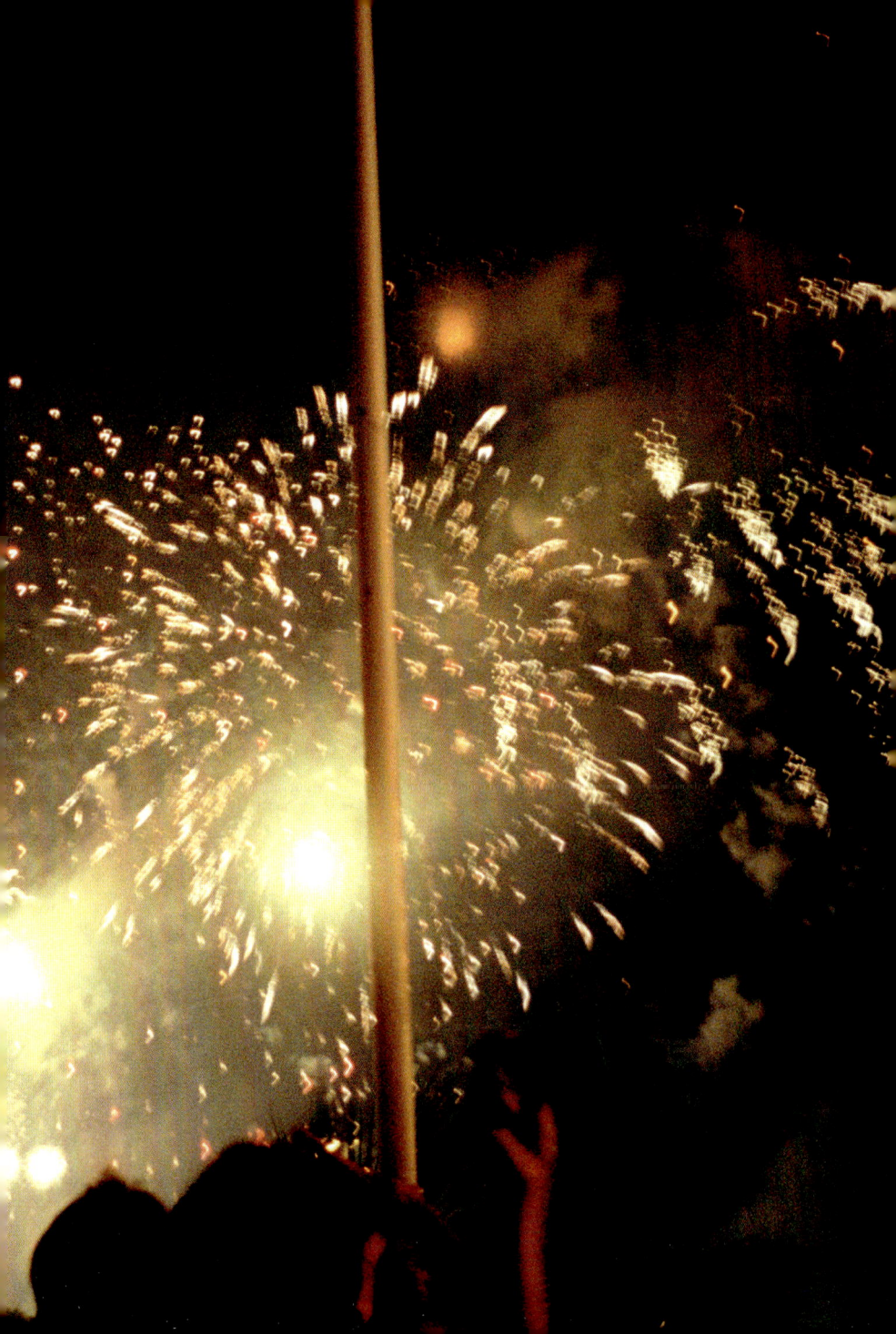

Fernando Fernandes

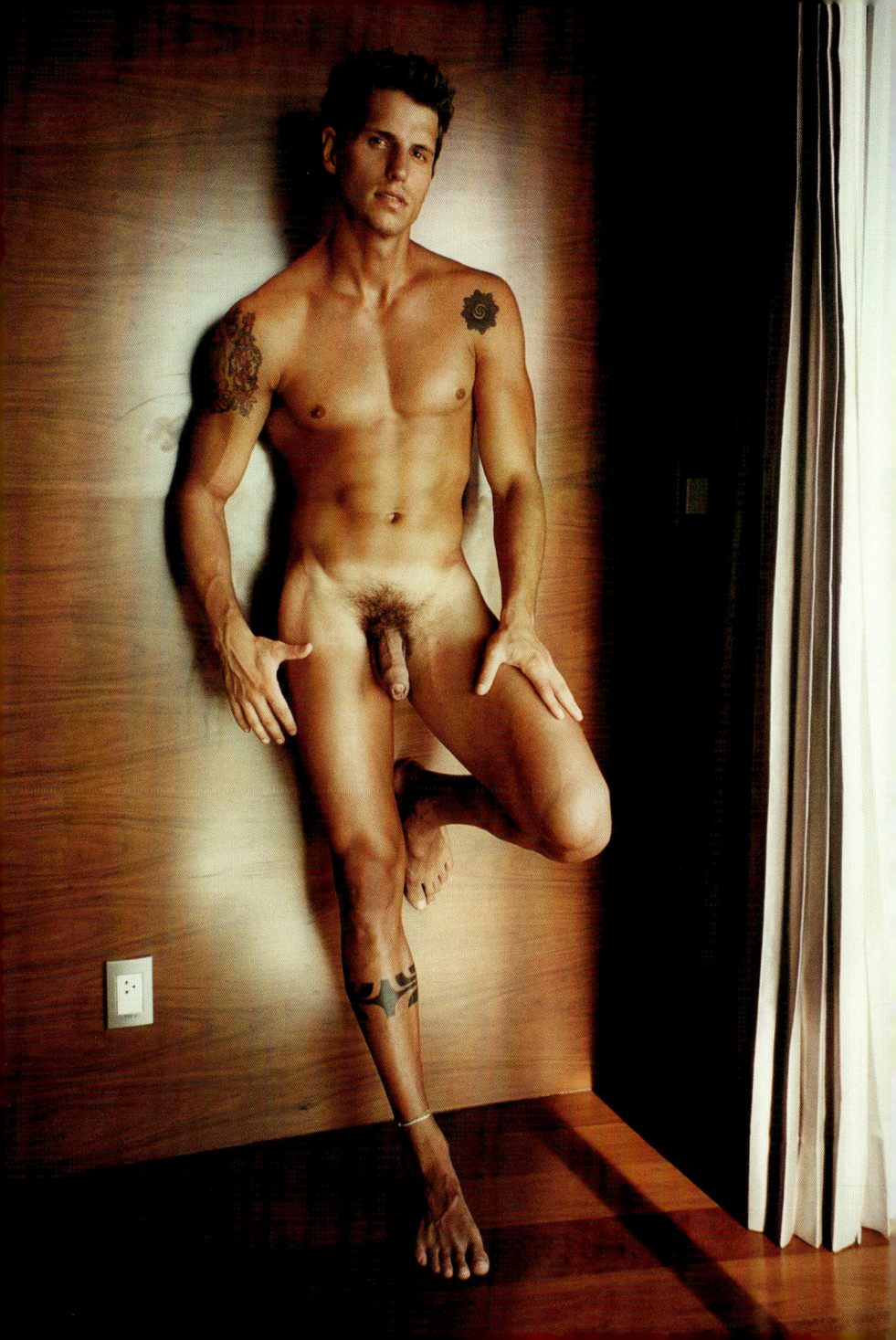

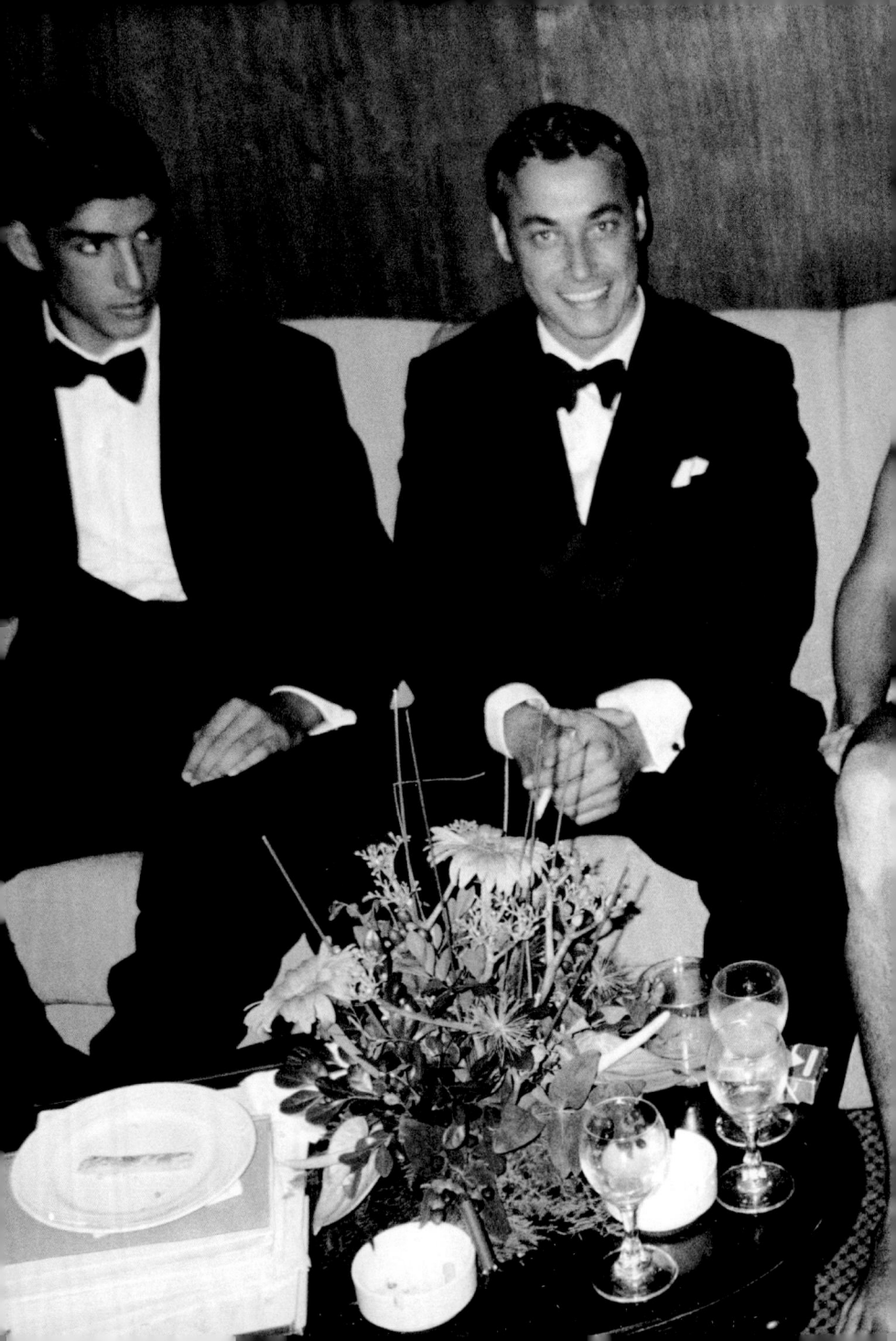

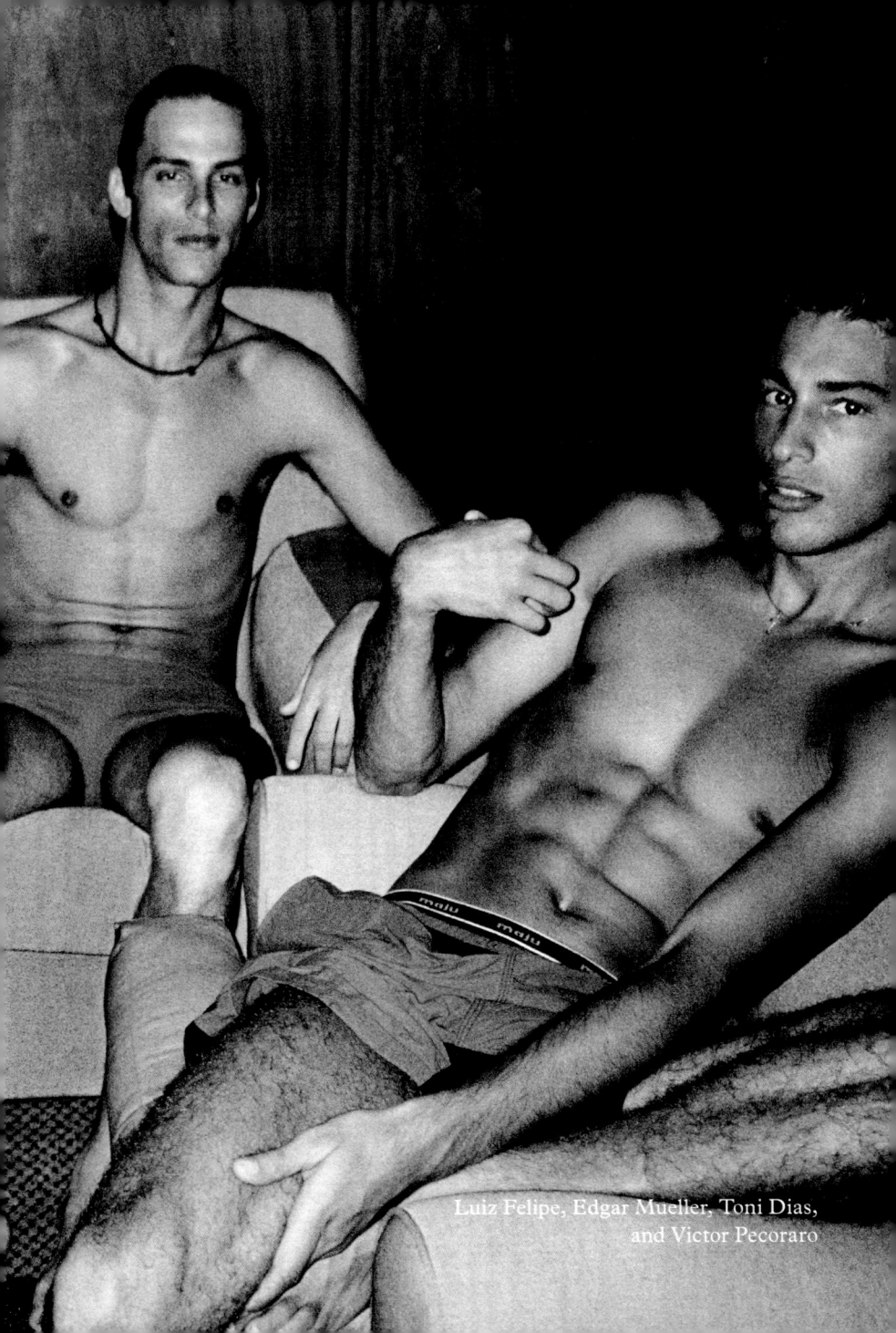

Luiz Felipe, Edgar Mueller, Toni Dias,
and Victor Pecoraro

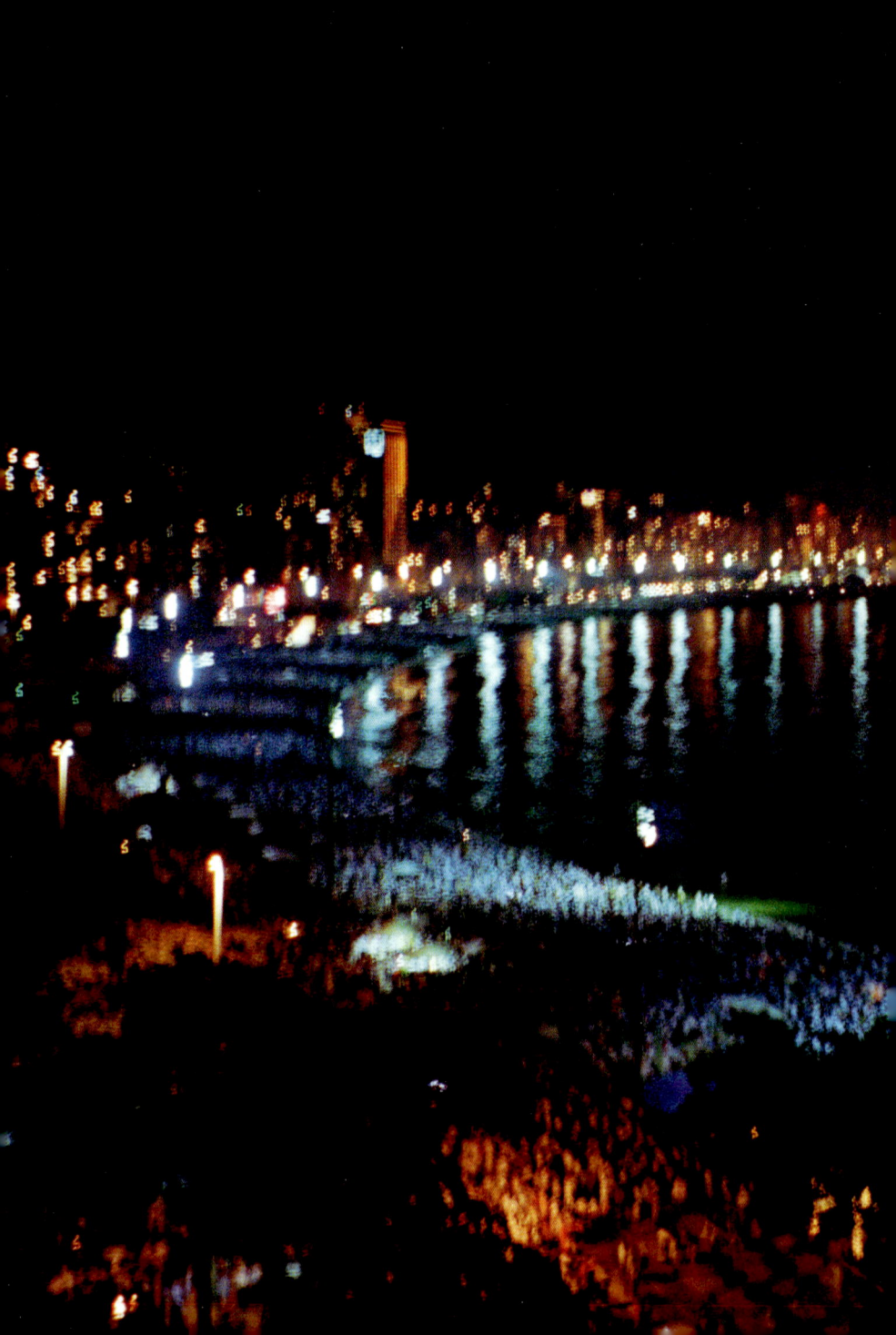

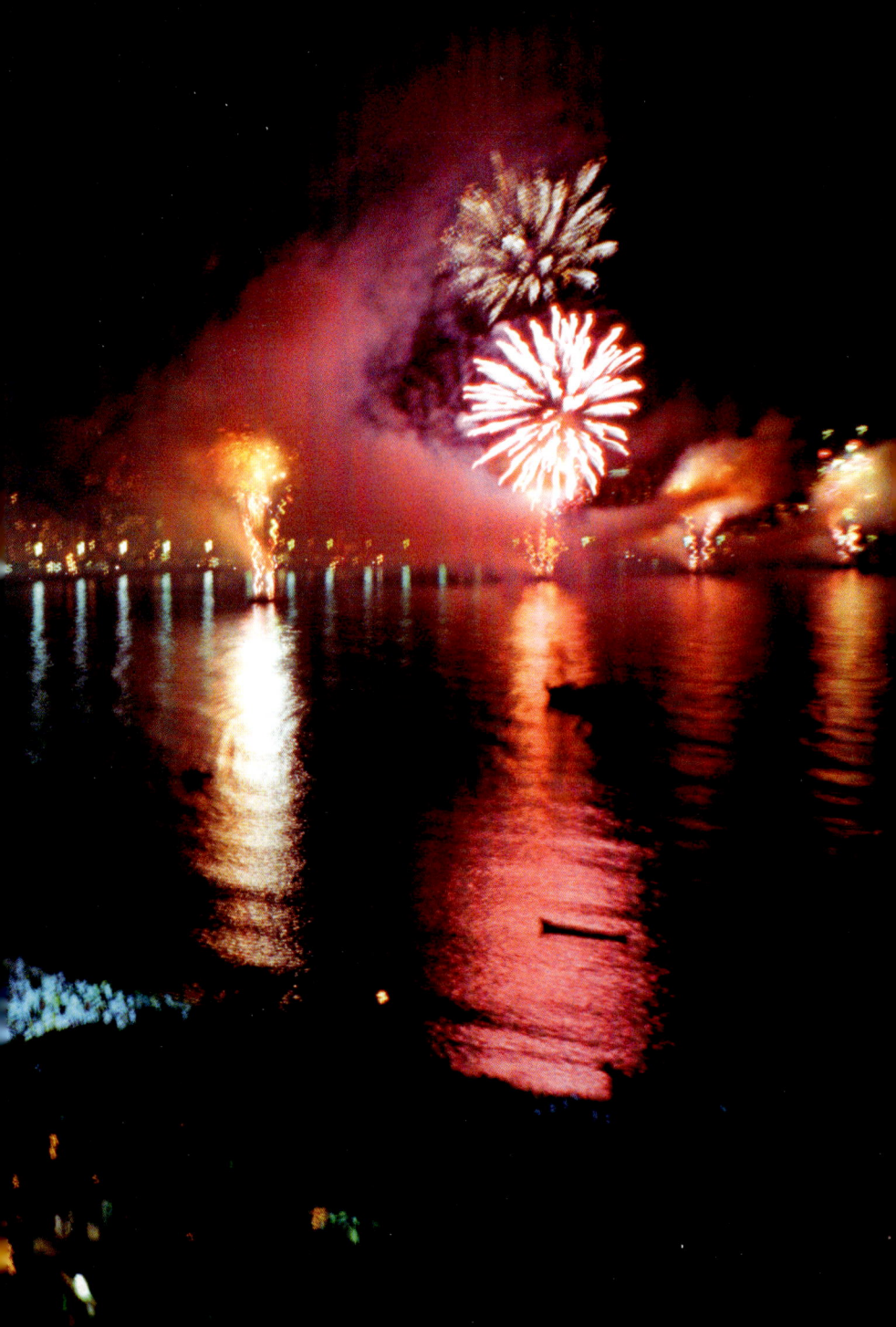

BIOGRAPHY

MARIO TESTINO

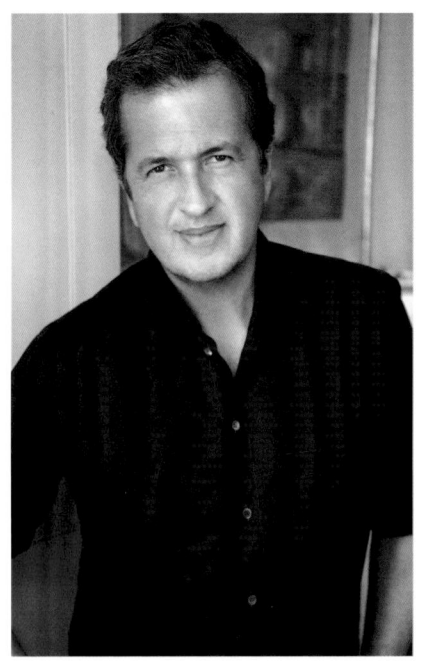

Mario Testino was born in 1954 in Lima, Peru. In the late 1970s, having completed his education in South America, he arrived in London to pursue a career as a fashion photographer. Over the following decades Mario Testino made his name internationally, becoming one of the most renowned fashion photographers of our time. Widely published in magazines such as *Vogue* and *Vanity Fair*, he is world famous for transforming the image of major fashion brands.

Mario Testino has been commissioned to photograph members of the British, Dutch, Greek, Jordanian and Norwegian Royal families. He has had a number of solo exhibitions around the world. His exhibition "Portraits" opened at the National Portrait Gallery in London in 2002 and continued to tour the world, reaching Italy, the Netherlands, Scotland, Japan, Mexico and Peru.

Mario Testino works closely with various charities. He has received the *My Hero* Award from the charity Aid for AIDS whilst also becoming the first man to receive the Commitment Award from the charity Women Together in conjunction with the United Nations. Mario Testino was awarded the Rodeo Drive Walk of Style Award for his outstanding contribution to the fashion industry. He was awarded the Order of Merit from the city of Lima, Peru, and is an Honorary Doctor of the University of the Arts London.

From an early age Mario Testino has been fascinated by Rio de Janeiro. He discovered the city in his early teens, and has since returned almost annually, unable to resist what he considers to be its "magical qualities." In 2007, in recognition of his continuous support of Rio de Janeiro he was awarded the Medalha Tiradentes from the city of Rio de Janeiro.

MARIO DE JANEIRO TESTINO is Mario Testino's ninth book.

THANK YOU

I would like to extend special thanks to all those who helped make this book possible.

Jan Olesen
Teresa Testino
Sergio Mattos
Alex Franco
Andrea Dellal
Antonio Pedro Fonseca
  Goulart Pereira
Caetano Veloso
Claudio Gomes
Giovanni Testino
Gisele Bündchen
Olavo Monteiro de
  Carvalho
Regina Casé
Sebastian Faena
Vicente de Paulo

Adam Whitehead
Adriana Varejão
Adriano Pedrosa
Alexandra Shulman
Alinne Moraes
Ana Beatriz Barros
Analu Montanaro
Andrew Tiller
Angelo Aguiar
Anna Wintour
Anne Nelson
Antonio Amancio
Argento
Art Partner
Assembléia Legislativa
  do Estado do Rio de
  Janeiro
Barwerd van der Plas
Beatriz Milhazes
Benedikt Taschen
Betsy Monteiro de
  Carvalho
Blanqui Navarre
Camilla Nickerson
Candé Salles
Carine Roitfeld
Carla Testino
Carlos Bockelman
Carlos Fernando Gomes
  de Almeida
Catia Lima
Cauã Reymond Marques
Celeiro

Cesare Lombardo
Chris Arvidson
Christopher Bailey
Ciara Parkes
Claudia Tannous
Cristhian Rosa
Cristine Franco
Daniella Sarahyba
Danni Camilo
Diogo d'Orey
Diogo Veiga
Domenico Dolce
Donata Meirelles
Donatella Versace
Drika Freire
Dudi Machado
Edgar Graça Mello
Edgar Mueller
EJ and Lili Jussen
Elena Petraco
Emanuela de Paula
Emanuele Mascioni
Eric Bergère
Estevão Ciavatta
Felipe Hulse
Felipe Roque
Felipe Sanguinetti
Felipe Veloso
Fernanda Lima
Fernanda Tavares
Fernando Fernandes
Francisco Lima Hilbert
Fundação Oscar Niemeyer

Gawain Rainey
George Perlman
George Yandell
Giuliana Testino
Giuseppe Stefanel
Grace Coddington
Graydon Carter
Graziela Alves
Grazielli Massafera
Guisela Rhein
Gustavo Carvalho
Hotel Arpoador Inn
Ian Hall
Icon
Isabeli Fontana
Jaime and Dora Jamarillo
Jay and Mimma Lovatelli
João Lima Hilbert
João Vellutini
John Allan
John Gnerre
Kalani
Kate Dewdney-Herbert
Lalá Guimarães
Leni Niemeyer
Leo Vieira
Loretta
Lori Bartlett
Lucas Brandão
Luciano Bossler
Lucinda Chambers
Luiz Felipe
Marc Lopez

Maria Teresa Oliveira
  Santos
Márcio Aguinaga
Márcio Garcia
Marcus Kurz
Marcus Vinicius Toscano
  Lopes
Mariana Ximenes
Marina Franco
Maysa Marques
Metro
Michael Howells
Michael Kors
Michael Roberts
Michele Norsa
Monica Nega
Monica Velando
Neelam Tikdas
Nizan Guanaes
Olivier Daube
Patricia Carta
Patrick Kinmonth
Paula Lavigne
Paulo Vieira
Pedro Buarque de
  Hollanda
Philippe Kliot
Phillip Williams
Raphael Ghedin
Raphael Lacchine
Renato Ferreira
Renato Kerlakian
Ricardo Jay

Riotur
Roberta Close
Rodrigo Calazans
Rodrigo Hilbert
Rodrigo Santoro
Rogério Fasano
Rômulo Arantes
Sabina Spaldi
Sacramento
Sicco Diemer
Sophie Chartres
Stefano Gabbana
Stephen Gan
Steve Macleod
Taiguara
Tanit Galdeano
Thais Botelho
Tiago and Daniel Lo
Tiago Marinho
Toby Knott
Tom Pecheux
Toni Dias
Tonne Goodman
Ulrich Eckhardt
V
Vanity Fair
Veruschka Baudo
Victoria Fernandez
Victor Pecoraro
Visionaire
Vogue

CREDITS

Project Coordination
Alex Bramall
Jemima Hobson

Design
Higher&Higher

Graphics
Tom Phillips

Printing & Retouching
R&D
Pietro Birindelli
Jono Patrick
Guillaume Dulermo
Paul Archer

Support Team
Brigitte Sondag
Candice Marks
Daniel Gorin
Georgina Godley
Harry Soames
Jan Olesen
John Gayner
Lucy Lee
Rafael D'Alò
Robert Kent

Travel
Frenchway Travel
Esther Davor
Yael Choukroun

Accommodation
Hotel Copacabana Palace
Andrea Natal

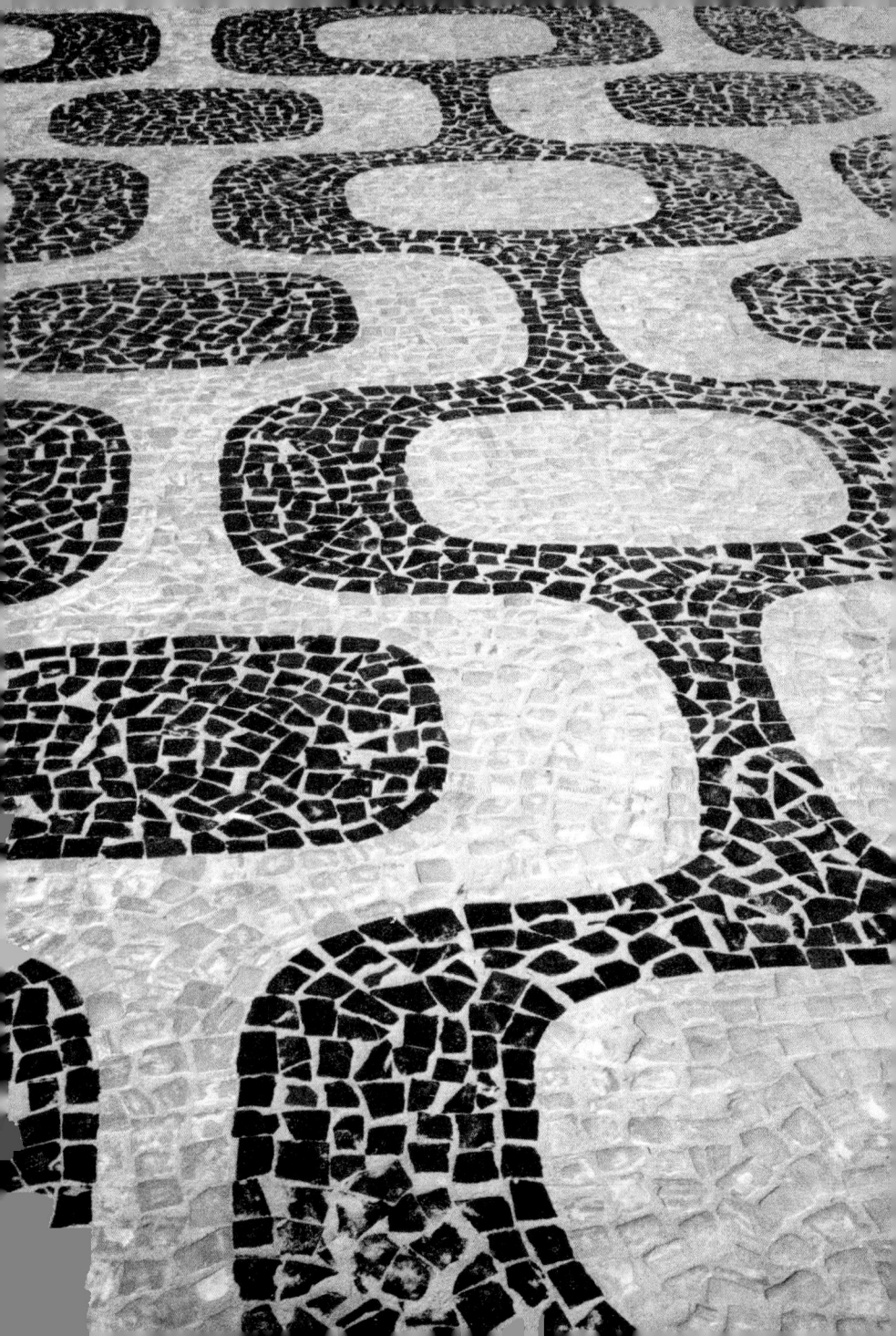